The Line Forms Here

Poets on Poetry   **Donald Hall, General Editor**

David Lehman

The Line
Forms Here

Ann Arbor

THE UNIVERSITY OF MICHIGAN PRESS

Copyright © by David Lehman 1992
All rights reserved
Published in the United States of America by
The University of Michigan Press
Manufactured in the United States of America
1995   1994   1993   1992   4   3   2   1

Library of Congress Cataloging-in-Publication Data

Lehman, David, 1948–
   The line forms here / David Lehman.
     p. cm. — (Poets on poetry)
   Includes bibliographical references.
   ISBN 0-472-09483-1 (alk. paper). — ISBN 0-472-06483-5 (alk. paper
: pbk.)
   1. Lehman, David, 1948– —Authorship.   2. American poetry—20th
century—History and criticism.   3. Poetry—Study and teaching.
4. Poetics.   I. Title.   II. Series.
PS3562.E428Z467   1992
811'.509—dc20   92-11679
                CIP

Acknowledgments

Grateful acknowledgment is made to the following journals and publishers for permission to reprint previously published material.

Cornell University Press for "Elemental Bravery: The Unity of James Merrill's Poetry," reprinted from *James Merrill: Essays in Criticism,* edited by David Lehman and Charles Berger. Copyright © 1983 by Cornell University Press. Used by permission of the publisher.

Newsweek for "Under the Influence of Harold Bloom," which first appeared as "Yale's Insomniac Genius" in *Newsweek,* August 18, 1986; "Poets Who Work for a Living," which first appeared as "The Practical Side of Poetry" in *Newsweek,* September 22, 1986; "Ambassadors of the Word," reprinted from *Newsweek,* November 3, 1986; and "Tales of the Oulipo," which first appeared as "Masters of Marvelous Mazes" in *Newsweek,* February 8, 1988. Copyright © 1986, 1988, Newsweek, Inc. All rights reserved. Reprinted by permission.

The New York Times Company for "The Pleasures of John Ashbery's Poetry," which first appeared as "The Creative Mind, John Ashbery: The Pleasures of Poetry" in the *New York Times Magazine,* December 16, 1984. Copyright © 1984 by The New York Times Company. Reprinted by permission.

Every effort has been made to trace the ownership of all copyrighted material in this book and to obtain permission for its use.

Introduction

The Line Forms Here is a selection of my essays and articles on poetry and the life of the poet.

At a writers' conference at Wesleyan University in 1984, I remember saying with some bravado that a single column about poetry in *Newsweek* made a bigger difference than all the writers' conferences in a year. I don't know if that's true, but I know that the thought excites me still. I have had the pleasure of writing about literature for a wider audience than is presumed to exist for it, and I do not concede that poetry has been, as the academics say, fatally "marginalized." The readership for poetry is there, and we oughtn't to condescend to it, and we certainly oughtn't to act as if it did not and could not exist.

Perhaps when we speak of the audience for poetry we should prod ourselves to speak of it in the plural; for besides that potential audience to which one wants to make an appeal, there is also the valued constituency of the confirmed and committed—the sort of people who go to poetry readings, browse through literary magazines in funky bookstores, and know by heart a dozen poems by Wallace Stevens. Everyone laments the neglect of poetry in our culture, but too few take notice of the readers who have proved their fealty to an art form that somebody is always, or annually, pronouncing dead. There must be a lot of life in the old muse-inspired trade if writers in *Commentary* or the *Atlantic* can get so vexed about it.

This book is divided into four sections. The pieces in part one concentrate on questions of poetic form. Part two, much the longest section of the book, treats seven individual poets at length. Part three widens the focus to include "Money and

Poetry," "Criticism and Crisis." Part four is the book's coda. As to critical principles: though I have gone on record endorsing Marianne Moore's position that poetry should be read "with a perfect contempt for it," I am by temperament something of an enthusiast and tend to favor a policy of generosity and inclusion. I have heard it said that "you cannot love both John Ashbery's poetry and Philip Larkin's." The editor of a highly regarded literary journal said this to me as if it were a self-evident truth instead of what it really is, an example of the kind of foolish consistency that Emerson warned against. There is a pleasure to be had in critical confrontation, and there are times when a binary opposition—between, say, Tolstoy and Dostoyevski—may occasion a masterly literary investigation. But the either/or logic is untrue to the experience of readers, who find it perfectly possible to respond with ardor to authors who may differ from each other in every other particular but share the quality of greatness that will make their works endure into the next century.

Most of the essays in this book were written as labors of love; some, for love and money; a few because of a beckoning controversy or an insistent editor. In every case the final shape of the piece was conditioned by its occasion. Writing for a newsmagazine or for the book review supplement in the Sunday paper imposes requirements quite different from those in effect for a leisurely piece published in a quarterly. In the writer's mind his journalism and his serious criticism are supposed to belong in two altogether different categories. In practice, however, and certainly in retrospect, it isn't easy to draw the line, and I am a passionate believer in the salutary effect of journalism—a profession with a strong sense of ethical standards and an insistence on accountability—on literary criticism.

Not having anticipated the making of this book, I had to rely on several bulging file cabinets and a system of filing that seems to get clumsier every year. In some cases all that survived was the printed version of the piece; in other cases I had the manuscript copy only. Where both were available I usually went with the printed version, but I have felt free to restore material cut to accommodate a magazine layout, and I have also combined articles that appeared in different magazines, or in different issues of the same magazine, and have made other revisions where it seemed important to do so.

Poetry is my first love. As one who writes the stuff, I have an emphatic (though not exclusive) interest in what my contemporaries and our immediate predecessors have done or are doing. As one who earns his living as a freelance writer and critic, I have indulged this interest whenever I could, priding myself on an ability to contrive a suitable occasion, format, and venue for my effort. Still, it took me by surprise to discover, when I put this volume together, material enough to fill several tomes, and I want to thank Donald Hall for helping me carve this book into its present form. LeAnn Fields, my editor at the University of Michigan Press, quickened the manuscript into existence with her anticipatory enthusiasm. Linda Howe lived up to her reputation for excellent copyediting. Lynn Chu, Roger Gilbert, and Glen Hartley made valuable suggestions. I am grateful to Nin Andrews for the work she did on the interview that concludes the book and for much else besides. The *Newsweek* piece on translators reflects reporting done by Barbara Rosen and Theodore Stanger. The essay on James Merrill appeared in *James Merrill: Essays in Criticism,* which I edited in collaboration with Charles Berger for publication by Cornell University Press. Finally, I must acknowledge the editors who published the pieces and shared a belief in the audience for poetry and the value of criticism: Kenneth Auchincloss, the late James Boatwright, Richard Burgin, Cecil Giscombe, John Gross, Herbert Leibowitz, Tom Mathews, William Phillips, Lloyd Schwartz, Harvey Shapiro, Annalyn Swan, and Michaela Williams.

Contents

I

Lines and Forms

Poetry, Verse and Prose
The End of the Line

*Monsieur Jourdain: Il n'y a que la prose
ou les vers?*

*Le Maître de Philosophie: Non, monsieur.
Tout ce qui n'est point prose est vers, et
tout ce qui n'est point vers est prose.*
—Molière, *Le Bourgeois Gentilhomme*

Whether as an act of rebellion against one set of conditions or of acquiescence to another, with conflicting intentions, amid intense pressures, the modern writer has willed a blurring of the line separating verse from prose; he has written poems that do not sound like poems, and look like them even less. This is undeniable, and we are right to be confused—it means the writer has done his work well, for the underlying impulse is to call into question our expectations as readers, our idea of poetic right and wrong. About the relative merits of some of the more extreme productions of recent years there is bound to be much debate, but the climate of confusion in which even our most traditionally minded poets participate is not one of misunderstanding pure and simple but of a calculated misunderstanding, a deliberate and radical process of exploration and excavation. An Ashbery poem that begins as a humorous meditation on some bad lines by Ella Wheeler Wilcox, moves on to couplets of poker-faced clichés in a calypso rhythm, and concludes with several seemingly inconsequential prose fragments spiked by stray lines of verse—this sort of confusion is intended, and has precious little to do with the long-standing

Published in *Shenandoah* (1982).

confusion, experienced by critics, scholars, and the reading public long before the age of experimentation, about the ever-fluctuating and uneasy relations between and among poetry and prose and verse. Of course, certain battles have long ago been fought and won, and the reader need no longer be especially enlightened to feel that Joyce's *Ulysses* is every inch as much a work of poetry as the verse *Ulysses* of Tennyson. A semantic confusion nevertheless remains inevitable in almost any conversation on the subject, simply because words like "poetry" and "poetic," "art" and "aesthetic," invite being taken in two, at times conflicting, senses: as descriptive terms, on the one hand, and as evaluative or judgmental terms on the other.

In *Principles of Literary Criticism*, I.A. Richards stated the problem succinctly:

> . . . at least two different sets of characters, due to different causes, are, in current usage, ambiguously covered by the term "aesthetic." It is very necessary to distinguish the sense in which merely putting something in a frame or writing it in verse gives it an "aesthetic character," from a sense in which value is implied. This confusion, together with other confusions, has made the term nearly useless.

In *Poetic Diction*, Owen Barfield offers a scheme to deal with the dilemma, suggesting a "spiritual distinction" between "poetic" and "prosaic" to complement the more exact opposition of "verse" to "prose." Barfield then goes on to give examples of "poetic verse," "prosaic verse," "prosaic prose," and "poetic prose." Yet even such an approach—designed to account for bad verse as well as for the prose poem—is not without its drawbacks, because all of these words are burdened with layer upon layer of conflicting connotations, and a proliferation of double meanings attends them all. Consider the opposition between "poetic prose" and "prosaic prose," which at first glance seems so attractive a way of differentiating the good from the bad, but which in fact turns out to be misleading to the point of being incorrect. For all its negative overtones, "prosaic" ought perhaps not to be a euphemism for bad or inconsequential. For Lionel Trilling, it is precisely a prosaic prose that is valuable and necessary in that form which he considers to be of the first importance, the novel:

> Mr. Eliot praises the prose of *Nightwood* for having so much affinity with poetry. This is not a virtue, and I believe that it will not be mistaken for a virtue by any novel of the near future which will interest us. The loss of a natural prose, one which has at least a seeming affinity with good common speech, has often been noted. It seems to me that the observation of the loss has been too complacently made and that its explanations, while ingenious, have had the intention of preventing it from being repaired in kind. A prose which approaches poetry has no doubt its own value, but it cannot serve to repair the loss of a straightforward prose, rapid, masculine, and committed to events, making its effects not by the single word or by the phrase but by words properly and naturally massed. I conceive that the creation of such a prose should be one of the conscious intentions of any novelist.

And as easily as "prosaic prose" can be used to praise, "poetic prose" can become a term of mild abuse, as when the French scholar Suzanne Bernard implies that the "poetic prose" of Chateaubriand is less valuable in its own right than in its evolutionary function as a primitive form that heralded the coming of the prose poem.

The semantic pitfalls are many. The prose of a Beckett or Stein must have struck its first readers as something else altogether from the Dickens they had been brought up on, and a reader today, notwithstanding the gift of superiority which hindsight bestows, will likely still be able to feel that shock the modernists took great pains to evoke. Further, a prose piece by William Burroughs—even if it consists entirely of a "cut up" of a given issue of *The Wall Street Journal*—is indubitably of another kind of prose from that proffered by the editors of that newspaper, and not because of the author's intention alone (although it may well be argued that intention, recognized and thus confirmed by the reader, or spectator, will suffice to differentiate *a urinal* from *the Urinal of Marcel Duchamp*). Again, the prose of even the most pedestrian of magazines differs dramatically in kind from a conversation between a waiter and his customers at a luncheonette. When Molière's "bourgeois gentilhomme" finds out he has been speaking prose all his life, it is a fine trick that Molière plays on him and on us; for inasmuch as M. Jourdain is a literary character, yes, he speaks prose and has done so unknowingly all along; but if we take him to represent a real-life personage, with a career offstage as it were, his statement is misleading and inaccurate. Scott Fitzgerald, Gertrude Stein noted in *The Autobiography of Alice B. Toklas,* "wrote naturally in sentences," a rare achievement—and rarer still the one who speaks naturally in sentences, who speaks in prose.

Nor is the word "verse" without its ambiguities and nasty overtones, of the kind that blunt our instruments of precision. One speaks of the "verses" of a minor poet as against the "poetry" of Wallace Stevens. "Verse" is sportsman's shorthand for the avocation of a spinster; "verses" belong on birthday cards. It is with this unhappy connotation in mind that Eliot says of a poem by Edgar Allan Poe, "It is, I am sure, 'poetry' and not 'verse.' " Yes, Pound admits, "prosaic" is used to damn, but "at the same time 'Poetry!!!' is used as a synonym for 'Bosh! Rott!! Rubbish!!!' " Or as Captain Lebyadkin in Dostoyevski's *The Possessed* remarks, slyly excusing an indiscretion of his, "Look on it as a poem and no more, for, after all, poetry is nonsense and justifies what would be considered impudence in prose." It is not surprising that a word imprecisely used and overused to refer to all things beautiful, sublime, tender, charming, and holy—by all romantics from Hazlitt to the rock singer of "Poetry in Motion"—should in the end be despised. We ought perhaps to be twice as cynical about bogus words as about the counterfeit emotions they instantly conjure up; this is the self-critical function every generation of speakers performs. Form becomes substance; sloppy language becomes foolish idea. Pound's famous declaration—that poetry ought to be at least as well-written as prose—is very much to the point.

The consternation a young critic feels when he realizes that his latest "original" profundity was uttered long ago by T.S. Eliot is only matched by the distress of learning that, whatever the given idea, Eliot in all probability contradicted himself at some other point in his career. The Eliot who called *Hamlet* a failure thought the prose poem an abomination, even though he had just added a remarkable one ("Hysteria") to the body of English literature. The later Eliot offers the following cogent summary of the problems of terminology I have just been describing. It occurs in the preface to his translation of *Anabasis,* by St. John Perse:

> I refer to this poem as a poem. It would be convenient if poetry were always verse—either accented, alliterative, or quantitative; but that is not true. Poetry may occur, within a definite limit on one side, at any point along a line of which the formal limits are "verse" and "prose." Without offering any generalized theory about "poetry," "verse," and "prose," I may suggest that a writer, by using, as does Mr. Perse, certain exclusively poetic methods, is sometimes able to write poetry in what is called prose. Another writer can, by reversing the process, write great prose in verse. There are two very simple but insuperable difficulties in any definition of "prose" and "poetry." One is that we have three terms where we need four: we have "verse" and "poetry" on the one side, and only "prose" on the other. The other difficulty follows from the first: that the words simply imply a valuation in one context which they do not in another. "Poetry" introduces a distinction between good verse and bad verse; but we have no one word to separate bad prose from good prose. As a matter of fact, much bad prose is poetic prose; and only a very small part of bad verse is bad because it is prosaic.

It is tempting to use "poetry" consistently as an evaluative term, and to use "prose" and "verse" as essentially descriptive terms, but it would be an ultimately self-defeating gesture, for language will doubtlessly always refuse to limit itself with scientific precision. A far more urgent task is the determination of what are the crucial and inescapable differences between verse and prose, and what are the peculiar attractions of each. Then, working inductively, we could try to locate the verbal gestures that convert the one or the other into poetry.

Some years ago, at a lecture delivered at Oxford, Christopher Ricks delighted in pointing out exceptions to the traditional distinctions separating prose from verse—such as the effort made by Robert Graves to set "the art of manifest statement" against "the rhythmic intoxication of verse." Having located the loopholes in the various definitions he quoted, Ricks threw a bomb at his rather inexperienced audience. The only real distinction between verse and prose, he asserted, is, because of its very obviousness, hidden, like Poe's purloined letter, in full view of everyone. Verse is in lines; prose runs to the end of the page. *C'est tout.* The effect on the audience was quite devastating. Most of the students resisted the notion at first, for it seemed somehow reductive of the high art into whose mysteries they had only just been ushered, but their arguments did not hold up. The logic is unassailable. Nor is it exactly a new idea. Northrop Frye has stated it:

> Jeremy Bentham is reputed to have distinguished prose from verse by the fact that in prose all the lines run to the end of the page. Like many simple-minded observations, this has a truth that the myopia of knowledgeability is more apt to overlook. The rhythm of prose is continuous, not recurrent, and the fact is symbolized by the purely mechanical breaking of prose lines on a printed page. Of course every prose writer knows that the writing of prose is not as mechanical as the printing of it, and that it is possible for printing to injure or even spoil the rhythm of a sentence by putting an emphatic word at the end of a line instead of at the beginning of the next one, by hyphenating a strongly stressed word, and so on. But the prose writer is largely the prisoner of his luck, unless he is willing to make the kind of revolt against luck illustrated by Mallarmé's *Coup de dés.*

If Mallarmé's oft-quoted remark, "Poems are made with words, not ideas," is as significant as we all seem to think it is, perhaps by similar logic we should, in our college classrooms, insist on repeating that verse is made of lines, rather than sentences. A look at the Latin roots of "verse" and "prose" confirms the radical truth of this observation. "Prosus" means "straight on"; "versus" denotes "turning," as our eyes turn at the end of a line. By definition, then, the writer of verse controls our turning, and thus our pace of reading and the emphasis we give to certain words; both sound and sense are affected, and sometimes actually governed, by this principle of lining, this revolt against luck. All truly that *vers libre* retained of traditional verse is its grammar of emphasis—for example, its potential for enjambment, the use of the turn at the end of a line for the purpose of emphasizing a word or disjointing a phrase into significantly separate parts. In his autobiographical *Early History of a Writer,* the Objectivist poet Charles Reznikoff charts the modern revolution of verse as a progression from metrics to "brand-new verse" distinguished only by its lining from "common speech":

I had been bothered by a secret weariness
with meter and regular stanzas
grown a little stale. The smooth lines and rhymes
seemed to me affected, a false stress on words and syllables—
fake flowers
in the streets in which I walked.
And yet I found prose
without the burst of song and the sudden dancing—
without the intensity which I wanted.
The brand-new verse some Americans were beginning to
    write—
after the French "free verse," perhaps,
or the irregular rhythms of Walt Whitman,
the English translations of the Hebrew Bible
and, earlier yet, the rough verse of the Anglo-Saxons—
seemed to me, when I first read it,
right:
not cut to patterns, however cleverly,
nor poured into ready moulds,
but words and phrases flowing as the thought;
to be read just as common speech
but for stopping at the turn of each line—
and this like a rest in music or a turn in the dance.

In such verse, Reznikoff adds in a parenthesis whose casualness makes a further point, the white space surrounding the writing, the pockets of air between the lines, give evidence enough of poetic intention and purpose:

(I found it no criticism that to read such verse as prose
was to have a kind of prose,
for that was not to read it as it was written.)

If, in an extreme of the plain style, lining could be held as the one formal requirement for verse poetry, the reason is that it is so often decisive in establishing the meaning of a poem. A pair of famous first lines will argue well for the significance of enjambment as a poetic device. Take the opening line of *Paradise Lost* away from what comes next, separate the fruit from the tree:

> Of man's first disobedience, and the fruit

Bordered on one side by a comma, and on the other by empty space, "fruit" is emphasized further, isolated further, by its position as the last word in the line, and by its metrical force, preceded as it is by a caesura and two unstressed syllables. The reader is asked to look at the fruit close up, to see it not only as the forbidden apple but as a word with various connected meanings, all of which come into play. "Fruit" suggests progeny and fertility, as in the biblical commandment "Be fruitful and multiply," God's first instruction to Adam. "Fruit" also suggests end-product or result, particularly a positive one, as in the phrase, "the fruits and evils of the Industrial Revolution," but it can also point to effects and consequences more generally, as when in the second act of *Hamlet* Polonius forbids his daughter from seeing the prince:

> "Lord Hamlet is a prince, out of thy star;
> This must not be": and then I precepts gave her,
> That she should lock herself from his resort,
> Admit no messengers, receive no tokens,
> Which done, she took the fruits of my advice. . . .

It is surely no accident that, upon inspection, the word "fruit" should prove so loaded. Within one context, it refers to "the fruit / Of that forbidden tree," the agent of man's fall, a specific moment in the history of the Garden of Eden, a single fruit of a certain, specific tree; in Book IX, Milton calls it "that fallacious fruit" (line 1046), which contains the fall of Adam and Eve even as the word "fallacious" does. Within another context, the word gestures back to the phrase that precedes it in the opening of the poem, completing that phrase; Milton announces his theme to be the depiction of the original sin and its aftermath, the act of disobedience and its fruits. One such "fruit" of the first sin is a punishment which contains the seeds of redemption; it is a fruitful fall, *felix culpa,* though at the most melancholic moment of the poem—the conclusion of Book IX—we are told of our initial parents that "they in mutual accusation spent / The fruitless hours" (lines 1187–88). Nevertheless, there is hope: from the forbidden tree comes wood for the cross, from suffering comes purgation and salvation. Labor is Adam's curse, but it is also the price of his readmission into paradise. As his labor in the fields will produce the fruit that will sustain him, so the fruits of Eve's womb—of the labor of childbirth—will include, many generations later, the one greater man who is the new Adam, Jesus Christ. If from evil the good is extracted, if God cheats Satan of his apparent victory by transforming the very mechanism of sin into the vehicle for man's redemption, then it stands to reason that the "fruit" in Milton's first line refers both to the cause and the effect of man's first disobedience. Paradise was both lost and regained in the eating of the apple, and it is only human time that separates the two events; the word unites them as they are united in the mind of the creator, it being the poet's mission to repeat a heavenly design. "Fruit" may thus be regarded as an example of textual self-reference, a word whose generative power poetically mirrors what it describes of God's workings.

The word "breeding" assumes a like significance in the opening line of *The Waste Land:*

> April is the cruellest month, breeding

Not by accident does the word occupy the strategic extreme of the line. Between "breeding" and "Lilacs from the dead land," between the participle and its object, falls what Donald Davie has called a "flicker of hesitation." "Breeding" hangs at the edge of space; a comma sets it off from

> April is the cruellest month

and blank space separates it from

> Lilacs out of the dead land.

"Breeding" gestures out to the whole poem, which may in fact be read as the death cry of a universe at whose metaphoric center is an abortion, a world that has bred failure and a world that has failed to breed at all. If Eliot uses the collage device to fragment the literary past in the same way that modern life has fragmented its cultural inheritances, and the familiar literary quotations are Eliot's way of marshalling the forces of tradition to mock an inadequate present day, then his use of "breeding" may be seen as wholly consistent with the strategy of the poem. The word creates its own context; it calls attention to itself for the purpose of signifying the very opposite of its customary denotation—just as April, which had signified rebirth and resurrection for poets from Chaucer to Shelley, has now become "the cruellest month."

For Eliot, the word carried a particularly negative charge and nasty valence. The word itself—and words of related meaning—occur throughout his work, of his late as well as of his early period, and always with a sting of contempt. The Jewish merchant in "Gerontion" wasn't born, but rather was "Spawned in some estaminet of Antwerp," amid sawdust and leftovers. "Spawned" is the first word of its line, capitalized emphatically, and emphatically stressed rhythmically—and behind it the reader senses something more general than anti-Semitism, something of a Coriolan complex, a disgust with the body and its demands altogether:

> My house is a decayed house,
> And the jew squats on the window sill, the owner,
> Spawned in some estaminet of Antwerp.

By eye and by ear the reader is led, by the effects of lining, to the word "Spawned," and so he cannot be surprised, when he turns to *Sweeney Agonistes*, to find the following summary of life on earth:

Birth, and copulation, and death.
That's all, that's all, that's all, that's all.
Birth, and copulation, and death.

Here the key word is the decidedly unromantic "copulation," which stands literally at the center of its line, as the tinny or thudlike part of the verse refrain. If Eliot could view the act that makes procreation possible in so unattractive a light— either because it expresses the tyranny of our bodies or because it exposes the psychic vulnerability of the human being—is it any wonder that he would seize on a failure of fruition as the theme that tied his own neuroses to the now hollow, now wasted, world of which he was, willy-nilly, a participant? (Eliot liked, not entirely because of his famous modesty, to attribute the composition of *The Waste Land* to the nervous breakdown that took him to Lac Leman, where he composed the poem.)

It is with an insistently pejorative connotation—not unlike that which Swift capitalizes on in "A Modest Proposal"—that Eliot intends us to regard our condition as "breeders." This is "the human condition" to which Reilly promises he can reconcile Celia in *The Cocktail Party*. It is a life of "the common routine," with

Two people who know they do not understand each other,
Breeding children whom they do not understand
And who will never understand them.

It is as if, in 1949, the world is still a waste land, and all that has changed for Eliot results from his recently acquired conviction that the condition of succumbing to despair is a curable one. The successful of us have succeeded as animals, as "breeders," rather than as parents made in the image of God; the only alternative held out to Celia, who wishes to escape from the common herd, is martyrdom and death. And if *The Waste Land* prepares us for *The Cocktail Party*—if the former is at all predictive of the spiritual career of its author—this too is suggested by the word "breeding" at the end of its opening line, with its suggestion that literature is still possible, that out of the chaos a poem may yet be bred, along with a tentative, verbal leap into salvation: "Shantih shantih shantih."

I have given several examples of how verse often depends for its effects on the manipulation of the space between and around the lines. A veritable inventory of examples, mostly culled from the blank verse of Milton and Wordsworth, is provided by Christopher Ricks in a remarkable essay on *The Prelude*. For Ricks,

> Reading should itself be a type of the proper relation of eye to ear; and the poet's lines—the relationships which he creates between the single line and its accommodating passage—must effect such a relationship of eye and ear.

Here is Ricks's gloss on these lines from *Home at Grasmere:*

> Dreamlike the blending of the whole
> Harmonious landscape; all along the shore
> The boundary lost, the line invisible
> That parts the image from reality;

The boundary is also that which we cross when we pass from one "line" to another; the "line invisible" is also that which separates one line from another, "invisible" because it is emblematised on the page by the white space. Invisible, but not non-existent; there is no thing solidly there, no formal punctuation, but there is nevertheless the parting—by means of a significant space, a significant vacancy—of one thing from another.

And here is Ricks's reading of these famous lines from "I Wandered Lonely as a Cloud":

> Continuous as the stars that shine
> Or twinkle on the milky way,
> They stretched in never-ending line
> Along the margin of a bay:
> Ten thousand saw I . . .

Not literally a "never-ending" line of daffodils, of course—any more than the line of verse itself is never-ending. Yet the fact that the verse line is not brought to an end by punctuation, the fact that it opens into unending space, allows the other aspect of the paradox to impinge on us too.

What a different effect would be obtained if a period were placed at the end of that line, Ricks rightly points out, and a comma were substituted for the colon that punctuates the line immediately following.

The argument is valid, too, for stanza breaks, on a yet more emphatic level. Witness the suspension of meaning that itself constitutes a meaning, achieved by the space and pause between the "forlorn" that ends the seventh stanza and the "forlorn" that opens the eighth and concluding stanza of "Ode to a Nightingale." And in everybody's favorite example of free verse, watch as the white space permits a sense of gradual and very deliberate unfolding, as of petals from a flower, without which Williams's famous poem could not possibly succeed:

> so much depends
> upon
>
> a red wheel
> barrow
>
> glazed with rain
> water
>
> beside the white
> chickens.

Williams's lining compels us to look very carefully and slowly at that which we might not otherwise see at all. A wheel turns into a wheelbarrow; we see white before we see the white chickens. If the poem instructs us on perception, it is the lining that drives the lesson home.

In turning his back on the line as the unit of composition, in choosing to rely fully on syntactical structure instead, the poet of prose has elected a different manner of punctuation, a less intrusive one, so that a certain tension is removed. A sentence of prose is a single cry, Herbert Read exclaimed, but compared with even the extended lines of Whitman, that cry can be a very long and loud one indeed, full of the complications of commas, which—to alter the metaphor—can act as "Stop" signs or as highway exits. In verse, the superimposition of line-structure onto sentence-structure creates an extra meaning; in prose, it is precisely the absence of this additional controlling device that accounts for a feeling of continuity in the writing, enabling the words to assume a different motion and direction. Between clauses within the one sentence, and between sentences—in the period created by the period—there occurs a vital tension, of thought acted upon by time. Prose might thus somehow seem more a matter of transition, juxtaposition, and transformation than of division and disjunction; a paragraph of prose is cumulative, whereas a verse stanza is integrative. So De Quincey saw it:

> The two capital secrets in the art of prose composition are these: 1st, The philosophy of transition and connection, or the art by which one step in an evolution of thought is made to arise out of another: all fluent and effective composition depends on the *connections;*—2dly, The way in which sentences are made to modify each other; for the most powerful effects in written eloquence arise out of this reverberation, as it were, from each other in a rapid succession of sentences.

To illustrate the first of these precepts, I shall offer as evidence sentences culled from Auden's *Age of Anxiety* and from Trilling's *Sincerity and Authenticity,* a volume of criticism. It is not my contention that Trilling's work be regarded as poetry, and I wish to avoid such a confusion; excellent prose need not aspire to the label of poetry to warrant our attention. I intend simply to delineate the effects good prose is capable of achieving, effects very different from those of verse, in the hope of arriving at a partial answer to why modern poets have felt an attraction to prose as a medium. Here, then, is the opening one-sentence paragraph of Auden's *Age of Anxiety:*

> When the historical process breaks down and armies organize with their embossed debates the ensuing void which they can never consecrate, when necessity is associated with horror and freedom with boredom, then it looks good to the bar business.

And here is the grand finale of *Sincerity and Authenticity:*

> The falsities of an alienated social reality are rejected in favour
> of an upward psychopathic mobility to the point of divinity,
> each one of us a Christ—but with none of the inconveniences
> of undertaking to intercede, of being a sacrifice, of reasoning
> with rabbis, of making sermons, of having disciples, of going to
> weddings and to funerals, of beginning something and at a
> certain point remarking that it is finished.

Notice how both sentences effect startling transformations—
of trope, of tone, and of thought—and how vital to the mean-
ing is the transition from one to the other. Shifting in mid-
gear from the language of philosophical abstraction to the
language of epigram and then from the elegance of the latter
to the language of the street, Auden achieves several things at
once. His prose enacts a tension between History with a capi-
tal "h" and the reality that defines itself as the precise intersec-
tion of an exact moment and a specific locale. The ironic way
he collapses his own eloquence is like a miniature of his in-
tended sense of the eclogue form employed in the book—as a
clash of artificial diction and "natural" setting, of alliterative
verse and a Third Avenue bar, of the "embossed" (meaning
"highly ornamented") and the unrefined. The commas here
function as intermediaries; the divisions of the thought are by
syntactical unit. Thus,

(1) When the historical process breaks down and armies orga-
     nized with their embossed debates the ensuing void which
     they can never consecrate,
(2) when necessity is associated with horror and freedom
     with boredom,
(3) then it looks good to the bar business.

The second clause modifies the first in two ways: it appears to
be a restatement of it in condensed form, and it reveals the
"ensuing" step in a sequence of events. The use of anaphora,
and the powerful parallelism in the second clause, make all
the more jolting the curt, surprising third clause, which con-

tains only one word of more than one syllable. The result is funny, as a nervous laugh is funny—the humor tempered by the ironic realization that there is no cause for merriment. For as much as there seems to be a causal relationship among the three clauses—which accounts for humor, that the "horror" of "necessity" should lead to a prosaic shot of whiskey—the three clauses can also be seen as translations of one another, as perfectly reasonable verbal correlatives of the same situation.

While Auden's sentence takes a dip, Trilling's moves from low to high, in rather a flight than a climb, as befits a concluding sentence. He begins by borrowing from the jargon of sociology and, in applying it to the matter of mental health—a matter for which it seems decidedly inappropriate—he enacts linguistically the tension that informs this last chapter of *Sincerity and Authenticity*. It is the tension between rivaling conceptions of madness and thus between what Trilling regards as a false and a true authenticity of being. The will to madness as a social value is presented in sociological terms, in a language as abstracted from human reality as the subject of Trilling's inquiry is "alienated" from "social reality":

> The falsities of an alienated social reality are rejected in favour of an upward psychopathic mobility to the point of divinity. . . .

Poetic, even as the above is deliberately anti-poetic, the grand, heroic closing metaphor is suggested by the simile ("to the point of divinity") which at first seemed of rather little importance; this is, in Harold Bloom's language, "the trope of a trope," a qualification that supersedes what it was intended to qualify:

> to the point of divinity, each one of us a Christ—but with none of the inconveniences of undertaking to intercede, of being a sacrifice, of reasoning with rabbis, of making sermons, of having disciples, of going to weddings and to funerals, of beginning something and at a certain point remarking that it is finished.

From the Christ-complex of the first half of the sentence, the reader moves to an absent actuality of Christ, in clear and precise human detail, the negative expression ("none") acting as a critique of what Trilling had earlier called the "form of assent which does not include actual credence" that underscores "the doctrine that madness is health . . . liberation and authenticity." The inventory effect, the rhythmic regularity of the repeated participle ending, creates speed, communicates urgency. This part of the sentence may be diagrammed thus:

> of the inconveniences
> > of undertaking to intercede,
> > of being a sacrifice,
> > of reasoning with rabbis,
> > of making sermons,
> > of going to weddings
> > > and to funerals,

This is followed by the text's artful self-reference, the boldness of saying "goodbye" matched by the boldness of comparing the task of literary composition to the project of an authentic Christ. That is the triumph of the final phrase in this summary life of Jesus:

> of beginning something and at a certain point remarking that it is finished.

Kafka's parable of "Abraham," admirably translated by Clement Greenberg, illustrates exceptionally well the second of De Quincey's "two capital secrets in the art of prose composition"—i.e., the modification of a sentence by its successor. Kafka has given us "An Abraham who should come unsummoned!" He is quite unlike Kierkegaard's latter-day Abraham, whose conference with God is dismissed as lunacy, whose sacrifice of Isaac is forbidden by his pastor. His dilemma is still an existential one, but it is hardly of a heroic character. The torments are those of a grade-school classroom:

> It is as if, at the end of the year, when the best student was solemnly about to receive a prize, the worst student rose in the expectant stillness and came forward from his dirty desk in the last row because he had made a mistake of hearing, and the

whole class burst out laughing. And perhaps he had made no mistake at all, his name really was called, it having been the teacher's intention to make the rewarding of the best student at the same time a punishment for the worst one.

In the pause between period and capital letter exists the pivotal point of the paradox, the space that permits the "either" to turn into "and," the mistake into intention, the mild schoolmaster into a god whose distinguishing feature is his *Schadenfreude*, the malicious joy with which he metes out judgment and exercises his authority. This twist of meaning, a wholly syntactic one, is as crucial to Kafka's cosmic jokes as it is to more conventional expressions of Jewish wit and humor.

Virginia Woolf opens an essay on "De Quincey's Autobiography" by remarking that

> It must often strike the reader that very little criticism worthy of being called so has been written in English of prose—our great critics have given the best of their minds to poetry. And the reason perhaps why prose so seldom calls out the higher faculties of the critic, but invites him to argue a case or to discuss the personality of the writer—to take a theme from the book and make his criticism an air played in variation of it—is to be sought in the prose-writer's attitude to his own work. Even if he writes as an artist, without a practical end in view, still he treats prose as a humble beast of burden which must accommodate all sorts of odds and ends; as an impure substance in which dust and twigs and flies find lodgment.

Woolf's own prose gives sufficient evidence of a change in "the prose-writer's attitude to his own work," of an attempt by the modernists to purify the dialect of the tribe in prose no less than in verse. All of the devices associated with "language charged with meaning"—Pound's definition of poetry—have been expropriated by the writer of prose: ambiguity and complexity, rhythmic richness, secondary meanings, irony, and what Blackmur has called "language as gesture." It is, however, also worth noting that to John Ashbery prose has seemed an inspiring medium precisely *because* it is "an impure substance in which dust and twigs and flies find lodgment." And as much as

Ashbery has successfully blended certain elements of prose into the verse poems of *The Double Dream of Spring* and *Self-Portrait in a Convex Mirror,* he has also unleashed the forces of verse into his prose poems, most notably in "Idaho," the final poem in *The Tennis Court Oath.* This work begins with—and at certain points it reverts to—a deliberately flat prose narration: "During the past few months, Biff had become quite a frequent visitor to Carol's apartment." After several paragraphs composed of descriptive sentences of this sort, the prose is interrupted, cut up, literally "spaced out." The typewriter itself seems to go wild, as Ashbery puts into poetic practice a method of erasure similar to that exemplified by Robert Rauschenberg's famous erasure of a de Kooning drawing. Underscoring the erasure is the knowledge that something of the original will indubitably survive the process, albeit in an altered and mysterious form. Here is an example, from "Idaho," of prose metamorphosed into verse, via what Ashbery elsewhere calls "this leaving-out business":

> Carol was aware today, however, that Biff had
> suddenly become obsessed with a sense of her;
> that he had caught fire. She was aware of
>
>   vast excitement,
>   apprehension,
>   a mental
>
> "Can I give you a hand?"
> She gave a little cry that was silenced by mouth on
>   uttermost tingling nerve
> "Carol!" he said. Can this be the one time
> ??????????????????????????????

It is as if the orderly universe of prose syntax has crumbled, confronted by impulses it cannot control.

Eliot's single prose poem, "Hysteria," is in many ways an exemplary work (though it receives scant attention in the many critical tomes devoted to its author) for its skilled manipulation of certain of the prose qualities that I have mentioned in this essay. The poem opens *in medias res:*

> As she laughed I was aware of becoming involved in her laughter and being part of it,

and the effect of the pronoun is to refer the reader outside of the poem, perhaps to an absent story from which this may be taken as an excerpt, perhaps to an inaccessible, irrecoverable life of hints and guesses behind the poem. Pointing as it does to a time before, the opening phrase takes cognizance of the problem of beginning (a metaphysical impossibility, equivalent to a fruitless search for a first cause) even as it begins. Eliot then translates the involvement with laughter into metaphor, supplying the concrete correlative of the abstract phrase, thereby renewing the latter by taking it surprisingly literally. Here, the matter-of-fact prose tone contributes significantly:

> until her teeth were only accidental stars with a talent for squad drill.

The mixture of military and celestial metaphors communicates with some urgency the ambivalence toward the feminine—"hysteria" derives from a word denoting womb—that characterizes the initial volume of Eliot's poetry, *Prufrock and Other Observations,* in which "Hysteria" appeared.

The second sentence of the poem takes us further inside, womb or mouth, in a repetition of gasps:

> I was drawn in by short gasps, inhaled at each momentary recovery, lost finally in the dark caverns of her throat, bruised by the ripple of unseen muscles.

The narrative reasserts itself, but the "trembling" repetition of a quotidian phrase works eerily to upset the order of a formal garden:

> An elderly waiter with trembling hands was hurriedly spreading a pink and white checked cloth over the rusty green iron table, saying: "If the lady and gentleman wish to take their tea in the garden, if the lady and gentleman wish to take their tea in the garden. . . ."

Notice how the ellipsis reinforces the feeling of fragmentation, a lack of resolution combined with a postponement of dread (akin to the effect achieved by the insistent "HURRY UP PLEASE IT'S TIME" in part two of *The Waste Land*).

The final sentence of "Hysteria" announces a plan of action that is contradicted by the poem's very existence, for it is very much an uncollected fragment:

> I decided that if the shaking of her breasts could be stopped,
> some of the fragments of the afternoon could be collected, and
> I concentrated my attention with careful subtlety to this end.

To end on such a note in verse might well be disastrous because too emphatic; but in prose it is subtle and wry—it works because the poem is so clearly without a true ending, having to content itself instead with an arbitrary end.

Notes on Poetic Form

I.

A distrust of received forms seems endemic to American poets. It is predicated on the conviction that depth or complexity of vision, force of passion, profundity of insight, or whatever it is that distinguishes art from mere craft will invariably precede rather than follow from a formal maneuver. This view found its first great exemplar in Whitman's "Song of Myself"—and its first great sponsor in Emerson:

> For it is not metres, but a metre-making argument, that makes a poem,—a thought so passionate and alive, that, like the spirit of a plant or an animal, it has an architecture of its own, and adorns nature with a new thing. The thought and the form are equal in the order of time, but in the order of genesis the thought is prior to the form.

That Emerson's edict continues to have its adherents is clear. Alice Fulton has restated the case: "During the act of writing, technique and meaning are inextricably linked, and it is only for the convenience of critical discussion that one could wish to separate them. The realization that craft depends on content leads to the concept of organic form and the idea that whatever elements help us experience a poem as a whole can be called its form."

Perhaps it betokens the rise of a new formalism that a rival

Adapted from the Afterword of *Ecstatic Occasions, Expedient Forms*, edited by David Lehman (New York: Macmillan, 1987).

notion—that "in the order of genesis" form may precede thought—seems on the ascendant. (By "a new formalism" I mean to designate the tendency as such rather than the specific group or movement of poets who have banded together under one or another label, issuing proclamations.) Certainly there has been a resurgence of interest in forms traditional or exotic—forms that can themselves create the occasion for poetry. Some regard this development as yet another manifestation of the back-to-basics spirit evident in other areas of cultural activity. Or is it that the emerging generation of poets is acting in filial rebellion against predecessors who valued nothing so much as what Whitman called the "barbaric yawp"? In any event, it is possible that the preoccupation with poetic form is precisely what distinguishes this generation from the last. A number of celebrated younger poets are clothing their poems in the traditional raiments of rhyme and meter. Others have embraced a principle of poetic form that follows from two key premises: that imaginative freedom can flourish amid self-imposed restrictions and that originality starts from a mastery of tradition, not an ignorance thereof. There are also those who remain solidly committed to free verse—they might write prose poems, but never a villanelle (never one that rhymes anyway)—but who are nevertheless engaged to the point of obsession with the form and appearance and design of their work. In this category one thinks of Jorie Graham, whose meanings are inextricable from the effects she obtains through her experimentation with form: for example, her substitution of blanks for words in several poems, or her unusual lining and punctuation—she may end a poem in the middle of a sentence with a dash instead of a period. These are formal choices, as crucial to the outcome in Graham's case as another poet's decision to write a double sestina using the same end-words that Swinburne used in *his* double sestina a hundred years ago.

II.

Subscribing to the traditional paradox that liberty most flourishes when most held in check, John Ashbery offers a shrewdly pragmatic explanation for his interest in the exotic pantoum. "I was attracted to the form," he writes, "because of its stricture, even greater than in other hobbling forms such as the sestina or canzone. These restraints seem to have a paradoxically liberating effect, for me at least." Ashbery concludes with sly deadpan: "The form has the additional advantage of providing you with twice as much poem for your effort, since every line has to be repeated twice."

To an important extent, such formal scheming casts the poet in the guise of problem-solver. In the course of working out the puzzle he has set for himself, a poem will get written—not as an afterthought, but as an inevitable by-product of the process. By this logic, the tougher the formal problem, the better—the more likely it is to act as a sort of broker between language, chance, and the poet's instincts. "And this may indeed be one way that 'form' helps the poet," Anthony Hecht observes. "So preoccupied is he bound to be with the fulfillment of technical requirements that in the beginning of his poem he cannot look very far ahead, and even a short glance forward will show him that he must improvise, reconsider and alter what had first seemed to him his intended direction, if he is to accommodate the demands of his form." This is desirable, notes Hecht, if the aim is—as Robert Frost said it was—an outcome that is both "unforeseen" and "predestined."

No doubt it's the prevalence of this aim that accounts for the sestina's unprecedented popularity among modern poets. The votaries in the sestina chapel may begin with Sir Philip Sidney ("Ye Goatherd Gods"), but there then follows a gap of three centuries before the procession is renewed by Rossetti and Pound, Auden and Elizabeth Bishop, and innumerable poets since. Allowing for maximum maneuverability within a tightly controlled space, the sestina has a special attraction for the poet in search of a formal device with which to scan his unconscious. Writing a sestina, Ashbery once remarked, is like riding downhill on a bicycle while the pedals push your feet. The analogy makes the whole procedure sound exhilarating, risky, and somewhat foolhardy, making it irresistible. Paradoxically, the very ubiquity of the sestina—it's a favorite in creative writing workshops—has recently begun to argue against it. The logic is Yogi Berra's: "Nobody eats at that restaurant anymore—it's too crowded."

III.

The question of measure and meter has been undergoing reexamination of late—inevitably, as poets discuss and dispute their ideas about form. Brad Leithauser, in a controversial essay entitled "Metrical Literacy," has argued that "poetry is a craft which, like carpentry, requires a long apprenticeship merely to assimilate its tools" and that meter is a true and perhaps indispensable implement in the trade. "Metrical illiteracy is, for the poet, functional illiteracy," Leithauser concludes. Nor is he alone in taking arms against plain speech: more than one poet has noted, with pleasure or alarm, that their contemporaries have brought back meter as a vital concern. The debate on the question is far from being one- or even two-sided. Douglas Crase, for example, doesn't place any the less value on finding a true measure even if he is little concerned with anapests and dactyls. What Crase wants is a meter suitable to an American vernacular and an American reality. He proposes "the 'civil meter' of American English, the meter we hear in the propositions offered by businessmen, politicians, engineers, and all our other real or alleged professionals. If you write in this civil meter, it's true you have to give up the Newtonian certainties of the iamb. But you gain a stronger metaphor for conviction by deploying the recognizable, if variable patterns of the language of American power."

Perhaps it would help to clarify the question of prosody, without simplifying it too much, if we rephrased it as an issue involving the desired amount of resistance that the poet wishes his medium to exert. Let two English poets argue the question for us. Here is Craig Raine defending his preference for unrhymed couplets in his book *A Martian Sends a Postcard Home:* "Technique is something you learn in order to reach a point where you're writing what you want with the minimum of interference. The unrhymed couplet interested me as something in which I could write fluently. Any verse, however, with a fair amount of freedom in it is actually much harder to write than strict verse." By contrast, Geoffrey Hill endorses "the proposal that form is not only a technical containment but is possibly also an emotional and ethical containment. In the act of refining technique one is not only refining emotion, one is also constantly defining and redefining one's ethical and moral sensibility." What Hill wants is more resistance, not less; he distrusts the very fluency that Raine prizes, and opts for a "harder" severity than "freedom" allows for. Hill endorses C. H. Sisson's remark: "There is in Hill a touch of the fastidiousness of Crashaw, which is that of a mind in search of artifices to protect itself against its own passions." Form as artifice or form as the path of least resistance, a maze or a straight line, a way of reining in the imagination or a method for letting it roam free, a container or a ceaseless stream: the permutations are endless.

Tales of the Oulipo

The unlikely protagonist of Georges Perec's *Life, A User's Manual* is an apartment house in Paris—with all its inhabitants, past and present, viewed from the vantage point of a single June evening in 1975. *Life* is a parade of beguiling tales, a festival of clever puzzles. There are brain-teaser detective stories, chess problems, bizarre contraptions and games ("electronic feedbackgammon") and Kafkaesque parables (a trapeze artist who refuses to come down from the air)—not to mention such artistic curiosities as a musical score in the pattern of a crossword puzzle, "with the across and down lines corresponding to sequences of chords and the blacked-out boxes serving as rests."

The novel's ultimate puzzle is designed by a wealthy English eccentric named Bartlebooth. After ten years of taking lessons in watercolor painting, Bartlebooth spends twenty years painting five hundred seascapes in as many ports around the world. Each is sent back to Paris, where a puzzle maker makes a 750-piece jigsaw out of it. For the next twenty years Bartlebooth plans to reconstruct each puzzle in turn. He will then return to the five hundred ports, bringing the original watercolors (there's a method for detaching the picture from the puzzle). Finally, he will apply a chemical to remove the paint from the picture—and end with blank paper. The concept of this self-erasing work of art is as suggestive as it is enigmatic; it implies that the artistic impulse expires in the act of being satisfied.

Perec, who died in 1982 at the age of forty-six, was simply

Newsweek (international ed.), February 8, 1988.

the most ingenious member of a Paris-based group of experimental writers and mathematicians called the Oulipo. The name is an acronym for Ouvroir de Littérature Potentielle, which translates as "Workshop for [or Sewing Circle of] Potential Literature." Its mission since its birth in 1960 has been to reconstruct rare literary forms or invent new ones—the stricter the better. Oulipians contend that constraints are necessary to the creation of literature, that inspiration is just a fancy name for linguistic gamesmanship. As Warren Motte notes in *Oulipo,* his excellent anthology of Oulipiana, these writers have likened themselves to "rats who must build the labyrinth from which they propose to escape." And what marvelous mazes they have constructed!

Raymond Queneau, the group's co-founder, contrived to write 10^{14} sonnets—*one hundred trillion sonnets*—by a procedure involving the interchanging of lines. Jean Lescure proposed the "N + 7" method of composition: for every noun in a given text, you substitute the noun seven places away in the dictionary of your choice. Perec revived the lipogram—a composition that deliberately excludes one or more letters of the alphabet—in *La Disparition* ("The Disappearance"). This three-hundred-page novel was written without the benefit of the letter *e.* Consider that the vowel occurs as frequently in French as in English and you'll recognize Perec's achievement as both heroic and monumentally eccentric. For the sake of symmetry, Perec later wrote a novel in which *e* is the *only* vowel.

Long a well-kept transatlantic secret, the Oulipo has begun to attract a dedicated U.S. following. Witness the wonderfully fresh and inventive plot machinations in Harry Mathews's *Cigarettes.* . . . Mathews, the only American member of the Oulipo, offers a daisy chain of linked lives centering on Greenwich Village and Saratoga Springs, among the posh and artsy racehorse set, in the late 1930s and the early 1960s. There are thirteen characters, but they come to us only two at a time. Each of fourteen chapters focuses on a different pairing—there's a destructive father-daughter relationship, a harrowing sadomasochistic affair, and so on. Only gradually and by implication does the full plot emerge. . . .

Mathews serves an uncompromisingly avant-garde muse. This is how he describes a central theme: "Language and what it cannot say, or: how poetic language says that it cannot say what it means and so succeeds in meaning what it doesn't say." The centerpiece of *Armenian Papers: Poems 1954–1984* is "Trial Impressions," a sequence of thirty versions of the text of an Elizabethan song. The song turns into a multiple-choice narrative here and an equivoque there; Mathews specializes in homemade forms as well as recondite ones. "Histoire" is a madcap and hilarious sestina whose repeating end words are "militarism," "Marxism-Leninism," "Fascism," "Maoism," "racism," and "sexism." None of them mean what you think they mean, and none will ever sound the same again.

Enchanted readers will want to check out Mathews's splendid early novels, *The Conversions* and *Tlooth,* available in new paperback editions. Both are picaresque adventures that beggar description. The point of departure in *The Conversions* is a rich man's capricious will. To gain his fortune, the successful heir must supply the answers to such riddles as "When was a stone not a king?" and "Who shaved the Old Man's Beard?" Thus begins this merriest of wild chases.

Exposure to Oulipo methods may well be the best kind of training for students of creative writing. Poet David Shapiro, an Oulipo admirer, jokes that he began to appreciate the lipogram "when my three-year-old son broke the 'T' on my typewriter." Shapiro discovered that the rigor of the form made possible an imaginative release. And what else is any form but an experiment with language? James Joyce was, in Oulipo parlance, a "plagiarist by anticipation." But not even Joyce ever managed the stunt Perec once pulled off: a palindrome—a phrase that reads the same in both directions—1,200 words long.

II

Seven Poets

Three Meditations on Wallace Stevens

I.

Dominant X

The vital, arrogant, fatal, dominant X.
—"The Motive for Metaphor"

X. distrusts action; he has his *is*,
His *was,* which shall be again, when
The jangle of change is spent, the jingle
Of jargon clicks off, and peace in the jungle
Reigns in the tiger's snore, as before.

He has the exact change in his pocket.
He deposits it in the small glass booth
Of the bus he boards on his way to work.
He distrusts action; he has his window,
His view, and there is nothing he can do

To alter the ego of the age except now
And then to turn poplars into cypresses,
Poppies into irises, Monet to Van Gogh;
To turn, and then, turn back again.

"Three Meditations on Wallace Stevens" was written in 1981, the year I held a fellowship at Cornell University's Society for the Humanities. The Society's theme that year was "culture versus nature." The piece was published in *Shenandoah* in 1981.

II.

Negativity

After the final no there comes a yes
And on that yes the future world depends.
No was the night. Yes is this present sun.

*

It can never be satisfied, the mind, never.
    —"The Well Dressed Man with a Beard"

Wallace Stevens seems nearly as fond of negative expressions, of nots and nevers and nuncles, as of jovial hullabaloos ("Such tink and tank and tunk-a-tunk-tunk") and state-of-being verbs. Three separate sentences in *Harmonium* negate the possibility of spring: "No spring can follow past meridian," the middle-aged lover sighs in "Le Monocle de Mon Oncle," and the same sentiment concludes both "Indian River" ("Yet there is no spring in Florida, neither in boskage perdu, nor on the nunnery beaches") and "Depression Before Spring" ("But no queen comes / In slipper green"). It is easy to see the attractions this rhetorical device would have for the autumnal Mr. Stevens, whose speculations on the nature and function of the imagination take as their starting point a condition of absence, "An absence in reality, / Things as they are." But in achieving their primary aim, that of indicating and specifying an absence, Stevens's negative expressions serve also as a means of inclusion, of making present in the text what is missing from the reality external to it, the reality defined as "things as they are." "There are no bears among the roses," Stevens writes in "The Virgin Carrying a Lantern," thereby compelling the reader precisely to juxtapose the bears and the roses, just as Eliot's Prufrock invites us to compare him to Hamlet when he says "No, I am not Prince Hamlet, nor was meant to be." The negative in both cases creates an ambiguity; put either statement in positive form and you diminish, if not demolish, its poetic impact.

For Stevens, here as elsewhere, the *no* acts as a pivotal point in the encounter or exchange between reality and the imagination. As in Samuel Beckett's *Watt,* whose eponymous hero is employed by the elusive Mr. Knott, the relations between *what* and *not* form a crucial subplot in Stevens's poetry, and we would do well to scrutinize some of his negative expressions for the light they may shed on his "motive for metaphor" and on the perpetual swinging of his poetic pendulum from absence to presence and back.

Stevens frequently uses *not* as a more accurate way of saying *like*—as a negative simile. A literalist of the imagination, he habitually dons his philosopher's hat in an effort to strip away from a "plain sense of things" those fictions that are merely falsehoods, that cheapen by sentimentalizing actuality. "The accuracy of accurate letters is an accuracy with respect to the structure of reality," he pronounces rather severely in *The Necessary Angel.* It is this side of Stevens that insists, even as he exuberantly metamorphoses a pineapple, that the poet "must say nothing of the fruit that is / Not true, nor think it, less." (One notes that the enjambment here compromises the face value of the injunction; the double negative makes a positive only after giving the misleading appearance of negative intent.) The "literalist" attitude is epitomized in the Williamsian title of Stevens's late poem "Not Ideas about the Thing but the Thing Itself." It is as though, preparatory to the imagination's redemptive activity, the poet must take pains to behold life unadorned and man unaccommodated, to oppose an empty spirit to a vacant place. Relentlessly he must distinguish the naked *is* from the mythic and no longer credible *was,* as in the World War I poem, "The Death of a Soldier":

> He does not become a three-days personage,
> Imposing his separation,
> Calling for pomp.

Heaven is empty; we live without a belief in nobility, let alone in miracles, and so the soldier's sacrifice is bereft of both the hope of resurrection and the power to impose itself upon the collective consciousness of humankind.

Nowhere does Stevens spell out with greater clarity the value of negativity as trope than in "Study of Two Pears," where, with Cézanne-like concentration, he affixes the beam of his gaze on an ordinary day's still life. The poem represents the turn to which "Someone Puts a Pineapple Together" provides the "tropically" sublime counter-turn. Like the latter, it bills itself as an "academic piece"—its first words are "Opusculum paedagogum"—but there the resemblance ends. To use the categories set up in Stevens's essay "The Noble Rider and the Sound of Words," "Study of Two Pears" is emphatically "favorable to what is real." "The pears are not seen / As the observer wills," the poem concludes; no, they must be seen "as in themselves they really are" (Matthew Arnold). Thus,

> The pears are not viols,
> Nudes or bottles.
> They resemble nothing else.

The "not" skirts the borderline separating metaphor from simile or, more exactly, it defines the essential difference between the two figures. The double negative serves to differentiate *seems* from *is,* in the name of letting "be be finale of seem." Two statements having equal validity are implied: "the pears resemble what they are not" and "the pears are not what they resemble." But in so distinguishing pears from "viols, / Nudes or bottles," has the poet not brought these very objects together? Has he not in fact shown us the pears "as in themselves they really are not" (Oscar Wilde)? The "not," then, effectively turns the sentence into the antithesis of its own thesis. It furthers an accurate perception of reality, reminding us that the identity of a thing involves the subtraction of all its *semblables.* At the same time, however, it admits into the picture plane the possibility of a proliferation of resemblances. Stevens has it both ways. He makes us see the fruits as simultaneously distinct from, and like, the things of their shape and climate.

In poems that celebrate the mind's ability to abstract the real and place it in an enchanted realm, the metamorphoses forbidden in "Study of Two Pears" take place, whether despite or because of an intervening "not" or its equivalent. The heliotrope, in "Gubbinal," assumes the guise of

> That strange flower, the sun,
>
> .   .   .   .
>
> That tuft of jungle feathers,
> That animal eye,
>
> .   .   .   .   .   .
>
> That savage of fire,
> That seed.

Here the place of the *not* is taken by the imagined reply of the skeptic to whom the poem is addressed, who would presumably reject such primitive magic. "Have it your way," Stevens tells this straw man; and if you do,

> The world is ugly,
> And the people are sad.

Such is the bleakness that comes from yielding without a struggle to "the pressure of reality." Nor does Stevens fail to let us know what kind of struggle he endorses. Among other things, it requires the assertion of an irrational myth-mindedness, the will to dissolve distinctions and to lift, by disbelieving, "the weight of primary noon." The naysayer in one must somehow be neutralized, the force of his negativity refocused, in order for things to break out of their confined limits, for them to conjugate and bring forth strange fruit, and for the tree they grow on to branch out in numerous metaphorical directions.

By its very title, "Study of Two Pears" had defined its project as an examination of what already exists. "Someone Puts a Pineapple Together," on the contrary, leaps from perception to construction and creation. In the course of the poem, "Someone" (the writer? the reader?) makes a mountain out of a pineapple; the poem charts

> The momentary footings of a climb
> Up the pineapple, a table Alp and yet
> An Alp, a purple southern mountain bisqued
>
> With the molten mixings of related things,
> Cat's taste possibly or possibly Danish lore,
> The small luxuriations that portend

Universal delusions of universal grandeurs,
The slight incipiencies, of which the form,
At last, is the pineapple on the table or else

An object the sum of its complications, seen
And unseen. This is everybody's world.
Here the total artifice reveals itself

As the total reality.

The pineapple has become an Alp, albeit "a table Alp"; the adjectival qualification has cushioned the force of negation sufficiently to permit the transformation to go on unimpeded. Whereas the "not" of "Study of Two Pears" warns the observer against seeing things as they might be, there is no such superego interference in the pineapple poem. The charm of this invitation extended to the power of possibility is that, far from effecting an unreal product, it leads to "the total reality." The fruit is "more truly" seen as "more strange." It is valuable precisely because it is "a fund" of images and because, in the words of another Stevens title, "Reality is an Activity of the Most August Imagination." Thanks to the fortuitous encounter of the pineapple and the imagination on the dining-room table, "the profusion of metaphor has been increased." In the Florida of the mind the pineapple has, through the agency of metaphor, transcended itself.

Traveling the road to metaphor, which is the road to a supreme fiction, the poet has had to hurdle the high posts of negativity. He has had to say "no" to "no"; he must, he knows, "divest reality / Of its propriety." How? By adding imagination, itself a part of reality; that is, by seeing the imagination as not incompatible with reality, which it means to complement not cancel. As a result of the process, "casual exfoliations" in the form of twelve pineapple plots, each "of the tropic of resemblances," each with the characteristic odor of the fruit, rise up into view, numbered for convenience's sake:

1. The hut stands by itself beneath the palms.
2. Out of their bottle the green genii come.
3. A vine has climbed the other side of the wall.

4. The sea is spouting upward out of rocks.
5. The symbol of feasts and of oblivion . . .
6. White sky, pink sun, trees on a distant peak.

7. These lozenges are nailed-up lattices.
8. The owl sits humped. It has a hundred eyes.
9. The coconut and cockerel in one.

10. This is how yesterday's volcano looks.
11. There is an island Palahude by name—
12. An uncivil shape like a gigantic haw.

Each of the twelve is an aesthetic prerogative, a potential starting block for a purely imaginary race around the track of an "abstracted" reality. In each case, the fiction is left for the reader to complete so as virtually to ensure that he or she become an active participant in the proceedings. Whether the volcano erupts again, whether the genii grant our wishes or confound them, whether the distant peak is reached, is immaterial; it is the possibility that counts.

In certain of Stevens's poems, the *not* cooperates quite amenably with the impulse toward divine, or at least exotic, potentiality. In "Disillusionment of Ten O'Clock," the negative expression permits the reader to behold something that is not there to compensate for the nothing that is. Only the first two lines of the poem concern themselves directly with inadequate actuality. The tone is sarcastic:

> The houses are haunted
> By white night-gowns.

The rest of the poem is given to lush alternatives to the drab and sterile suburban night:

> None are green,
> Or purple with green rings,
> Or green with yellow rings,
> Or yellow with blue rings.
> None of them are strange,
> With socks of lace
> And beaded ceintures.

> People are not going
> To dream of baboons and periwinkles.
> Only, here and there, an old sailor,
> Drunk and asleep in his boots,
> Catches tigers
> In red weather.

We see, in effect, as on a split screen—things as they bleakly are, intimated by the reiterated negatives, off to one side, and things changed upon the blue guitar on the other side. The crucial words in the poem are *none* and *or* and *not,* for they make possible the multiplication of illusions. And by the poem's conclusion, no "no"—only an "only"—is needed to modify the figure of the poet as an old but virile sailor. What is absent from the real night has been made present in the poem, while what is present in the night becomes a shadowy "not," an absence, in the poem. We began with the disillusionment of the title and we end with fresh "illusionment" and the promise of more. This is entirely in line with Stevens's objections, made at several points in *The Necessary Angel,* to the "disillusory" enterprise of Freud's *The Future of an Illusion.* Such zealous rationalism, Stevens argues, is "inimical to poetry."

"Things as they are," then, frequently amount to embodied nothingness. Seeing them that way becomes an exercise in negative capability and as such is an indispensable preliminary to the sleight-of-hand man's main act. "The Snow Man" is only the most devastating example of the equation of *what* and *not* in Stevens's poetry:

> For the listener, who listens in the snow,
> And, nothing himself, beholds
> Nothing that is not there and the nothing that is.

The weight of the definite article, both here and at the end of "The Man on the Dump," has occasioned much comment, but the double sense of "nothing" is equally worthy of consideration. The word is primal in the sense Freud intends in his essay "The Antithetical Sense of Primal Words": it means itself and its opposite. All that is necessary to separate one "nothing" from another—the imagination's sweet nothings from the bitterly cold nothings of the day—is the *the*. Something and nothing reverse roles, and nothing is all. One thinks, in this connection, of the uses to which Henry Green put the word in his novel *Nothing*. One thinks too of the last line of A. R. Ammons's prefatory poem to *Sphere: The Form of a Motion*. "Nothing will ever be the same again," he writes, indicating either that a complete change has occurred or that, on the contrary, nothing stays itself, and "ever" shall.

The "bodiless" serpent in the opening section of "The Auroras of Autumn" is, Harold Bloom argues, a symbol of Ananke, goddess of dread necessity, third in line after Eros and Dionysus for the Orphic poet to embrace. It may also be read as a trope for poetry which, by relentlessly transforming its materials, sheds defunct versions of the self, as the snake discards successive skins. In Stevens's last poems, the discarding process advances to a final affirmation of the nothing that remains. To be sure, Stevens continues to rely on negative expressions for the old purpose of bridging the gap between absence and presence, mediating between reality and imagination. There is, for instance, the characteristic use of the negative simile in "Reality is an Activity of the Most August Imagination":

> It was not a night blown at a glassworks in Vienna
> Or Venice, motionless, gathering time and dust.

But the end to which "the visible transformations of summer night" leads is

> An argentine abstraction approaching form
> And suddenly denying itself away.
>
> There was an insolid billowing of the solid.
> Night's moonlight lake was neither water nor air.

As a way of first making distinctions and then transcending them, the negative expression has served as the perfect "dialectical" instrument. Now, having cleared the air of everything, it proposes itself as the one suitable linguistic forum for approaching the ultimate in "mere" being, "without human meaning, / Without human feeling." The invisible is the negative of day's photograph, and it can be developed only in the dark room of the imagination, the shadow of god. Here is the conclusion of "A Clear Day with No Memories":

> Today the air is clear of everything.
> It has no knowledge except of nothingness
> And it flows over us without meanings,
> As if none of us had ever been here before
> And are not now: in this shallow spectacle,
> This invisible activity, this sense.

III.

Stevens and Freud

> *Not as a god, but as a god might be.*
> —"Sunday Morning"

In "The Noble Rider and the Sound of Words," Stevens cites "Boileau's remark that Descartes had cut poetry's throat" and suggests substituting Freud's name for that of Descartes. Stevens had particularly in mind *The Future of an Illusion,* which he calls "inimical to poetry" because it advocates "a surrender to reality." Like Nabokov, another aesthete and illusionist *par excellence* who displays considerable irritation at the drop of Freud's name, Stevens adopts a somewhat cantankerous tone in registering his objections, but this is misleading: in both cases the dissent is intellectual and not merely temperamental. Indeed, upon inspection, the quarrel between the American poet and the founder of psychoanalysis delineates itself quite logically into a pair of rival columns. On the left hand side, under Stevens's banner, value adheres to the imagination and to the irrational element that nourishes it; on Freud's side of the ledger, the voice of reason counsels us sternly to brave the terror of existence without recourse to placebos or narcotics in the form of fond wishes, fairy tales, daydreams, imaginings. Both would agree that religious beliefs, having lost all credibility, amount to illusions, and neither would dispute the other's definition of the word. Freud puts it for both of them when he stresses that "illusions need not necessarily be false—that is to say, unrealizable or in contradiction to reality." The crucial point is that, whether they prove erroneous or accurate in the long run, illusions derive "from human wishes" and flourish with a complete disregard for scientific verification. Precisely so, Stevens would say. No, it is over the ground of value not meaning—over the worth and necessity of fictions, as Stevens prefers to call them—that the two writers engage in their tug-of-war.

At the center of Freud's enterprise is an identification of the rational intellect with civilization itself. Our instincts, though we must be kind to them, are not to be trusted. Like a child come of age, the culture as a whole must, by an act of rational choice and enlightened will, renounce such pleasure-promising instincts as stand in the path of the civilizing impulse, the progress of science translated into the exigencies of the social world. Science conceives of itself as the archenemy of illusions and, by extension, of the imagination that contrives them, often enough as part of a self-delusion, a neurotic soap opera of the psyche.

At the heart of Stevens's mystery is the conviction that the zero degree of reality does not provide nourishment enough for the human spirit upon which we who pursue happiness have no choice but to depend. Stevens exalts the mind's illusion-making capacity even as Freud admonishes against it. Nor would the poet shrink from recognizing, and accepting, a religious aspect to the poetics he propounds. "After one has abandoned a belief in god, poetry is that essence which takes its place as life's redemption," he writes in his "Adagia," a Nietzschean compendium of epigrams, thus providing the perfect prose trot to these lines from "The Man with the Blue Guitar":

> The earth, for us, is flat and bare.
> There are no shadows. Poetry

> Exceeding music must take the place
> Of empty heaven and its hymns,
>
> Ourselves in poetry must take their place,
> Even in the chattering of your guitar.

Stevens says much the same thing in the rambunctious high spirits of "A High-Toned Old Christian Woman," where he opposes a wink to the devout widow's wince. In that poem's terms, peristyle and saxophones—a conjunction of images that combines Greek aestheticism and jazz "primitivism"— differ from the nave and "windy citherns" of an outmoded Christianity not so much in their desired goal as in their effectiveness in reaching it. "We agree in principle," Stevens tells the old woman, about the need to "project a masque / Beyond the planets." Where we take our separate paths, he adds, tweaking her pious nose, is in our attitudes toward "bawdiness"; far from unholy, as madame would have it, it in fact helps one trace a route to the sublime, to a paradise renewed.

For organized religion, then, Stevens has as little respect as Freud. Heaven is haunted, we are told more than once, and "the darkened ghosts of our old comedy" must go the way of that "old catastrophe," the crucifixion. But Freud aspires to a utopian nowhere; he brandishes his sword at the gate and banishes the ghosts from their ghostly paradise and into a world of forced labor. Stevens, on the contrary, envisions a sensuous New Jerusalem in Eden's stead, an imagined land where spirit and sense will replace spirits and shadows. Where Freud, under no illusions as to the discontents reality generates, resolutely stands as realism's champion, Stevens's visionary mission leads him to wonder quite candidly whether he has "lived a skeleton's life, / As a disbeliever in reality," as he writes in the late poem "As You Leave the Room." The doubt endures a momentary existence: the "elevation" the poet experiences is, he maintains, "part of a major reality, part of / An appreciation of a reality." Yet, speaking for Freud, we can seize upon that flicker of doubt and say that the imagination's high priest must, by the very nature of things, lapse into the domain of the unreal or, at least, the unreasonable. Stevens accepts this danger in stride. If, after all, the imagination alone can furnish a satisfactory response to the dilemma of reality, and if the imagination remains a natural instinct rather than a culturally acquired value, so be it. Like a religion, indeed, "poetry must be irrational."

As I have mapped it out, the conflict between Freud and Stevens seems made to order for the perennial university symposia that pit culture and reason against nature and instinct in a philosophical debate of universal application.

But perhaps the most interesting feature of Stevens's quarrel with Freud is that, in the bold strokes I have drawn to summarize the confrontation, neither party is being completely fair to himself; their attitudes are far more complex than the positions the logic of the argument compels them to take. In fact, each is heroically ambivalent about the very articles of his faith; the uneasy relations between reality and the imagination call forth paradoxical responses from both authors. It is that area of overlap to which I want to give some attention, for reasons that will, I hope, become clear in the process.

Consider Freud first. The opinion put forth with such vigor in *The Future of an Illusion* faintly contradicts other of his assumptions and premises. Of this Freud himself seems, one could say, subconsciously cognizant. Beginning with the fourth chapter of his book, he transforms his "monologue" into a putative dialogue with "an opponent who follows my argument with mistrust." This is a familiar if no less efficient rhetorical device; it is nothing else than the dialectical method employed by Socrates, with whom Freud shares the dual credo that "the unexamined life is not worth living" and that reason is the proper baton to conduct the examination. But the very ease with which Freud adopts an adversary stance—only to knock it down, to be sure—does testify to his sympathetic identification with the rival point of view. It would not be going too far to say that he contains his own enemy, in both senses of *contain:* he has it inside him, like a mutinous id, and he repels its military advance, or at least limits it to a slice of mental territory set within well-defined borders. Like Stevens, Freud is an adept naysayer, and what he says no to he includes, albeit in a shadowed form.

No one had done more than Freud to present as a legitimate source of knowledge what his own and previous generations dismissed as the irrational. No one succeeded as he did in expanding our sense of reality, conferring ontological and epistemological status on the unconscious, the mythic, the products of fancy and fantasy, wit and "the diseased imagination," whether these manifested themselves in dreams, in jokes and errors, or in texts and tales. From the theater of illusions came the Oedipal paradigm that Freud made the cornerstone of his new science. To that complex of behavior patterns he affixed the phrase "the family romance"; the phrase suggests the extent to which Freud cast the character of the psyche in terms derived from aesthetic (primarily dramatic) categories. (He was also, it should be added, quick to own up to his indebtedness to the poets who, as he put it, got there first.) Freud operated rather like a literary critic in his scrutiny of the psyche's poetic inventions. It is not at all difficult to see why a contemporary of his might have looked upon him as a witch doctor, for in a quite literal sense he believed himself to be a mind reader. To the degree it provided him with a text to interpret, clues to track down, defenses to "deconstruct," the neurotic imagination was capable of remedy; its concealments themselves would foster revelation, just as poetic figures such as metaphor and irony disguise (or repress) the truth in order to express it in all its intricacy.

How then could the doctor in good conscience attack the system of signs that was all that stood between him and, in Yeats's phrase, "a fabulous, formless darkness"? The obvious answer is that, for Freud, the signs are symptoms, metaphors of malaise. The function of criticism is not to foster an appreciation of illusions and enchantments but to debunk them, and to insist that a new script in a new, diagnostic language supercede the old one. Freud would, by writing about a myth, replace it, to extend the parallel with literary criticism, much of which seems determined at present to dispatch into oblivion the kind of writing on which presumably it used to feast. By rechristening poems "texts," which title also designates their own critical writings, literary theorists seem to want to substitute abstruse research for primary imagination, the prose of reason for the uncommon-sense of poetry. To be fair to Freud, he eschews the exaggerations that plague some of our most advanced critics. Like Plato who banished poets from *The Republic* and yet wrote as one, employing parables and elaborate figures to chart out his thought and staging the proceedings as a comedy of ideas whose purely formal possibilities (as Oscar Wilde showed in *The Decay of Lying* and *The Critic as Artist*) still obtain, Freud was himself a spellbinding poet and masterly mythologizer. What's more, he believed the myth *was* truth; he himself acted the part of the Tiresian proof-giver in demonstrating that our lives enact and reenact, compulsively repeating, parts mythically played by Oedipus and Jocasta and Laius. Inasmuch as his writing often took the form of a refiguring of ancient myth and literary metaphor— one thinks, for example, of his analysis of the three caskets in *The Merchant of Venice*—Freud's procedures have something vital in common with those of modern poets such as Eliot, Rilke, Joyce, and Cocteau, to name but a few who conceived the present in mythic patterns and consciously sought to "update" their sources. Edmund Wilson, in a striking phrase, called Karl Marx "the poet of commodities"; as the poet of the psyche, the poet of Cupid and Psyche, Freud likewise speaks the voice of prophecy—with the added virtue that, like Adam's dream, it seems a waking truth.

Certainly the poet no less than the critic owes an obligation to Freud. James Merrill's poetry would in its general contours and specific details—the weight given to dreams and to the dream-language of the pun, for instance—argue a close affinity with Freud's questioning of reality. It is pertinent, too, that John Ashbery should publish a poem entitled "Civilization and Its Discontents," while Kenneth Koch weighs in with "The Problem of Anxiety." And going back a generation, Auden's poetry, from the time of his American sojourn onwards, is virtually predicated on a holy alliance between Kierkegaard and Freud.

By touching thus briefly on the poetic base (and the poetic attractions) of Freud's scientific structures, I think we can discern a latent heroism in his renunciation of an instinctive myth-mindedness. It could even be argued that this constitutes the secret autobiographical message of *The Future of an Illusion,* if we read that work as a poem: in some important way the argument there mirrors the life.

It is as easy to detect the philosopher in Stevens as the poet in Freud. Like Shelley, Stevens grounds his vision in a deep skepticism; his assent is invariably prefaced by denial. In poem after poem Stevens speaks in the accents of the skeptical ironist; he is a rationalist by diction, a metaphysician by temperament. Where Eliot's *Four Quartets* are philosophical in content but structured on the model of a musical composition, Stevens's poems suggest the structure of an argument to go with their philosophical concerns. Reading "Le Monocle de Mon Oncle" or "Sunday Morning" requires one to follow an argument whose terms are metaphorical and whose propositions add up by dint of a definite if parabolic logic. The sense of a dogged progression through contraries is as strong in these poems as it is in *The Future of an Illusion.*

Moreover, Stevens resembles Freud closely in the pronounced approval he gives to Nietzsche's exposé of the tyranny of heaven. From both Stevens and Freud we can derive a clear understanding of the process by which

> The people grow out of the weather;
> The gods grow out of the people.
> ("Loneliness in Jersey City")

Like Freud, Stevens would subscribe to Voltaire's assertion that "man invented god in his own image and god instantly returned the favor." The logic here, incidentally, illustrates Harold Bloom's exposition of the necessary belatedness of all poetic activity. If the primitive mind perceives what it projects, an angry god in a lightning storm, if, from the image of "the fire eye in the clouds," he imagines a deity, then clearly the divinity he beholds must be made in man's own image. Thus, by insisting that man is made in the image of his maker, the religious mythologizer wishes precisely to reverse the priority, to make the belated seem early—an example of Bloom's trope of *metalepsis.* Man's worship is at root an acknowledgment of his weakness in the face of the savage forces of nature; giving birth to a god that he can, by propitiating, control, he has transmuted the very measure of his weakness into an avenue of power, a "shadowed strength" in Bloom's phrase.

Stevens is after a myth of divinity that is original in both senses, that achieves its priority not by a confidence trick but by visionary intelligence. He wants to recover the myth that survives the obsolescence of myths; he knows he must go back to the source to find food for the fictive imagination. As he writes in "The Sense of the Sleight-of-Hand Man,"

> It is a wheel, the rays
> Around the sun. The wheel survives the myths.
> The fire eye in the clouds survives the gods.

In pursuing his supreme fiction, in prophesying a savage "chant of paradise" so at odds with Christian austerity, Stevens would deny that he forfeits his right to the title of realist. Or, rather, he would assert that "realism is a corruption of reality"; he would remind us that a fiction, if believed in, is no longer a fiction. Still, in order to command our belief and our allegiance, poetry must be founded on the real; there is that crucial distinction to be made between fiction and falsehood. "The real is only the base," Stevens writes in the "Adagia." "But it is the base." The imagination must call our attention to what is actually there—"The empty spirit / In vacant space"— before we can possibly presume to go beyond it.

Where does all this leave us? The confrontation between Stevens and Freud can now, I think, be seen "more truly and more strange." In brief, Stevens would "abstract reality, which he does by placing it in his imagination"; Freud would do the exact reverse. Perhaps one should say "the lateral reverse" and communicate thereby the idea that Freud and Stevens have, in effect, swapped mirrors. Just as Freud's nobility is apparent in his attempt to surmount the "infantilism" of "religious consolations," so is there nobility in Stevens's ambition to surmount his native rationalism in the name of the sublime. And one somehow wants not merely to navigate between the two points of view but to include them both. It has frequently been observed that with the advance of civilization the prose impulse becomes stronger and the verse impulse correspondingly weaker; that idea is disturbing indeed, not least because poetry has historically brought with it a species of redemptive enchantment of which we today are sorely in need. Rather than succumb to so costly an "advance," Stevens holds out the possibility of a sublime transcendence; to say no to "the pressure of reality," to cancel it out, is to pave the way to that possible yes on which "the future world depends." As a stay against the tide, a possibility preserved, Stevens's defense of "imagination as value" is exemplary. It seems, finally, a value that the humanist must keep in the forefront of consciousness even as he puts into practice Freud's program of an "education to reality."

Elizabeth Bishop's Prison Sentences

Traditionally, poets have dwelled in paradoxical prisons. To enter bonds of queen and country is to affirm one's freedom, Donne seductively argued; Lovelace, equally extravagant if less playful, insisted on liberty as a function of spiritual innocence. He denied not the actuality of stone walls and iron bars, just their right to cohere into prisons and cages, in a passage that schoolchildren were presumed once upon a time to know by heart:

> If I have freedom in my love,
> And in my soul am free,
> Angels alone, that soar above,
> Enjoy such liberty.
>
> ("To Althea, from Prison")

If Lovelace could look upon imprisonment as "an hermitage," a time to rededicate himself to a courtly ideal, Hamlet's princely mobility could scarcely preclude a bout of claustrophobia. "Denmark's a prison," he announces, and follows with a characteristic verbal gesture, robust hyperbole collapsing into poignantly prosaic understatement:

> O God, I could be bounded in a nutshell and
> count myself a king of infinite space, were it not
> that I have bad dreams.
>
> (Act II, scene ii)

This piece was written for *Elizabeth Bishop and Her Art,* edited by Lloyd Schwartz and Sybil P. Estess (Ann Arbor: University of Michigan Press, 1983).

It is, as Hamlet acknowledges, a classic opposition of mind and matter. Whatever his present difficulties, he does not doubt the mind's supremacy over the world it beholds: "There is nothing either good or bad but thinking makes it so." As far as Hamlet is concerned, man's potential to breathe the infinite space of angels is, despite the narrow dimensions of his cell, still available, though not right here, not just now.

It would be interesting to determine when *despite* in that last clause turned into *because of,* when the emphasis shifted and poets actively sought a species of imprisonment because only there would the soul learn true freedom, or goodness, or the peace that passeth understanding. The argument, a recurrent one in medieval Christian theology, has in effect been rewritten, its paradox completed, by agents of the Romantic imagination. In the same spirit in which he commends duty as the "Stern Daughter of the Voice of God," Wordsworth solemnly wills a curtailment of his freedom, identifying form as a necessary jail in his sonnet on the sonnet:

> In truth the prison, unto which we doom
> Ourselves, no prison is: and hence for me,
> In sundry moods, 'twas pastime to be bound
> Within the Sonnet's scanty plot of ground;
> Pleased if some Souls (for such there needs must be)
> Who have felt the weight of too much liberty,
> Should find brief solace there, as I have found.
> ("Nuns Fret Not at Their Convent's Narrow Room")

To Paul Pennyfeather, the beleaguered hero of Evelyn Waugh's *Decline and Fall,* prison ironically allows for the autonomy of the self, its independence from social pressures, its release from "the weight of too much liberty":

> The next four weeks of solitary confinement were among the happiest of Paul's life. . . . It was so exhilarating, he found, never to have to make any decision on any subject, to be wholly relieved from the smallest consideration of time, meals, or clothes, to have no anxiety ever about what kind of impression he was making; in fact, to be free. . . . There was no need to shave, no hesitation about what tie he should wear, none of the

fidgeting with studs and collars and links that so distracts the waking moments of civilized man. He felt like the happy people in the advertisements for shaving soap who seem to have achieved very simply that peace of mind so distant and so desirable in the early morning.

A comic gloss on Lovelace's "To Althea, from Prison," the chapter in which this passage appears has the title "Stone Walls Do Not a Prison Make"; not surprisingly, a later chapter is called "Nor Iron Bars a Cage."

As we proceed from *despite* to *because,* we move as well from a conception of the imagination as that which redeems reality to a conception of the imagination as, in the last analysis, sufficient unto itself. A clear statement of this last analysis is found in J. K. Huysmans's *À Rebours,* which develops the logic of the prison paradox into an aesthetic principle. The protagonist of that novel ingeniously devises a means by which to travel without ever having to leave his room, secure a passport, book passage, pack bags, or say farewell—without, in short, any of the inconveniences of actuality. "Travel, indeed, struck him as being a waste of time, since he believed that the imagination could provide a more-than-adequate substitute for the vulgar reality of actual experience." Two poets upon whom Elizabeth Bishop has exerted a powerful influence, James Merrill and John Ashbery, offer inspired variations on this theme of the stationary traveler. More a *récit* than a short story, Merrill's "Peru: The Landscape Game" describes a trip to the land of the Incas; the poet plans to go there, but it is his anticipation of the place that he records, a Platonic reality too good not to be true. The imagination acts in self-defense as it spins out an eternal possibility, proof against the disappointment Wordsworth experienced when he saw Mont Blanc:

> How to find the right words for a new world?
> One way would be to begin, before ever leaving home, with some anticipatory jottings such as these. Then, even if the quetzal turns out to be extinct, if sure-footed grandmothers from Tulsa overrun the ruins, and Porfirio's baby has a harelip and there are cucarachas in the Hotel Périchole, the visitor may rest easy. Nothing can dim his first, radiant impressions.

Such "jottings," intended for perusal on the ride down to Lima, give new meaning to the idea of flight insurance.

Ashbery, too, would seem to subscribe to Verlaine's notion that every landscape is a state of mind. From his vantage point in an office building more than a thousand miles away, the speaker of Ashbery's "The Instruction Manual" takes us on a guided tour of Guadalajara, "city I wanted most to see, and most did not see, in Mexico!" The task of writing "the instruction manual on the uses of a new metal" serves as the unlikely launching pad for this mental flight. "How limited, but how complete withal, has been our experience of Guadalajara!" the speaker can exclaim upon his return to the desk he never had to leave. Amusing as that statement is, it tells its sober truth about the poetic process. On paper the poet flies to Peru or Guadalajara not as places but as names, words, sounds; one arrives at "the imagination of the sound—a place." This is the conclusion reached by A. R. Ammons in his poem "Triphammer Bridge":

> *sanctuary, sanctuary,* I say it over and over and the
> word's sound is one place to dwell; that's it, just
> the sound, and the imagination of the sound—a place.

By delineating the progression from "wanted . . . to see" to "did not see" to "I fancy I see, under the press of having to write the instruction manual," Ashbery's poem makes a further point. It is as though a condition of absence were a prerequisite for the adventurous imagination. So we are directly told in another of Ashbery's early poems, "Le Livre est sur la table":

> All beauty, resonance, integrity,
> Exist by deprivation or logic
> Of strange position.

The proposition that the imagination varies directly with deprivation and isolation, that imaginative need mothers invention, and that physical confinement is conducive to spiritual freedom, receives full treatment in Elizabeth Bishop's early and remarkably prescient short story (or *récit*), "In Prison." This account of an ideal "life-sentence" contains the seed Ashbery would cultivate in "The Instruction Manual," even as it makes the case for creative misreading, for what Harold Bloom, like Bishop a mapmaker, calls "misprision":

> I understand that most prisons are now supplied with libraries and that the prisoners are expected to read the *Everyman's Library* and other books of educational tendencies. I hope I am not being too reactionary when I say that my one desire is to be given one very dull book to read, the duller the better. A book, moreover, on a subject completely foreign to me; perhaps the second volume, if the first would familiarize me too well with the terms and purpose of the work. Then I shall be able to experience with a free conscience the pleasure, perverse, I suppose, of interpreting it not at all according to its intent. Because I shary with Valéry's *M. Teste* the "knowledge that our thoughts are reflected back to us, too much so, through expressions made by others"; and I have resigned myself, or do I speak too frankly, to deriving what information I can from this—lamentable but irremediable—state of affairs. From my detached rock-like book I shall be able to draw vast generalizations, abstractions of the grandest, most illuminating sort, like allegories or poems, and by posing fragments of it against the surroundings and conversations of my prison, I shall be able to form my own examples of surrealist art!—something I should never know how to do outside, where the sources are so bewildering. Perhaps it will be a book on the cure of a disease, or an industrial technique,—but no, even to try to imagine the subject would be to spoil the sensation of wave-like freshness I hope to receive when it is first placed in my hands.

In Bishop's later work, an explicit echo of this passage occurs in "The End of March" where, in a tone more wistful than whimsical, the writer describes her "proto-dream-house," a "dubious" structure that tallies in a great many particulars with her earlier version of prison as paradise:

> I'd like to retire there and do *nothing*,
> or nothing much, forever, in two bare rooms:
> look through binoculars, read boring books,

old, long, long books, and write down useless notes,
talk to myself, and, foggy days,
watch the droplets slipping, heavy with light.

For the way it prefigures attitudes and motifs that we encounter not only in *Geography III* but throughout the poet's career, "In Prison" commends itself to critical inspection over and beyond its intrinsic merits, considerable though these are. Here we find, at however ironic a remove, a defense of Bishop's "mentality," her faith in "the power of details" as momentary stays against confusion, her stance as quiet nonconformist, whose individuality of style is able somehow to flourish within a regimented order. The insouciance of "One Art," the ironic process by which defeat turns into victory, is anticipated in the story; here is an initial statement of the dialectical tension between autobiographical disaster and artistic mastery, a tension central to the villanelle and one that lurks beneath the surface of the prose poem "12 O'Clock News" with its military metaphors for the act of writing. Moreover, "In Prison" contains information helpful for us to understand the painterly disposition of a poet who continually derived inspiration, as well as subject matter, from objects and apparitions, large bad pictures and tiny ones ("About the size of an old-style dollar bill"), and seascapes disguised as animated "cartoon[s] by Raphael for a tapestry for a Pope."

The strategy for reading that Bishop proffers points to the governing conceit of the story, "the pleasure, perverse, I suppose, of interpreting it not at all according to its intent"—*it* standing here for prison, which willful misinterpretation renders to mean the inner life of the imagination, the "real life" of the soul. The narrative starts with a flip reversal of Joseph K.'s predicament in *The Trial*. Like Kafka's protagonist, Bishop's persona has committed no crime, but there the resemblance ends. He positively wants what Joseph K. dreads; nor does he suffer from irrational guilt seeking to justify its existence. Once arrested, Joseph K. never doubts his guilt, even while ostensibly seeking to prove his innocence; Bishop's nameless character runs no risk of arrest since, in order to attain the imprisonment he "can scarcely wait for," he seems prepared to do precious little and certainly nothing criminal, unless criminality be defined in the singular way attributed to Edgar Degas in "Objects & Apparitions": " 'One has to commit a painting,' said Degas, / 'the way one commits a crime.' " But if the poet adopts this position, it is without political intent or fanfare. The pun on "sentence" in the phrase "life-sentence" may get us nearer the truth; from one point of view the writer may be said to serve successive "sentences." Be that as it may, the author of "In Prison" strikes the pose of a young Hegelian, wishing literally to make a virtue of necessity. Our hero has been chosen by prison, he would say; the will is needed not to act upon this destiny but to acquiesce before it, to accept what he conceives as "necessity." Given his definition of freedom, only an attitude of passive non-resistance will do, only the passive voice will be strictly accurate. Notice the grammatical ambiguity that closes the story:

> You may say,—people have said to me—you would have been happy in the more flourishing days of the religious order, and that, I imagine, is close to the truth. But even there I hesitate, and the difference between Choice and Necessity jumps up again to confound me. "Freedom is knowledge of necessity"; I believe nothing as ardently as I do that. And I assure you that to act in this way is the only logical step for me to take. I mean, of course, to be acted *upon* in this way is the only logical step for me to take.

Justice is beside the point. It is clear we are talking metaphorically, not about guilt and punishment, but about the self and its need to make peace with the certitude of loss. To volunteer for prison is to plan a journey into the interior, confident that in the exchange of physical liberty for imaginative freedom one has, philosophically speaking, struck a good bargain, given up the apparent, embraced the real. Like Ashbery's dreary office building, prison affords both the opportunity and the motive for metaphor, but a far more urgent task also confronts the prisoner. It will be his audacious enterprise to establish an idealized dwelling place within the least likely, least congenial, of quarters; like Crusoe on his island, he will attempt to convert an alien landscape into one that responds to his humanity. It is almost as though he (or his author) were consciously designing a test for "one" art—singular, definitive of the poet's identity—an art that feeds on what might otherwise consume it, that thrives on loss, that welcomes limits in order to transcend them. We are, in sum, solidly within the walls of a conceit, a paradox regained, a cliché renewed in surprising ways. At one point at least, prison metaphorically dramatizes the situation of the writer, any writer conscious of his belatedness. Thus, referring to the "Writing on the Wall," our would-be prisoner announces his intention to

> read very carefully (or try to read, since they may be partly obliterated, or in a foreign language) the inscriptions already there. Then I shall adapt my own compositions, in order that they may not conflict with those written by the prisoner before me. The voice of a new inmate will be noticeable, but there will be no contradictions or criticisms of what has already been laid down, rather a "commentary." I have thought of attempting a short, but immortal, poem, but I am afraid that is beyond me; I may rise to the occasion, however, once I am confronted with that stained, smeared, scribbled-on wall and feel the stub of pencil or rusty nail between my fingers.

The sense of postponement here as elsewhere in the piece reinforces our impression of it as an initial statement of purpose, a warm-up for the main event yet to come, the time of confrontation, pencil stub in hand, "with that stained, smeared, scribbled-on wall" of poetic tradition.

What makes "In Prison" work so well is that, having subtly and very quickly established the figurative nature of the writing, Bishop ironically becomes a literalist of the imagination, specifying the exact dimensions of the cell, describing its walls and window and the view from the window with painterly precision, ruling out such surrogates for prison as monasteries. To live, in a shabby hotel room, "as if I were in prison"? No, the narrator says, that won't do. Nor will what we now call a country-club prison, the sort of place that temporarily housed persons of a certain class convicted of wrongdoing with relation to the Watergate burglary and cover-up. Joining the navy is likewise eliminated from consideration, though on different grounds: not so much because it would parody "my real hopes," but for the telling reason that "there is something fundamentally uncongenial about the view of the sea to a person of my mentality." Why? Because, we may infer, it is the very symbol of the lawless and limitless and as such must clash with the mentality that yearns for fixed borders; also because the sea's vastness and essential unity threaten to drown out all details, all the "slight differences" that strike the poet as inherently valuable. The sea's great expanse is a needless luxury, a point implicitly made in that portion of the story given over to a mock-review of the literature of incarceration. Oscar Wilde is rebuked for the self-pitying note that mars "The Ballad of Reading Gaol." " 'That little tent of blue, Which prisoners call the sky,' strikes me as absolute nonsense. I believe that even a keyhole of sky would be enough, in its blind, blue endlessness, to give someone, even someone who had never seen it before, an adequate idea of the sky." The "romantic tunnel-digging" of *The Count of Monte Cristo* is also rejected by this early spokesman for Bishop's views, this hard-liner impatient with sentimental formulae. What is desired, after all, is not an escape from, but an escape into, the unadorned cell of consciousness.

As in "Crusoe in England," it is a persona and not the poet who does the talking in "In Prison." To make sure we realize this, Bishop takes pains to distinguish the speaker's gender from her own. (He has thought of enlisting in the armed services—and of playing on the prison baseball team.) The distance thus created between writer and text sets ironies in motion, but these seem otherwise directed than at the speaker's expense. Rather, they work to effect a delicate interplay between order and chance, limitation and space, determinism and free will, the philosophical dualities that energize the story. If one's reading consists of a single book, and that a boring one, one can multiply it by a theoretically infinite number of misreadings, magical as lies. If one's view is restricted to a bare cobblestone courtyard, framed by the window so that it takes on the aspect of a painting, its boundaries severely defined, its activity therefore rescued from disorder, it is nevertheless a series of paintings in one, and within its order there is plenty of room for chance; vagaries of weather ensure the possibility of variations galore, as Monet demonstrated with his cathedrals and haystacks, products of the changing light. The confinement, then, is meant not to eliminate dealings with the external world but to circumscribe the relations and, by doing so, to put them on an aesthetic plane. What one sees becomes an ever-changing picture, what one reads, an occasion for the imagination to roam free. If, for the aesthete's ends, what barely suffices ("a keyhole of sky") is deemed better than a surfeit, that is partially because it underscores an important truth about poetic knowledge. All that we can know are parts and fragments; by the same token, each part, each detail, acts as a synecdoche, pointing to a potential whole, a design the mind must intuit or invent. "I expect to go to prison in full possession of my 'faculties,' " the speaker says. "In fact," he adds, "it is not until I am securely installed there that I expect fully to realize them." In short, the prison of his aspirations is nothing like a place of asylum, refuge from trouble, a rest cure; on the contrary, his sentence will tax, and reward, his powers of imagination. And one can go further: one can say, too, that he plots his prison itinerary for reasons similar to those that elsewhere impel Bishop's "I" and fellow travelers to undertake journeys to unfamiliar places that call "home" into question. A fantasized excursion to prison can give rise to such "questions of travel" as Bishop will pose in a memorable poem:

> *"Is it lack of imagination that makes us come*
> *to imagined places, not just stay at home?*
> *Or could Pascal have been not entirely right*
> *about just sitting quietly in one's room?*
>
> *Continent, city, country, society:*
> *the choice is never wide and never free.*
> *And here, or there . . . No. Should we have stayed at home,*
> *wherever that may be?"*

Such interrogations yield no answers, only suasions, and these subject to change. "In Prison" leans one way, *Questions of Travel* the other. But whatever the differences in their attitudes to travel, the restless geographer and the secluded inmate have an ultimate direction in common, an ultimate task their opposing inclinations will equally culminate in—the making of the map of an identity.

As a theory of imagination that is necessarily a theory of absence, "In Prison" prepares us well for the projects of Bishop's mature poetry. It is remarkable how often she turns to imagery of room, cell, cage, and box, and usually within the context of an aesthetic inquiry; she has a penchant for illustrating her sense of art by postulating constructions the shape of boxes or made of them. Take "The Monument," which traces the growth of a work of art from "piled-up boxes" to "a temple of crates." Its external appearance seems to some extent a subordinate value; it functions to safeguard "what is within," about which it is protectively reticent:

> It may be solid, may be hollow.
> The bones of the artist-prince may be inside
> or far away on even drier soil.
> But roughly but adequately it can shelter
> what is within (which after all
> cannot have been intended to be seen).

A "crooked box," the dream house of "The End of March" is prisonlike in more way than one, a rough but adequate shelter with constraints enough to provide the stimulus, if not the necessity, for creative action. And in "Objects & Apparitions," Bishop's translation of Octavio Paz's homage to the boxes of Joseph Cornell, the paradox of a nutshell's infinite space is immediately articulated:

> Hexahedrons of wood and glass,
> scarcely bigger than a shoebox,
> with room in them for night and all its lights.
>
> Monuments to every moment,
> refuse of every moment, used:
> cages for infinity.

Cornell's boxes have been characterized as "monumental on a tiny scale"; the phrase has its relevance to Bishop's art. The impulse toward this peculiar brand of monumentality combines with the conceit of the "enormous" room most notably, perhaps, in "12 O'Clock News," in which the writer's desk and the objects on it are magnified (and mistranslated), seen as through the eyes of a Lilliputian, with results at once humorous and touching.

Paradise as Elizabeth Bishop with tongue-biting irony conceives it has a precedent in "The Great Good Place" Henry James described, as these sentences from James's story make clear: "Slowly and blissfully he read into the general wealth of his comfort all the particular absences of which it was composed. One by one he touched, as it were, all the things it was such rapture to be without." The tone (and much else) is different, but the sentiment the same, in "One Art." There the disaster-prone are advised to "lose something every day" and then to "practice losing farther, losing faster." The imperative seems at first purely ironic, a way to keep anguish and dread at bay, to avoid giving in to self-pity. But the ironist's supreme gesture is to mean just what she says, contrary to appearances as well as expectations. Bishop does, at least in one sense, recommend that we go about losing things, not so much because this will prepare us for the major losses inevitably to follow, but because the experience of loss humanizes us; it shows us as we are, vulnerable, pathetic, and yet heroic in our capacity to endure and to continue our affirming acts amid conditions less than propitious. When Bishop talks of losing as an art she does not mean losing well, being a good sport. In one sense, she means less: it isn't hard to master what comes naturally to us: we are always losing things, from our innocence to our parents to our housekeys: that is why *lose* was the perfect syllepsis for Alexander Pope. Yet "the art of losing" is a wonderfully ambiguous phrase, and the ability to reconcile its two meanings— to experience loss as itself a remedy for loss—constitutes a powerful poetic gesture, whose success may be measured by the poet's skillful handling of the villanelle's intricate form in the face of all that militates against order and arrangement.

In "The Poet," Emerson wrote that "every thought is also a prison; every heaven is also a prison." Not the least virtue of Elizabeth Bishop's poetry is that, from the start, it shows us the truth that remains when Emerson's terms are reversed.

Delmore, Delmore
A Mournful Cheer

He looked onto the world like the act of an aged whore.
Delmore, Delmore.
He flung to pieces and they hit the floor.
                                                    —John Berryman, *The Dream Songs*

There's a moment in Delmore Schwartz's best-known and best-loved story—"In Dreams Begin Responsibilities"—that the captivated reader is not likely ever to forget. The story's protagonist is sitting in a darkened movie theater, watching one of his primal dreams on screen: the courtship of his future parents, "dressed in ridiculously old-fashioned clothes," several years before his birth. Their leisurely stroll along the Coney Island boardwalk is in ironic counterpoint to the terrifying sense of inevitability with which the boy watches. When at last the father proposes marriage, and the mother tearfully agrees, their son suddenly stands up and shouts, "Don't do it. It's not too late to change your minds, both of you. Nothing good will come of it, only remorse, hatred, scandal, and two children whose characters are monstrous." But of course it really is too late; the wish that one had not been born can never be gratified. Resignation, which in Schwartz's vocabulary is another name for maturity, comes in the form of the spectator in the next seat, an old woman who yanks the boy back into place: "Be quiet. You'll be put out, and you paid thirty-five cents to come in."

This essay appeared in *Parnassus* in 1979 as a review of *Delmore Schwartz: The Life of an American Poet,* by James Atlas; Schwartz's *In Dreams Begin Responsibilities and Other Stories,* edited by James Atlas; and *Last and Lost Poems of Delmore Schwartz,* edited by Robert Phillips.

It is precisely this sequence of emotions that attends our reading of Delmore Schwartz's biography. His life describes the parabolic curve of a model Greek tragedy, and tormented by our helplessness, we in the audience can offer nothing but an abundance of belated pity for that marvelous boy as, with youthful gladness, he takes his first irreversible steps down the well-worn path leading to despondency and madness and finally self-annihilation. "Not to be born surpasses thought and speech," the chorus sings in *Oedipus at Colonus.* "The second best is to have seen the light / And then to go back quickly whence we came." Our reluctance to abandon our seats before this melancholic finale has less to do with our having paid, with the costly emotions of hope and admiration, to get in, than with our worry that the life may have been a paradigmatic one, that by its very nature a talent such as Delmore's could not have survived intact the various shocks of modern American life—the feeling of being an alien in an eerily familiar place, for instance, or the withdrawal pains that are so much a part of an addiction to the narcotic of success. To his credit, James Atlas refuses to sentimentalize the case, refuses to hold "the system" conveniently to blame for the poet's lapse from grace into wretched paranoia, a condition to which he was susceptible in the best of times:

> Do they whisper behind my back? Do they speak
> Of my clumsiness? Do they laugh at me,
> Mimicking my gestures, retailing my shame?
> I'll whirl about, denounce them, saying
> That they are shameless, they are treacherous,
> No more my friends, nor will I once again,
> Never, amid a thousand meetings in the street,
> Recognize their faces, take their hands,
> Not for our common love or old times' sake:
> They whispered behind my back, they mimicked me.

A soberingly lucid account of Schwartz's "desolate condition and the vengeful irrationality that issued forth to conceal it" constitutes a necessary corrective to "a myth that has given Delmore's tragic life a spurious symbolic value for which he was himself in part responsible"—the myth of suicidal nihilism as ultimately the only valid (and "poetic") response to an overtly hostile or merely hostilely indifferent cultural environment. Nevertheless, Saul Bellow and John Berryman are not alone in having seized the occasion of Schwartz's calamitous end as a moment for more general lamentation and for ironic reflection about the nature of the survivors in a cultural regime in which poets cannot "make a living." It is hard not to see Schwartz as an emblematic figure, capable of stirring us in his ravings no less than in his brilliant and original literary creations, meant to reproach and admonish us with the purity and grandeur of his aspirations as well as with the unbanished image of his demise, in the elevator of a seedy Times Square hotel, unshaven, his shirt torn, while taking out the garbage at three in the morning. "It was his misfortune to be metonymous," Atlas notes, "the very embodiment of an entire generation's traumas and opinions."

"In Dreams Begin Responsibilities," written when its unknown author was still shy of his twenty-second birthday, catapulted him to early prominence. So impressed were the editors of a revived, newly anti-Stalinist *Partisan Review* that they printed it as the lead item of their first issue, ahead of contributions by Lionel Trilling, Edmund Wilson, Wallace Stevens, Picasso, *et al.* Messrs. Rahv, Phillips, Macdonald, and Dupee (and later Vladimir Nabokov) were among those who recognized it as a masterpiece; on the strength of its impact, Schwartz gained entrance into the sophisticated intellectual and literary milieu whose manners he chronicled with sardonic splendor in the fine story "New Year's Eve." A young man in a big hurry, Schwartz was soon to distinguish himself as the author of penetrating critical essays—on, for example, Auden, Eliot, Hemingway, Faulkner, and Hardy—and of that significant document entitled "The Isolation of Modern Poetry," an analysis of the causes and consequences of the gulf separating poets "from the lives of other men, who, insofar as they could be considered important characters, were engaged in cultivating money or building an industrial society . . . human beings in whom culture and sensibility had no organic function." With "Coriolanus and His Mother," his verse retelling of Shakespeare's play, as interpreted by an audience consisting of Freud, Marx, Aristotle, Beethoven, and Kant, and punctuated by five exhilarating *entr'acte* prose poems, Schwartz displayed the kind of inventiveness and facility for making a poetry of ideas that would prompt James Laughlin, his editor at New Directions, to refer to him as "the American Auden." Other of the poems he was publishing at the time also manage to swim out from under the suffocating influence of Yeats and Eliot, and reach a "terror firmer" (to borrow a pun from John Hollander), but it was in his creative prose that Schwartz achieved greatness; it was as a poet that he conceived his short stories, which developed a flair for high-class gossip into vivid social commentary ("The World Is a Wedding," "New Year's Eve") and recorded with pathos and humor the New York of Jewish immigrants and their American-born children ("The Child Is the Meaning of This Life," "America, America").

Having assumed the burden of being the most promising poet in America by the time he was twenty-five, only to be betrayed by "the beautiful American word, Sure," well might the young man have awakened one morning and muttered that "a glorious future is behind me." In Delmore's case—evidently, no one who knew him ever called him Schwartz, a pleasurable familiarity that extends to the anonymous reader—the supernal ambition to be a great poet was necessarily accompanied by a sense of displacement, anxiety, and loss. The ambition was self-defeating in more ways than one. Mastered by his obsessions, he became, with every last investigation into the mysteries of his personal ontology, no less deracinated and homeless, no less perplexed by the face which stared at him in the lake of Narcissus. Delmore's stories confirmed, rather than ameliorated, a sense of irremediable rupture from the ethos they memorialized with such stunning accuracy and insight. It was as if the act of writing consumed his material, leaving no nourishment for the life; more exactly, any effort at recovery would be sabotaged by the instinctive loathing the poet could not overcome. As Schwartz writes in one of his most moving stories, "America, America," "the lower middle-class of the generation of Shenandoah's parents had engendered perversions of its own nature, children full of contempt for everything important to their parents."

With consummate self-consciousness, amusing and intrusive by turns, Delmore habitually measured himself by the loftiest of standards, projecting his own countenance onto the portraits of Dante and Keats and Rimbaud. "Where was Tolstoy and where was Shakespeare and Dante just before their 28th birthday?" he wondered as his own approached. His intimate awareness of the lives and works of his literary forebears proceeded from "the presumption / That all are like myself / And that I am *like* all," a sympathetic identification that may help explain the charming half-ironic display of learning that informs his poetry; but it was also responsible for the ponderous attempt he made in the overlong and overwrought *Genesis* to produce a modern *Prelude,* applying the insights of Freud to the task of recollecting the first seven years of his life in extravagant detail. "Nothing is worse than a bad poem which was intended to be great," Auden has written, and the remark is of special appositeness for this and other of Schwartz's excruciatingly grandiose projects, examples of psychoanalysis gone haywire, generally abandoned in fragmentary form.

Delmore was a casualty of the paradox that amounts almost to a credo among modern artists, the tendency—which Trilling eloquently describes, seeking to discredit it, in *Sincerity and Authenticity*—to overcome alienation by completing it, to reject "the falsities of an alienated social reality . . . in favour of an upward psychopathic mobility." Schwartz himself acknowledged the dangers of this tendency in "The Isolation of Modern Poetry," regarding as a development to be resisted rather than welcomed the divorce agreement between culture and society, the estrangement of poetry from "the common language of daily life, its syntax, habitual sequences, and processes of association." Yet it was also tempting to make a virtue of one's neuroses, inasmuch as these "marks of weakness, marks of woe" themselves implied a powerful indictment of society's cruel exigencies; according to this formulation, the artist is akin to a wounded Philoctetes, denying the service of his bow to his countrymen. This conception of art as defiant exile received inspired treatment in the verse play *Shenandoah,* which, like much of Schwartz's imaginative writing, comes by way of an excavation into a preconscious zone of feelings, that exotic territory on the border between anguish, borne of futility, and a curious nostalgia for what one could know about only by hearsay.

The alarming details of his family life, and what might be termed the unseen presence of a prenatal shadow—his mother used the pregnancy as a species of blackmail, to lure the wayward father home—are problems that never ceased to haunt the poet, and his unlikely name seemed to Delmore an apt metaphor for the singularity of his origins and, he would have liked to believe, his calling. Variants of the name occur throughout his works: Shenandoah Fish, Hershey Green, Cornelius Schmidt, Faber Gottschalk, Richmond Rose. Inveterate mythologizer of himself, Schwartz concocted numerous anecdotes accounting for his first name; depending on the story, he was named after a local delicatessen, an actor named Frank Delmore, a Pullman railroad car, a Tammany club, a Riverside Drive apartment house. Delmore possessed, as Atlas says, "a genius for eliciting general laws from the particular scenes of his life," and so, in *Shenandoah,* the naming of a child is presented as "the small event"

> Which gave my mind and gave my character,
> Amid the hundred thousand possibilities
> Heredity and community avail,
> Bound and engender,
>   the very life I know!

In the play, a suitable name, "distinguished and new and American," must be found for their offspring by Mr. and Mrs. Fish, assisted or hindered by relatives, friends, and local authorities. Each makes a suggestion; to each there are objections. From time to time their arguments are interrupted by a grown-up version of the child, whose speeches exhibit Schwartz's considerable powers of condensation and synthesis. One such soliloquy proffers a summary description of Delmore's literary heroes, the great modernists who "find in art / What exile is: art becomes exile too, / A secret and a code studied in secret, / Declaring the agony of modern life." Shenandoah will join them; he will wear his name like a wound. It makes him one of the chosen, as does the rite of circumcision with which the play appropriately ends: "for with a wound / —What better sign exists—the child is made / A Jew forever! quickly taught the life / That he must lead, an heir to lasting pain."

James Atlas has a keen eye for the macabre entertainment value of Delmore's career; there is an element of voyeurism in our reading of his biography, as though Schwartz were an inspired combination of Oscar Levant, Lenny Bruce, and the lunatic newscaster of *Network*. In fact, had Schwartz been able to overcome the stage fright that plagued him throughout his life, or managed to convert his social awkwardness into a performing asset, he would have been a media natural, alternately going to pieces in flamboyant and bizarre ways and giving us the lowdown on the cultural figures he knew—and he appears to have known all the right people, having cultivated "an unerring talent for becoming acquainted with whatever person or idea happened at the time to be just on the verge of prominence." An indefatigable monologist, whose Borscht Belt delivery Bellow captures nicely in *Humboldt's Gift*, Delmore moved with bewildering ingenuity from the liberalism of Adlai Stevenson to the married and domestic lives of pederasts, from Trotsky's literary theories to Rommel's military strategies, from Dante to the scandal sheets. About Eliot, whom he called "a literary dictator," Schwartz was particularly fascinating, mixing shrewd insights with fantastical gossip and fabrication. It is no accident that the pages devoted to "Von Humboldt Fleischer" are far and away the most stirring in Bellow's novel, for above all else Delmore Schwartz was a presence, inspiring at times and at other times maddening, and the unwritten text of his life must have struck his biographer as itself an extraordinary literary creation.

One might usefully compile a compendium of the witty sayings and rhetorical flourishes in Delmore's stories, letters, and peripatetic conversations. The sexual act, he wrote, "begins everything and ends nothing, and often, as everyone knows, produces as aftermath the most unutterable sadness, even in those so self-delighting that they are intoxicated by the comeliness of their shadows." In a similar vein he announced that "our adult lives are a long suffering and chiefly unsuccessful attempt to free ourselves from the utter corruption of childhood, infancy, and the egotism contracted in the womb." Philip Rahv was called a "manic-impressive"; "Philip does have scruples, but he never lets them stand in the way." Of the prose style of Lionel Trilling, Delmore commented, "I wish he would not make the most obvious remarks in the tone of one who has just discovered a cure for cancer," and notwithstanding its hysteria, "The Duchess' Red Shoes" remains one of the few insightful critiques of Trilling's liberal ideology. Combining an academic career with a literary vocation at a time when the creative writing workshop was still a novelty, Schwartz recorded some priceless examples of a new genre, that of the inadvertent *bon mot,* such as the Radcliffe student's remark that "a liberal education makes a girl broader" or another girl's misreading of a line from "Prufrock": "Shall I part my bare behind?" Schwartz was also a master of the paradox ("Even paranoids have enemies"), the pithy paraphrase ("Rilke endures / Of silence and of solitude the unheard music / In empty castles which great knights have left"), the vaudeville routine ("Existentialism means that no one else can take a bath for you"), and the parodic renewal of famous quotations. Consider this couplet from one of the dozen dream songs, "one solid block of agony," which Berryman dedicated to his friend's memory: "I am the Brooklyn poet Delmore Schwartz / Harms & the child I sing, two parents' torts." Aping Stephen Dedalus, he defined history as "a nightmare during which I am trying to get a good night's rest"—an aim that always eluded him, insomniac that he was, with a lifelong dependence on sedatives; the situation is dramatized in the frequently anthologized poem "In the Naked Bed, in Plato's Cave."

If it is amusing to imagine Schwartz correcting his analyst on fine points of Freudian theory, that is as nothing beside the supreme irony of the note scribbled by Delmore's mother on the back of a typescript of "In Dreams Begin Responsibilities"—a letter as poignant as Naomi Ginsberg's final message to her son in "Kaddish":

Dear Delmore

If there is another word besides wonderful I don't know I
don't remember telling you all these so accurate. Please save
this story and bring it home for me. There are moments in my
life, thet I believe all my struggles are worth while.

Mother

This was the same mother whose marital stratagems, and ef-
forts to pit her son against his father, Delmore could never
quite forgive, though he did vow to forget

the speech my mother made
In a restaurant, trapping my father there
At dinner with his whore. Her spoken rage
Struck down the child of seven years
With shame for all three, with pity for
The helpless harried waiter, with anger for
The diners gazing, avid, and contempt,
And great disgust for every human being.

Shame, pity, anger, contempt, and disgust—children all of his
mother's rage—made up the emotional baggage the poet felt
impelled to drag along beside him on his daily travels and
encounters. Attempts to reconcile himself to humanity (and
therefore to himself) were like labors of Sisyphus for Del-
more, and one way to read his poems is as a chronicle of his
losing battles. Looking at "Seurat's Sunday Afternoon along
the Seine," Schwartz could participate at second hand in the
benedictory impulse of the painter and at the same time be-
moan the critical remove that stood between him and the
blessed "Sunday people." Understandably, Schwartz felt an
intense attraction to the character of Coriolanus; and it is
characteristic of the author of "Coriolanus and His Mother"
to reverse himself, after a Homeric catalogue of earthly plea-
sures, by turning Baudelaire on his head: "Let us require of
ourselves the strength and power to view our selves and the
heart of man *with* disgust."

It is a measure of Atlas's biographical skill that he allows the
facts of the case history to speak for themselves, and they are

chilling: persecution delusions, marital disasters, erratic be-
havior. Constant anxieties about money led Schwartz to hatch
intricate plots to win academic tenure (though he always felt
uncomfortable in the classroom). Then there was the wild sce-
nario that began with the suspicion that Nelson Rockefeller
was having an affair with Elizabeth, Delmore's second wife,
and ended in Bellevue. (The poet hired a detective to harass an
art critic who has since become an influential member of the
New York art establishment.) In all this Atlas provides valuable
corroboration to the account given in *Humboldt's Gift* of the
friendship between Bellow and Schwartz, its vagaries and
points of stress, and its attractions withal for the Chicago-based
Nobel laureate. Indeed, Atlas is as coolly exact on the details of
Delmore's emotional career as he is on the interlocking lives of
his literary associates and the external facts about his publish-
ing history. Yet it is precisely as a case history that Schwartz is
presented to us, as though his writings were incidental and not
by themselves a justification for the biography. And here I
must register my one objection to a book that deserves in the
main the many accolades it has garnered. As a literary biogra-
phy, *Delmore Schwartz: The Life of an American Poet* is also per-
force a work of criticism; in the absence of adequate apprecia-
tion and practical criticism, this function is all the more vital.
But for all the sympathy he displays for the writer, Atlas is also
somewhat passionless, and his praise of Schwartz's poetry
seems perfunctory at times. Perhaps this is why some reviewers
of the biography have waxed moralistic, castigating Schwartz's
failings, or in other ways concentrated on the man or the pre-
dicament to the exclusion of the work, which they dismiss. Un-
fortunately, unless readers of the biography arrive equipped
with a prior awareness of Schwartz's writing they are unlikely
to come away with an interest in consulting it now. And this is a
shame, for the occasion does not call for closing the book on
Schwartz but for renewing the pleasures of his texts.

A lasting readership is merited for such poems as "The
Ballet of the Fifth Year," in which Romantic motifs are bril-
liantly revitalized, and "The Heavy Bear Who Goes with Me,"
about the Caliban in Everyman, "a swollen shadow, / A stupid
clown of the spirit's motive," who

Perplexes and affronts with his own darkness,
The secret life of belly and bone,
Opaque, too near, my private, yet unknown,
Stretches to embrace the very dear
With whom I would walk without him near,
Touches her grossly, although a word
Would bare my heart and make me clear,
Stumbles, flounders, and strives to be fed
Dragging me with him in his mouthing care,
Amid the hundred million of his kind,
The scrimmage of appetite everywhere.

Or take "An Argument in 1934," unaccountably omitted from the new edition of Schwartz's stories and available only to readers with access to the Winter 1942 issue of the *Kenyon Review*. Written in what he called biblical prose—"It is as if the senses were stained glass windows, and one only saw the light through the stained glass windows of one's senses"—with the sentences numbered in the fashion of scriptural verses, "An Argument in 1934" breaks down the distinction between story and prose poem in an original and inspired way. The piece is "about" the Depression, "the pyramid in the shadow of which these young men were walking." A visit to the New York Public Library supplies the occasion for heated debate about topical matters (the New Deal, the working class) and about the dangers and delights of solipsism, that perennial collegiate quandary, which Schwartz handles as deftly as Forster had in the opening pages of *The Longest Journey:* "You have just been punched by the external world."

Consider, too, the blending of the interpretive and creative modes of expression in "Coriolanus and His Mother." In "New Year's Eve," Schwartz referred fancifully to this work as "a satirical dialogue between Freud and Marx in which Freud comes to agree that capitalism is organized anal eroticism when Marx agrees in return that the oedipal complex is rooted in the ownership of the means of reproduction." This description is not quite accurate, though it does allude to the chief conceit of the work, the viewing of a play through the eyes of a compound familiar ghost. In using literature itself as metaphor, and in the specific appropriation of a Shakesperean text for modern metamorphosis, Schwartz furnished a precedent here for Auden's *The Sea and the Mirror;* and as is true for that work, it is the prose poetry that enables the critique to transcend its source. Donning the guise of "the most belated Shakespearean fool," the poet seizes the pause between acts to relate the proceedings to "an abstract picture postcard of the wounded nudity about which all things whirl, that is to say, the soul":

> In the precise center of this oblong postcard a human being is shown, possessing hair, eyes, hands, feet, arms, belly, genitals, and the other parts which make possible thought, movement, and love. This human being might be mistaken for Joseph, who had a many-colored coat; Moses, for whom God burned; David, who threw stones so well; Ulysses, who wished to go home; Orestes, who was hunted; Oedipus, who destroyed his own eyesight (perhaps secretly desiring the vision of Tiresias); Peter, betrayed by the cock; Dante, the greatest traveler; or the remorseless Morning Star, John Milton, who seduced our first mother. He might be mistaken for any one of these famous gentlemen. For look you! he undergoes the pain of all vertebrates, the labor of standing up. He endures the loneliness of all conscious beings. He ties his shoelaces in his own style, which merely shows that like those famous heroes, he is betrayed by his body, his feet hurt him and he must blow his nose. . . . No one, not the most precise counterfeiter, can duplicate his handwriting, for no one writes with precisely such curls. His handwriting is, however, merely a symptom of his nervous system. He is original.

Like the Bellow novel two years before it, the Atlas biography has spawned a proliferation of articles on Schwartz, many of which take a curiously condescending view of his poetry. Certain of the commentators are frankly writing memoirs, adding to the saga, while some of the critics whose concern is with currency seemed not even to bother reading or rereading the poems, having apparently decided that this mess of a man could not have anything to say to us—a grievous error in the face of a history of writers whose lines are wiser and nicer than their days. It is, to be sure, an error easy to succumb to, considering the profound interest in the moral imagination, the attention paid to the intersections of life and art, which the author's early writing displayed. And if the preaching at Delmore's ghost seems ungenerous, it does provide us with ready explanations for what went wrong—how narcissism turned into *acedia,* how melodrama was mistaken for tragedy. Like a man possessed by unfriendly demons who knows his lucid moments but cannot sustain them, Schwartz could from time to time reach an oasis in the desert of his confusion but could not prevent its fading into mirage; he gradually surrendered the shaping power necessary for his art.

It is dismaying nevertheless to think that the end result of such analysis might be to consign the poet to the ever widening shelf of unread sources of chatter and rumination. Virtually alone among recent reviewers, Robert Towers (in *The New York Review of Books*) went back for a thorough look at the poems and came away emptyhanded, disappointed. Part of the problem, perhaps, is that Schwartz is still in need of an editor to erase the dross and surround the gems with white space, not an uncommon predicament for a poet who could not manage his talent. He is a marvelous poet in passages and parts—he delights not so often with a finished, well-made poem as with passages of power and beauty, tucked in the pockets; his very failures seem spectacular, if only because a sense of overwhelming ambition seems somehow to stand apart from the works themselves. *Summer Knowledge,* the volume of selected poems that Towers consulted, contains enough that is mediocre, mannered in style, and archaic in diction to obscure the vitality of imagination that an "aficionado of his mess" (in Frank O'Hara's phrase) finds scattered here and there within the volume, or in old copies of the *Kenyon* and *Partisan* reviews, or indeed in the quotations sprinkled throughout Lila Valenti's helpful article, "The Apprenticeship of Delmore Schwartz" (in *Twentieth Century Literature,* July 1974).

Now there appears the *Last and Lost Poems of Delmore Schwartz,* designed, its editor tells us, as a "rescue mission," a companion volume to *Summer Knowledge,* meant to save from oblivion unpublished poems found among the poet's papers as well as a sampling of published works previously uncollected. It is intended as a "rescue mission" in a polemical sense also. Robert Phillips would like the book to rescue Schwartz from his numerous detractors and from such of his admirers—the majority—who mourn with Berryman the great falling off there was in Delmore's career as a poet. In the latter aim, Phillips cannot be said to have fully succeeded. He offers, in his preface to the volume, few reasons beyond his enthusiasm for his repeated contention that the last poems radiate "energy and delight." While his enthusiasm is genuine and therefore affecting, it does not prevent Phillips from citing, with apparent disapproval, some slightly misquoted lines from Frank O'Hara's "Memorial Day, 1950," with its jubilant reversal of Schwartz's most famous title ("Our responsibilities did not begin / in dreams, though they began in bed"). Phillips holds up the O'Hara poem to throw into relief the "lyric talent" of Delmore's last period, the "refreshing" celebration of "the natural, the lovely, the beautiful, and the harmonious." Under the circumstances, however, it is a most unfortunate comparison in which the older poet comes off a bad second best. O'Hara's poem, a breakthrough effort in his career, is remarkable for its life-affirming elation and bravura as well as for its successfully realized aesthetic— pursued by Schwartz but never completely mastered—which combines the lyrical impulse with the concrete and incongruous particulars of modern city life. For all their euphony— the gift of melody never deserted their author—many of the *Last and Lost Poems* seem tired by contrast, written in a kind of forced ecstasy, a gush of words contrived to create an artificial happiness that Schwartz could feel only when transported out of himself.

Brought up on Eliot as he was, Delmore Schwartz had always engendered new ideas for his poetry out of the past's great examples, but as his end drew near his sounds grew less distinct than their echoes. This is from the "Overture" to "The Studies of Narcissus":

> "Call us what you will: we are made such by love."
> We are such studs as dreams are made on, and
> Our little lives are ruled by the gods . . .

Later, in the same work,

> . . . After utter forgiveness, what knowledge
> Can be possessed by consciousness?
> Forgive: do not forget. Remember and live,
> For life is rooted in memory's damnation and blessedness.

The instinct to paraphrase Shakespeare's Sonnet 116, retaining as structural elements certain key phrases, is a good one, but the poem produced thereby suffers from sheer verboseness:

> Love is not love
> Nor is the love of love its truth in consciousness
> If it can be made hesitant by any crow or dove or
> seeming angel or demon from above or from below
> Or made more than it knows itself to be by the
> authority of any ministry of love.
> ("Sonnet Suggested by Homer, Chaucer, Shakespeare . . .")

On the other hand, one can see in "Spiders," which is a kind of wry meditation on the subject of Robert Frost's "Design," the wit that Kenneth Koch found so enchanting in his Harvard mentor. The poem anticipates the jolly didacticism that Koch brings to perfection in *The Art of Love:*

> Sometimes the male
> Arrives with the gift of a freshly caught fly.
> Sometimes he ties down the female, when she is frail,
> With deft strokes and quick maneuvers and threads of silk:
> But courtship and wooing, whatever their form, are informed
> By extreme caution, prudence, and calculation,
> For the female spider, lazier and fiercer than the male suitor,
> May make a meal of him if she does not feel in the same
> mood, or if her appetite
> Consumes her far more than the revelation of love's
> consummation.

In another late poem, the theme of Keats's "In a Drear-Nighted December" receives a treatment that is noble in its simplicity. "They" are birds, in the morning rain:

> They did not think at all
> Of the great red and bursting ball
> Of the kingly sun's terror and tempest, blazing,
> Once the slanting rain threw over all
> The colorless curtains of the ceaseless spontaneous fall.
>
> ("Poem")

On the whole, however, it is to the poems dated 1937 and 1941 that we are likely to respond with pleasure, for the precocious intelligence and sharp prosodist's ear that they reveal:

> The bubble-dancer, the deep-sea diver,
> The bureaucrat, the adulterer,
> Hide private parts which I disclose
> To those who know what a poem knows.
>
> ("What Curious Dresses All Men Wear")

One wonders why *Shenandoah,* missing from *Summer Knowledge,* has here again been omitted.

A comparison of the two longer works with which the new volume closes spells out the difference between what might have been and what was to be. Labeling itself "An Entertainment," "Paris and Helen" (1941) begins with an epigraph from Pope's translation of *The Iliad* juxtaposed with the naming of an ideal cast—Robert Montgomery as Paris, Madeleine Carroll as Helen, Greta Garbo, Myrna Loy, Hedy Lamarr, and Dame May Whitty taking turns as Venus, in her various guises. It is a verse play in the Yeatsian manner, and its burlesque of Hollywood is an effective counterpoise to the weight of final reflections:

> Is it not right
> And just that strong divinity
> Should intervene so much in human life
> And help poor Paris, help the human heart,
> Otherwise so ignoble, mean, and starved?
> —He has a shallow view of God's strange ways
> In Heaven and Earth, who thinks the just alone
> Deserve His charity.

"Kilroy's Carnival" (1958) similarly wishes to conflate high culture and low, this time in the form of "A Poetic Prologue for TV." But here the voice turns shrill, the humor without sufficient subtlety. Much of "the show" is devoted to the reading of letters and queries sent in by viewers. "You are a nut: a complete nut: that's why your program keeps becoming more and more popular," one writes. Another asks, "Are you a conscientious objector to life like the inspired novelist Count Leo Tolstoy?" The answer conveys the full pathos of Delmore Schwartz. "The answer is that I am conducting an interminable filibuster against the death of the heart in the little death of each day."

In his poem "At the Grave of Henry James," Auden prays for the many writers "whose works / Are in better taste than their lives," and if we remember to trust the poet rather than the man, we will not fail to experience a pleasurable intellectual commotion upon reading the works of Delmore Schwartz. And in that spirit we will, when reviewing the sad facts of his life, look on him not as a failure or an object lesson on the perils of egotism but as the sleepless "veteran of childhood" who wanted his eyes to "burn like the street-light all night quietly, / So that whatever is present will be known to me," but who could not transcend the profound nervousness that gnawed "at the roots of the teeth of his being." "Let no activity / mar our hurrah of mourning," John Berryman urged. "Let's all be Jews bereft, for he was one."

Elemental Bravery

The Unity of James Merrill's Poetry

. . . break, blow, burn, and make me new.
—Donne, "Holy Sonnets"

For nothing can be sole or whole
That has not been rent.
—Yeats, "Crazy Jane Talks with the Bishop"

With the visionary gleam that informs his cosmic commedia, James Merrill appears to have taken a great many readers by surprise. The critic who might once have damned Merrill with faint praise—by extolling him as "merely" a master craftsman—no longer has that luxury, if luxury it is to deny oneself the pleasures of texts in which, as in the novels of Jane Austen and Henry James, an education of the feelings takes place under the tutorship of language. "The Book of Ephraim," *Mirabell,* and *Scripts for the Pageant* are as elegant of surface, as fastidiously well-wrought, as any of Merrill's previous writings, but there should now be less room for misunderstanding. The "poems of science" Merrill has fashioned achieve a remarkable synthesis of levity and gravity; their gay, buoyant atmosphere contrapuntally sets off the seriousness of their hieratic intent. If Merrill's tone remains that of the dandy, his attitude that of the aesthete abroad (who feels "American in Europe and exotic at home"), one can scarcely ignore the news he now brings us from heavenly circles of limitless circumference, whose centers are everywhere.

"Mind you, it works best as metaphor," Merrill's vision

From *James Merrill: Essays in Criticism,* edited by David Lehman and Charles Berger (Ithaca: Cornell University Press, 1983).

does, as he himself remarks of his model of "the psychic atom." Still, the wedding of science fiction and poetic truths for the sake of dealing with ultimate questions as well as with the pressures of an immediate reality—this is a larger ambition than we are accustomed to, and an ambition largely brought off. And surely one must admire the performance, the skill with which Merrill has approached a problem memorably defined by one of his voices from beyond:

> DANTE'S LUCK LAY IN HIS GULLIBLE
> & HEAVENLY WORLD   WE MY BOY DRAW FROM 2
> SORTS OF READER: ONE ON HIS KNEES TO ART
> THE OTHER FACEDOWN OVER A COMIC BOOK.
> OUR STYLISH HIJINKS WONT AMUSE THE LATTER
> & THE FORMER WILL DISCOUNT OUR URGENT MATTER

Uncomprehending or dismissive responses are indeed inevitable. With his Ouija board apparatus, lost continents, and black holes, this most urbane of poets has made himself vulnerable on several counts. But I would argue that it is precisely thanks to the taking of this risk, to the fusion of "stylish hijinks" and "urgent matter," of comic book and art, that Merrill's great breakthrough has occurred. It seems to me, moreover, that the breakthrough has come not as an about-face but as the culmination of a lifetime of trials and tremors; there is, I will undertake to show, an essential unity to Merrill's career. Toward the "lessons" of *Mirabell* and *Scripts,* Merrill began doing his homework long ago. He has schooled his sensibility to aim at high romantic ideals, or at a network of them: the apprehension of angels on earth, the recovery of paradises misplaced or extinct, the redemption of time, the outwitting of mortality.

In securing Merrill's place as an American original, the trilogy compels us to take a retrospective look at his career and, in doing so, to question our biases, to wonder how so many could fail for so long to recognize as virtues this poet's metaphysical wit and his prodigious formal resources; a melancholy conclusion points to the devaluation, in our time, of the verbal gestures that give Merrill's poetry its distinctive finish. Like Emerson's Rhodora, these gestures are their own excuse for being, but their existence is far from gratuitous. To the contrary, Merrill's formal choices and his visionary insights present a classic chicken-and-egg problem in causality. His "means" and his "meanings" coincide; the pun, so characteristic of its author, is as much an instrument of truth as an element of style or a quirk of mind. From the start Merrill's reflexive attentiveness to a word's multiplicity of meanings signaled a concomitant interest in the overtones of an action or event: what life proposed, language disclosed. Pleasurable in itself, Merrill's wordplay is thus inseparable from the tasks his sense of poetic vocation demands of him. The trilogy represents an apotheosis of the effort to extend the scrutiny of self to the point that the examined consciousness—no less than "the life lived" and "the love spent"—acquires the shape and clarity of a work of art. By the same token, the earlier books may now be seen to chart the progress of the poet toward a vision as difficult to endure as to earn, the living record of one who transformed himself from "maker" to "creator" with no consequent loss of craft, whose outbreaks from the jail of form result in new forms every bit as exacting as those they supplant, designed to enhance poetic freedoms rather than diminish them.

To call the trilogy a comedy is to fix its mode, not to circumscribe its flight. It might be argued that the comic impulse derives much of its energy from the perceived push-and-pull between gravity (or gravitation) and levity (or levitation), and Merrill's poetry is indeed poised between the thrill of escape from the earth's magnetic force and the relentless insistence of our corporeal natures, dragging us back to earth. The pattern is defined in the comic archetype of the stargazer who falls into a ditch, although in the versions of this motif found in Chaucer, Sidney, and Swift the accent falls on the assertion of our "clayey lodgings" that make a mockery of all spiritual aspiration. Not so in Merrill's poetry. There the "erected wit" stands a good chance of rescuing the "infected will": never has Merrill excluded the possibility of a true transcendence, beyond even the project of uniting sense and soul, Cupid and Psyche, the Sultan and Scheherazade. Even before "Ephraim," his work is rife with intimations of an immortal world in which, at a stroke, two clichés renew themselves—"whatever will be, will be right." (Not for nothing is JM said to be the "faithful representative" of an obscure nineteenth-century editor of the works of Alexander Pope.) "Form's what affirms," Merrill affirms in "The Thousand and Second Night," and so, finally, does the comic impulse, with its hope of order restored, its happy ending implicit from the start. It holds out the promise that buoyant chatter can redeem weighty matter, that wit is everlasting and dust but for a time, that the stuff of tragedy, endured and absorbed, can be transmuted—by a conceit Rilke would have enjoyed—into the musical "scale of love and dread" played on a "thinking reed" by "the great god Pain."

In his poetry, Merrill characteristically cuts the figure of the suave host whose conversational brilliance and fondness for camp humor disarm the invited guest, so that the pouring of spirits at dinner's end finds him half-drugged already "in laughter, pain, and love" or "wit, affection, and despair," as the case may be. In "A Tenancy," the poem that closes *Water Street*, Merrill makes this tight-lipped pronouncement:

> If I am host at last
> It is of little more than my own past.
> May others be at home in it.

As "The Book of Ephraim" gathers momentum, the "others" who make their home in Merrill's salon include Zulu chieftains and "pallid Burne-Jones acroliths": like a friendly organism, the poem harbors and offers nourishment to all who call. But I do not mean to dwell overlong on this biological sense of "host"; it is pertinent that *hospes,* the Latin root of the word, signifies "host," "guest," and "stranger," for each fairly describes an aspect of the poet. He has ever been his own "perfect stranger"; he now plays host to a host of spirits, "familiar" and strange at once, while he himself is the guest in a heaven Ephraim defines as "THE SURROUND OF THE LIVING." To be host is not to deny other duties: from his privileged position at "the angelic secretariat" he takes dictation from Auden and other "ghostwriters": but then, Merrill's sense of hospitality is hardly conventional.

An additional sense of host can help correct a common misconception of readers who, upon opening *Mirabell,* will instinctively suspect the poet of pulling their legs. Such a reader will wonder whether Merrill gave strict credence to the messages spelled out by the willowware cup on his Ouija board; perhaps he or she will associate the work's otherworldly population with the mock-heroic machinery of *The Rape of the Lock,* will question the "scientific" basis of the poem, or will simply think the whole thing rather silly. Next, reassured by the way the poet has anticipated these reactions, impressed by the skepticism that marks the poet's persona, the reader will decide that Merrill consulted the board in much the same way that Yeats took note of his wife's sleeptalking, as a kind of Jungian trick, a way of coaxing the imagination. No doubt several of these responses have something to commend them, but committed readers will go further. They will begin to see that for Merrill the Ouija board is no more a trick than the Eucharist would be for devout Catholics. I draw my simile not only from the ecclesiastical sense of "host" but from the value Merrill everywhere places on the forms of ritual, the processes that prepare one to receive a vision of, and communion with, divinity. To be sure, Merrill's religiosity is quite explicitly that of the aesthete. Asked how "real" his "new mythology" seemed to him, Merrill has given this reply: "Literally, not very—except in recurrent euphoric hours when it's altogether too beautiful not to be true." If the relation between beauty and truth proposed here should strike familiar Keatsian chords, that is no accident; the romantic element in Merrill's work—its Platonic confidence, its sensuality of language—will prompt many to see Keats's capable hand pushing Merrill's pen in pursuit of his theme, "an old, exalted one: / The incarnation and withdrawal of / A god."

Reviewing Merrill's career, one is struck by the consistency with which the poet has turned to this theme, by the frequency with which his poems function as rituals designed to welcome and witness the divine visitation and to mourn over its aftermath. Not since Rilke has a poet trained his vision with such determination to explore the realms of the angels, confident that superior eyesight can discern their presence here on earth. "Life was fiction in disguise," and as a corollary proposition, "the stranger is a god in masquerade": subscribing to the defense of masks and fictions mounted by Oscar Wilde in *The Critic as Artist,* Merrill never forgets that the purpose of the disguise is to foster ultimate recognition, that the unmasking scene crowns the masquerade ball. Consider these lines from "A Dedication," the poem that serves as the valedictory close to *The Country of a Thousand Years of Peace;* the poet is communing with the newly-dead Hans Lodeizen, a figure of importance in the trilogy as well:

> These are the moments, if ever, an angel steps
> Into the mind, as kings into the dress
> Of a poor goatherd, for their acts of charity.
> There are moments when speech is but a mouth pressed
> Lightly and humbly against the angel's hand.

Significantly, the angel is rendered as a Shakespearean monarch, bearing a likeness to Henry V in disguise among his troops. His state is kingly, we are meant to see, and his charity a form of *caritas;* standing and waiting, the poet is struck speechless in his praise.

The "evidently angelic visitor" returns twice in *Water Street,* both times in the context of a work of art half-perceived and half-created by the poet. In "Angel," the figure appears "in finely woven robes, school of Van Eyck," in the painting hanging "above my desk"; in the angel's gestures and "round, hairless face," the poet reads a text "demanding praise, demanding surrender," forbidding profane speech. In "A Vision of the Garden," the poet recollects the childhood incident when, using his breath for ghostly writing on a chill windowpane, he drew the features of an angel doomed to "fade in mist"— features that will someday, he adds, be embodied in a flesh-and-blood "you." Nor is the figure absent from succeeding volumes; if anything there is a proliferation of guises by which he may be apprehended. An unlikely reincarnation occurs in *Braving the Elements,* in "Days of 1935": the poet's remembered fantasy of being kidnapped at age nine by "Floyd and Jean," gangster and moll. To them he becomes, in one of the poem's poignant reversals, deeply attached; and in an eery echo of the "mouth pressed / Lightly and humbly against the angel's hand," the boy struggling with his captor leaves "my toothprints on his hand, / Indenture of a kiss."

David Kalstone reports on a hidden agenda to Merrill's career, to which the titles of his volumes attest:

> It would be interesting to know at what point Merrill saw a larger pattern emerging in his work—the point at which conscious shaping caught up with what unplanned or unconscious experience had thrown his way. In retrospect a reader can see that *Braving the Elements* (1972) gathers behind it the titles—with full metaphorical force—of Merrill's previous books. In *The Country of a Thousand Years of Peace, Water Street, Nights and Days,* and *The Fire Screen,* he had referred to the four elements braved in the book which followed them. (*Divine Comedies* extends it one realm further.)

The elements thus braved resurface in *Scripts for the Pageant,* only now they have been elevated into a quartet of angelic essences. "Samos," the magnificent canzone at the heart of that volume, weaves a pattern of the "Promised Land" out of the elements and our ability to engage them; the poem's five recurrent end words are "water," "light," "fire," "land," and "sense." If there is a teleology at work here—if "sense" somehow leads to "ascents"—one way to measure it is by reference to the poet's progressively more successful attempts at prolonging his brief encounters with those divinely appointed messengers who came at first unbidden and eventually by way of response to his conscious summons. Perhaps the most extraordinary change in Merrill's poetry since *Divine Comedies* is its scale, its epic extension of a lyric impulse; by dint of an arduous soul-making, vessel-breaking progress, Merrill has managed to sustain the epiphanies that had previously proved as delicate and evanescent as Walter Pater's privileged moments or those of Stephen Dedalus.

It had always seemed an implicit truth in Merrill's poetry that the god's incarnation must be followed by his withdrawal.

Hence, in works preparatory to "The Book of Ephraim"—in the past that serves as prologue—the ecstatic occasion is tinged with regret at its imminent loss. Beauty, as Stevens put it, is momentary in the mind; the word "moments" occurs no fewer than three times in the nine lines of "A Dedication." Alas, the poet seems to lament, the vision cannot endure—to paraphrase Auden, it does not seriously intend to stay; more exactly, we can endure it only briefly. Yet even in defeat the poet takes away such knowledge as heralds future victory.

"Charles on Fire" comes close to making a parable from the (necessarily) interrupted vision, the blaze of brightness that blinds the viewer back into the cave but, once seen, ignites the determination to gain a return match, to stage a second showing. The poem records precisely the sort of epiphany Pater had in mind when he wrote, in *The Renaissance:* "A sudden light transfigures a trivial thing, a weathervane, a windmill, a winnowing flail, the dust in the barn door; a moment—and the thing has vanished, because it was pure effect; but it leaves a relish behind it, a longing that the accident may happen again." Like "A Narrow Escape," "Charles on Fire" has a *Symposium* setting—somewhat ironically, given the wise man's reticence at dinner's end. By the time of *Scripts,* the party will have grown into a full-fledged banquet, an ongoing and movable feast that numbers Plato himself among the gregarious "guest-hosts"; but here we are granted only an isolated moment of illumination bracketed by darkness. In a second respect as well, "Charles on Fire" resembles "A Narrow Escape" and the seven other poems Merrill published in 1954 under the title *Short Stories:* it tells a tale in little, claiming the stuff of short fiction for the province of verse, just as "The Book of Ephraim" would later perform the functions of a novel. I quote the poem in full:

> Another evening we sprawled about discussing
> Appearances. And it was the consensus
> That while uncommon physical good looks
> Continued to launch one, as before, in life
> (Among its vaporous eddies and false calms),
> Still, as one of us said into his beard,

"Without your intellectual and spiritual
Values, man, you are sunk." No one but squared
The shoulders of his own unloveliness.
Long-suffering Charles, having cooked and served the meal,
Now brought out little tumblers finely etched
He filled with amber liquor and then passed.
"Say," said the same young man, "in Paris, France,
They do it this way"—bounding to his feet
And touching a lit match to our host's full glass.
A blue flame, gentle, beautiful, came, went
Above the surface. In a hush that fell
We heard the vessel crack. The contents drained
As who should step down from a crystal coach.
Steward of spirits, Charles's glistening hand
All at once gloved itself in eeriness.
The moment passed. He made two quick sweeps and
Was flesh again. "It couldn't matter less,"
He said, but with a shocked, unconscious glance
Into the mirror. Finding nothing changed,
He filled a fresh glass and sank down among us.

In "little tumblers finely etched" and "filled with amber
liquor," the poet's alter ego serves up a trope for poetry, for
that kind of poetic making whose desired end is the burnished
artifact, frozen in its elegance, into which go a few rare and
expensive drops of "spirits." It is a poetry that keeps up ap-
pearances; and, in the sense of "physical good looks," "appear-
ances" are what the after-dinner conversation turns to. At one
time, we learn, these may have sufficed, as the delicate objet
d'art might once have satisfied its maker. Indeed, the group
agrees, uncommonly handsome physiognomy might still be
said "to launch one." At this point in the poem, Merrill instinc-
tively renews the somnolent metaphor in "launch": having
been christened, having had the queen break a bottle on his
hull, the initiate is now sailing somewhat against the current,
through the "vaporous eddies and false calms"—the mislead-
ing appearances of calm—that are all that stand between him
and turbulent waters. The figure is extended in the beat dic-
tion of the bearded young man, who issues a crucial proviso:
"Without your intellectual and spiritual / Values, man, you are

sunk." Both *sunk* and *man*, the two slang words in the statement, work overtime. Looks might launch the man, but staying afloat is a "spiritual" matter.

No sooner has our host poured the liquor than the same young man—ironically, since he has been the one to insist upon the "spiritual" side of things—takes a sudden interest in appearances and fashion, flaming the brandy as is done "in Paris, France." (A lovely touch, naming the country conveys a sense of the speaker's innocence and enthusiasm; he has the arrogance of youth—of one who has only recently been "launched.") His action results in an appearance of a wholly unexpected kind, an emblem of the angelic realm; in lieu of a toast, there is a divine hush:

> A blue flame, gentle, beautiful, came, went
> Above the surface. In a hush that fell
> We heard the vessel crack. The contents drained
> As who should step down from a crystal coach.

These lines do more than conduct us to the story's denouement. If, in the poem's terms, the sea represents that element of flux upon which our material lives toss and turn, fire is the agency of the spirit, of all that "couldn't matter less." Dancing "above the surface," the "blue flame" comes as a revelation; it has all the attributes of an epiphany, that is, a flashing forth of divinity, of darkness made visible. Extending the poem's sailing metaphor, the "blue flame" also suggests the bluish aura or glow visible around the masts of a ship during an electrical disturbance: the phenomenon known as St. Elmo's Fire, after the patron saint of sailors. The ship in question is no longer seaworthy, however; it has metamorphosed into an altogether different sort of vessel, one that cannot weather the storm. The glass, though it collaborated with the flames and the brandy to make the epiphany possible, can neither survive the moment nor contain it. The glass cracks; the fire that purifies destroys. But in its flickering instant a social occasion has turned into a religious mystery, as physical appearances have given way to a spiritual apparition. From circumstances that must, at least at first, seem unlikely, Merrill has extracted "the makings of a miracle," in Elizabeth Bishop's phrase; from the milieu of manners, he has derived the forms of ritual and ceremony so dear to him because they connect the realms of art and of spirit. And if, as a result, the host's serving of "spirits" may be taken as a trope for the poetic process, it is the vessel-shattering flame that has turned an inconsequential anecdote into a parable.

Harold Bloom has demonstrated that, as found in the doctrine of the Lurianic Kabbalah, the theme of the cracking of vessels furnishes an antecedent myth for the literary artist's "breaking of forms," an account of creation that the secondary or "belated" artist must reenact. According to the Kabbalah, God first created "*kelim*, 'vessels,' of which the culminating vessel was *Adam Kadmon* or primal Man." But the creative light was too strong, or the vessels too fragile, for the majority of them shattered instantly to pieces. It is axiomatic—the very products of holy energy cannot contain it, cannot stay whole. Fortunately, by stages one can grow to absorb such heavenly light as, in its original force, cannot but burst the beholder, splintering his vision as if it were no sturdier than a child's eyeglasses lying smashed and forlorn on a worn gymnasium cinderpath. Creation can be restored, the dispersed light gathered, only by a process of restitution that, in Bloom's words, calls for "acts of meditation, acts that lift up and so liberate the fallen sparks of God from their imprisonment in the shards of the *kelippot* [broken vessels of evil]." That these acts of meditation are "at once psychic and linguistic," that "defense mechanisms and rhetorical tropes" accomplish the work of restitution, hammers home (for Bloom) the pertinence of the analogy for an understanding of poetic creation. It would be impossible, in so brief a summary, to do justice to Bloom's reasoning. But even as I have sketchily described it, the myth of blinding light, broken receptacles, and redemptive meditation cannot fail to illuminate a vital aspect of "Charles on Fire" and the tendency it exemplifies in Merrill's poetry.

Indeed, whether or not the allusion lay beyond the poet's conscious intention, "Charles on Fire" seems invested with a knowledge of kabbalistic doctrine. Just as "God's name was too strong for his words" and therefore smashed the *kelim*, so here the "blue flame" shatters one of the "little tumblers finely etched"; just as the divine sparks of light disperse, so here the "contents" drain from the glass. The destruction is holy nevertheless, for it yields the glimpse of an angelic presence, "as who should step down from a crystal coach." The very syntax of this royal simile recalls the moment of Merrill's first angelic encounter:

> an angel steps
> Into the mind, as kings into the dress
> Of a poor goatherd, for their acts of charity.

The visitation has taken place, however unseemly the circumstances, and it has swiftly made itself felt. Precisely where the vessel has cracked, a lane to the spiritual realm has opened—we remember that these lines from Auden's "As I Walked Out One Evening" occur in the "Quotations" section of "The Book of Ephraim":

> *The glacier knocks in the cupboard,*
> *The desert sighs in the bed,*
> *And the crack in the tea-cup opens*
> *A lane to the land of the dead.*

Now Charles, "steward of spirits" in both senses, experiences a momentary transfiguration, even as he resumes his duties as host; preparatory to sweeping up the spilled "contents," his "glistening hand" has "gloved itself in eeriness," has added an invisible layer to his skin. Only for a moment, to be sure: and it passes, as the flame itself "came, went," pausing only for the length of a comma. The change in Charles does not survive "a shocked, unconscious glance / Into the mirror," which confirms our host's return to flesh and to the world of looks and appearances; the other "host," the sacred guest, has departed, if he was ever there—he existed by intimation alone, by the proxy work of a simile. And now, with the conclusion of the poem, the metaphor of shipwreck is brought to port: "He filled a fresh glass and sank down among us."

I have analyzed "Charles on Fire" in such detail not only because Merrill's intricate conceits demand and reward the closest possible attention but because this paradigmatic epiphany mirrors so many of the concerns and habits we encounter in the trilogy. There, as here, the consuming wish to entertain the angels (in the additional sense of entertaining an idea) is as fundamental as Merrill's penchant for elevating social gestures, parlor games, apparent accidents, even a guest's gaucheries, into acts and activities of mystical significance, performed, pondered, repeated as rituals, as invitations extended to the divine unknown. Thus from figures on wallpaper, demoniac beings spring to imaginative life; thus a photocopying machine can supply the requisite mirror and flash of light that, in an ironic update of Proust's memory triggers, bring spirits rushing to the scene. Nor does the question of appearances go away after "Charles on Fire." Merrill is still asking it in the celestial context of *Mirabell:* "Will it ever, ever solve itself, / This riddle of appearances in Heaven?" "This riddle," which can be solved by paradox alone, refigures the diners' dilemma in "Charles on Fire"; it revises that poem's gloomy conclusion on the uneasy relations between spirit and corporeal form. How, JM wonders during one of the early lessons, can his bodiless tutors be said to resemble the bats on his wallpaper? His skepticism merits an "A PLUS" from the spirit of Maria Mitsotáki, who exposes "THE FICTION THAT THEY HAVE APPEARANCES   THEY DO NOT." Nevertheless, though he exists "in the realm of no appearances," JM's favorite bat promptly turns into a peacock and manifests himself as such. From "Charles on Fire," whose mirror signaled a failed metamorphosis, we have arrived at a place where mirrors—and where the mind's mirrorlike systems of reflection and speculation—enable spirits to "appear," allow contact to be made with them, and can even revamp bat into peacock, "741" into foppish "Mirabell," a number into a name.

In the journey of his making, the Merrill of *Nights and Days* seems in retrospect to have been governed by Hölderlin's wistful observation (in "Brod und Wein"):

> Denn nicht immer vermag ein schwaches Gefäs sie zu fassen,
> Nur zu Zeiten erträgt göttliche Fülle der Mensch.

> [For not always can a frail vessel contain them,
> Only from time to time can man bear the plenty of the gods.]

But he has also learned that he must endure—and more, he must work to bring about—the shattering of vessels, the *shevirah hakelim,* before he can embark upon those redemptive acts of meditation that will restore his blissful seat at "the angelic secretariat." He will have to subject to a visionary blaze the vessels of his craft; he will have to stretch to the breaking point the sculptured verse forms that resemble "little tumblers finely etched." In the books that lead up to *Mirabell* and *Scripts for the Pageant,* Merrill has taken just this course. His poetry seems to have burst out of contours lovingly etched; the forms he has mastered he shatters, and out of a gathering of splinters a new heavenly order has emerged. It is surely appropriate that the epigraph of *Scripts* contains a reference to the delicate glass the groom must shatter with his foot during the Jewish wedding ceremony: for the climax of that book occurs when JM and DJ, scribe and hand, break a mirror in order to release the imprisoned spirits of Auden and Maria. It is also to the point that the word "break," in conjugated or participial form, recurs throughout *Mirabell* and more than once signals an actual break in the flow of words, a rupture between verb and object. Two examples:

> Broken—for good?—of its imperious
> Slashing at capitals, our cup points out
> A gentler dictum . . .

And, two pages earlier, in an italicized letter addressed to DJ:

> *How about breaking (remember*
> *that old dream?) the trip with a glimpse of Stonehenge*
> *& Avebury?*

It is a rupture, we learn, that necessitates the surgery DJ must undergo. He had suffered it when—no accident!—he carried up some flights of stairs the immense Victorian mirror that proved indispensable to the Ouija ceremony; the pain of the breakage constitutes the cost, for him, of admission to the celestial seminars. JM, for his part, has been told he will have an "ARTISTIC BREAKTHRU." But inevitably the message containing this prophecy or promise itself "Breaks off. Is broken off," mid-sentence, before the speaker could complete the thought. Some sort of fragmentation must, it seems, precede or accompany a vision of unity. After all, the author of "The Broken Home" was also, and first, the product of one. No accident: there is a special providence in the fall of a sparrow—or in the breaking of a trance, a limb, a code, a home. "Nothing can be sole or whole," said Crazy Jane to the Bishop, "that has not been rent."

Of this pattern Merrill's story "Peru: The Landscape Game" takes charming notice. An account of a trip to Peru, the story was conceived and composed *before* the trip took place, in the writer's effort to provide proof against disappointment, anticipatory imaginings to compensate for the inadequacies of actuality. The story's generative conceit is "that psychological game in which each person describes a house he then leaves in order to take an imaginary walk. One by one he discovers a key, a bowl, a body of water, a wild creature, and finally a wall. Free association is invited at any stage, and nothing explained until the last player has spoken." What kind of bowl springs to Merrill's mind as, the night before flying to Lima, he plays the game? Not golden but a "mixing bowl, cracked—fearing botulism, I kick it out of my path." A humorous translation of the line occurs a page later, in this exchange:

> "What was it your bowl meant?" K yawned, up in the room.
>
> "I'm a good mixer. But liable to go to pieces."

In the Jungian code the story proposes as an interpretive key, the bowl stands for Art.

II.

Merrill brings to "The Book of Ephraim" a novelist's ambition and sense of scale; elsewhere as well his imagination gravitates toward narrative form. But in Merrill's most ambitious narrative experiments the characters break ranks, the sequence of events snaps; the friction between double-meaninged words causes flames to flare, threatening to disrupt the proceedings. Such disruptions are intentional and inevitable. What makes them so? The ironically self-deprecatory tone Merrill uses when referring to his "unrelenting fluency" hints at an answer. Here is a poet who, mistrustful of his gifts, harbors the suspicion that, as he puts it in "The Thousand and Second Night," "fluent passages of metaphor" undermine the text, falsify the experience. Since his events of insight occur as disjunctions, violations, even fractures, the interrupted narrative has emerged as a favored strategy.

For Merrill, breakdown leads eventually to breakthrough. Laboring to find a form that will stretch to assimilate interruptions and intrusions, he has made the most of these threats to his poetic coherence; they present, after all, a fit challenge to his shaping powers, a stimulus toward the construction of new and larger wholes, houses that can stand though divided against themselves. Between the whole and its parts, between the expansive impulse and the contractions of form, between lyric endings and narrative ends, there is at best an uneasy truce. We would do well to keep this complicated dialectic in mind. A poem pauses to make room for a subversive patch of prose; quatrains drift toward and away from sonnets; sonnets, in a poem composed of a series of them, reassert their individual integrity even as the boundaries between them begin to blur. Thus the poems formally enact their underlying tensions. The marvel is that their "unrelenting fluency" prevails despite the wandering rocks and other obstacles blocking the way.

It is possible to read certain of Merrill's poems as chapters of a life in progress, a *Künstlerroman* in the making; "The Book of Ephraim" is, in Kalstone's words, "only the most explicit and extended of these efforts" toward "a kind of autobiography in verse." In supervising the relations between autobiography and "fiction in disguise," Merrill turns frequently to Proust for guidance. Already in *Water Street*, where a poem "For Proust" has "Scenes of Childhood" for a neighbor, Merrill's devotion to this master is brought to the surface; "The World and the Child," the volume's moving villanelle, features that most primal of Proustian scenes, "the child awake and wearied of," stoical in his dark bedroom while parents and others in the room below talk about him. The influence has deepened in the course of Merrill's career; the poet has even, in the willowware cup he and his partner use as a Ouija pointer, found a worthy substitute for the teacup from which, thanks to Marcel's madeleine, "towns and gardens alike" sprang into being. It is to Proust that, in "Days of 1971," Merrill attributes the "twofold" law said to govern human desire. From Proust, too, Merrill derives one of his distinctive procedures: "To overlook a subject for its image, / To labor images till they yield a subject." He rebels against this tendency momentarily in "The Book of Ephraim," but the struggle only confirms the extent of the influence, Proust being the kind of necessary angel with whom the poet must sometimes wrestle, in overnight combat, to emerge the next morning limping into a new name—Jacob's fate in the Bible.

With the instincts of a novelist, whose detached omniscience asserts itself even in a first-person narrative, Merrill enjoys playing shrink to his own analysand, refusing to stay put on the couch. Curiosity and not complaint is this poet's driving force. Accordingly, after the example of Proust, Merrill endeavors to read his days, as though they constituted an unwritten text; he would determine what valences the elements of his life might be said to have; he would leap to poetry from exercises of the involuntary memory. Time is the joker in the deck, the great variable in the formula chalked on the blackboard. Consciousness of a fourth dimension leads the writer to depart freely from accepted chronology, juggling past and present events (and future forebodings) instead of imposing a linear sequence on them:

> Too violent,
> I once thought, that foreshortening in Proust—
> A world abruptly old, whitehaired, a reader
> Looking up in puzzlement to fathom
> Whether ten years or forty have gone by.
> Young, I mistook it for an unconvincing
> Trick of the teller. It was truth instead
> Babbling through his own astonishment.

As Proust did, Merrill relies on his fictions to guide him past astonishment to the truth. He avails himself of the error, the joke, the slip of the pen or pun, the dream: all the subterfuges of the psyche, the witticisms of the soul, as Freud described them in *The Psychopathology of Everyday Life, Jokes and Their Relation to the Unconscious,* and *The Interpretation of Dreams.*

Jung is given a more prominent place in "The Book of Ephraim," but the trilogy's debt to Freud is arguably the profounder one. So Mirabell acknowledges, honoring Freud for having married myth to science:

> FREUD'S WORK WAS TO ILLUMINE FOR
> SCIENCE THE DELICATE ENVELOPE OF SOUL: THE PSYCHE:
> MANIFESTATION OF SOUL ENERGIES   IF BREATH IS THE
> SOUL OF THE BODY THEN PSYCHE IS THE BREATH OF THE SOUL

What else is Mirabell's "no accident" clause but an uppercase version of Freudian determinism, with myth and metaphysics layered on? At one point in "Ephraim," however, Freud seems to have a special nay-saying part to play: it is JM's shrink, cast in the role of doubting Thomas, who furnishes the skeptical counterturn to the Jungian or Stevensian equation of God and the imagination. Tom would have JM and DJ regard their Ouija sessions as a "harmless" folie à deux; he even prompts the former to come up with a textbook explanation for "these odd / Inseminations by psycho-roulette." The trilogy overcomes such denials—Freud puts in a personal appearance to override Tom—but by including them, attributing some of them to himself, Merrill manages to anticipate possible objections to his work and thereby to deflate them. This foresight is more than a shrewd rhetorical strategy. As much as his insouciance under pressure, his reluctance to believe what his celestial informants have to say contributes to the tension between matter and manner (or antimatter) that is one of the trilogy's abiding sources of energy. The result is a species of the comic sublime, the assertion of wit and cultivated sensibility in the very throes of an ecstatic seizure. Such clashes of impulse are fundamental to the enterprise. "The two pioneering forces of modern sensibility are Jewish moral seriousness and homosexual aestheticism and irony," Susan Sontag observes in her "Notes on 'Camp,' " and judging by his treatment of these "forces" in *Mirabell,* one imagines Merrill would concur. The one impulse constantly tests and tempers the other, as the poetry performs the work of reconciliation, housing them under one head just as Ephraim, taking after Joyce's Bloom, embodies a synthesis of Hellenism and Judaism.

Between one Scylla and another Charybdis—between novel and poem, or fiction and life, or artifice and nature—the poet seems often to be navigating. While it causes him some anxious moments, the real or merely apparent antagonism implicit in these dualities can turn into a fruitful exchange, especially when Merrill makes the evolution of a work one of that work's subjects. This he does with wry self-consciousness (as in "The Thousand and Second Night") or by intimation (as when, in "The Friend of the Fourth Decade," the ritual washing of a postcard collection, in the manner of a philatelist eager to dislodge stamps, suggests the process by which a novel "dissolves" into a poetic solution.) By the time of "The Will," in *Divine Comedies,* writing and living have become so bound together as metaphors for one another that Valéry's *il faut tenter de vivre* seems to have evolved into *il faut tenter d'écrire.* In several of these poems Merrill very nearly adopts the posture of novelist manqué that marks his experimental novel, *The (Diblos) Notebook.* It is almost as though he conceived of such works as surrogates for the shipwrecked "big book" that Mallarmé regarded both as the desired destination of all existence and as its vehicle. Merrill's strength of versification, his ability to load every rift with ore, is such that what might appear a liability—the need to predicate a work on an absent but prior text—is converted into an asset: language takes the place of incident, and the writing of a longer prose narrative seems an uneconomical superfluity. Yet such works do seem to lurk somewhere in the background; "The Thousand and Second Night" and "From the Cupola," for example, both include excerpts from *Psyche's Sisters,* a spurious novel by the pseudonymous A. H. Clarendon, whose similarly unwritten *Time Was,* quoted in "The Book of Ephraim," reinforces our impression of him as a stylist in the manner and mode of E. F. Benson.

Among the poems that seem to have presented themselves to Merrill, at least initially, as the stuff of prose, "The Book of Ephraim" is unquestionably the most notable. Its opening section delineates the trilogy's prose origins and poetic alchemy, beginning with an admission of error or weakness:

> Admittedly I err by undertaking
> This in its present form. The baldest prose
> Reportage was called for, that would reach
> The widest public in the shortest time.

Defeated by deadlines, the poet then considers the novel to be the proper form for his "novel" material, and when here too the attempt is aborted, again he blames himself:

> My downfall was "word-painting." Exquisite
> Peek-a-boo plumage, limbs aflush from sheer
> Bombast unfurling through the troposphere . . .

Along the way Merrill complains of the inadequacy of "Our age's fancy narrative concoctions"; supernal punmanship engenders psychoanalytical insight as he explains why he dismissed from consideration "the in its fashion brilliant / Nouveau roman," which

> Struck me as an orphaned form, whose followers,
> Suckled by Woolf not Mann, had stories told them
> In childhood, if at all, by adults whom
> They could not love or honor.

The form of "Ephraim" would appear, then, to have been contrived at last resort, all else having failed. And we are right to assume that something other than modesty, something beyond rational planning, accounts for this version of the work's origins. The point is that, in its final state, the poem gathers together various discarded or unrealizable selves: it functions as reportage, fairy tale, novel, even nouveau roman. The flotsam and jetsam of at least one abandoned novel bob up to the surface of "Ephraim"; from details given here and there, an enterprising reader can extrapolate the entire plot of this shipwrecked work. But (to switch metaphors) in doing so he will have visited but one story in a multitiered structure. For the poem also asks to be read as history, as a recollection of the twenty years preceding it—and as a chronicle of 1974, the year of composition, which supplies its share of metaphors:

> Impeachment ripens round the furrowed stone
> Face of a story-teller who has given
> Fiction a bad name (I at least thank heaven
> For my executive privilege vis-à-vis
> Transcripts of certain private hours with E.)

But in order for "The Book of Ephraim" to make a present of its several pasts, to recover and to redeem its broken pieces, there had to have been something to wreck—something to break, to burn, and to be made new. As a necessary prelude to the final composition, a novel had to be drafted, if not inscribed, then not simply shelved but thrown away, "accidentally on purpose," as children like to say. In *Divine Comedies,* "The Will" documents this crucial transitional phase—the loss or rejection, the loss that is a rejection, of the abandoned novel that became "Ephraim."

Among Merrill's poems "The Will" is scarcely unique in being concerned with the salutary effects of loss. As befits the author of "Midas among Goldenrod," an early poem, Merrill participates in the mythic pattern that Richard Howard sees as central to his generation of poets: he would dissolve his golden touch in water, longing to lose what he had labored to acquire. In fact, it might be equally helpful to use Prospero as his foil, for he vows to drown his book and break his magic staff after having first unleashed and then resolved his tempest in a teacup. For Merrill, the impulse to bring order out of wreckage seems ever accompanied by the desire to reverse the process, to crack the well-wrought urn; within his completed design, there persists a lingering distrust of artifice and design. Consider the punning relation of numbers to words in *Mirabell: Books of Number.* Stephen Yenser explains:

> Thus section 0 begins "Oh very well then," and section 1 echoes its number in both French and English: "UNHEEDFUL ONE."

3's "Trials and tremors" make use of Greek and the reader's choice of several other languages, 4's "Fear" of German, 5's "Go" of Japanese, 6's "She stood" of Russian, 7's "CHILDREN" of Chinese, 9's "NO VEIL" of Italian and Portuguese. 2 and 8 ring changes on the device, the one beginning with the second letter of the Hebrew alphabet (sometimes used in place of the number) in "Bethinking," the other with "8."

What could speak more eloquently of the value this poet attaches to design—and of his steadfastness and ingenuity in keeping to one? Nor are the results merely ornamental; the conceit signifies. It dramatizes the notion that an alphabet of numbers gave birth to the writing; it suggests that language has a mind of its own, an autonomy of genius. Yet, though the correspondences are blessed, though they are produced by imagination and not by mere fancy, the poet reports that he is "sickened by these blunt stabs at 'design' " when, in *Scripts for the Pageant,* he looks back at the numbered portals he had erected for *Mirabell* and sees that book itself as a "Tower of Babel."

The trilogy has its share of deliberate breakdowns, characters stopping in mid-speech, interruptions, abandonments, misgivings, turnings against the self. The fragments do coalesce and cohere; the set pieces fit together, puzzle perfect; yet something about them militates against that sense of completion, of "design." The hybrid form and blend of styles exhibited by the work argue for a poetry of movement, process, and flow, as if for the sake of vitality the poet had to be a quick-change artist. "The Book of Ephraim" presents Merrill at his most protean, constantly changing shape, modulating from the narrator's pentameter to Ephraim's telegraphic style, hopping from sonnet sequence to terza rima. One ingenious section takes the guise of an annotated dramatis personae; another, taking a cue from its initial letter, consists entirely of quotations, mostly in prose, from real or imagined sources. Expediency would seem to be Merrill's rule of thumb:

> Since it had never truly fit, why wear
> The shoe of prose? In verse the feet went bare.
> Measures, furthermore, had been defined
> As what emergency required.

As Marianne Moore put it, "ecstasy affords the occasion and expediency determines the form"; form, in effect, follows function. The garments available to the cunning seamstress are various enough to assure that for each speaker, for every situation, the appropriate dress will be found. But clothes are doomed to stay shapeless until worn—it takes a living body to make them come to life, and an "emergency" (in the sense of "an emergent occasion") to bring the wardrobe out of the closet.

"The Thousand and Second Night" prefigures "The Book of Ephraim" with respect to its expedient form. Like the latter, if on a smaller scale, it combines narrative and reflection upon narrative, interrupting its flow to accommodate a sonnet here, a prose paragraph there; there is visible evidence of split seams, but these have been skillfully mended. The poem's controlling image is its final one: an ethereal Scheherazade who merges with her fictions, a lusty Sultan liberated from her spell, left in the dark as to what his own tale might mean. The pair can stand for the soul and the senses, night and day, moon and sun, fiction and action, mother and father, even Psyche and Cupid. Can the poet negotiate a peace these estranged or quarreling couples can live with? Or, as Merrill puts it in *Mirabell*, will "Sultan Biology" come to love nature as Scheherazade, and if so, to what effect? The questions linger in the air long after the crisis that prompted them has found resolution and acedia has given way to resolve. "Form's what affirms," then, without actually settling anything; there is at best a half-rhyme between *form* and what it means to *affirm*. The remark appears in the poem's penultimate section, garbed in one of life's nonfiction disguises, the instructor's trot through a poem:

> Now if the class will turn back to this, er,
> Poem's first section—Istanbul—I shall take
> What little time is left today to make
> Some brief points. So. The rough pentameter
>
> Quatrains give way, you will observe, to three
> Interpolations, prose as well as verse.
> Does it come through how each in turn refers
> To mind, body, and soul (or memory)?

The tension between narrative "forward motion" and poetic closure establishes itself immediately in "The Thousand and Second Night." The three "rough pentameter / Quatrains" that open the poem lead us to expect a fourth to follow, and it does; but it breaks off abruptly after two clipped lines, forcing us to revise our reading, to regard the opening fourteen lines as a sonnet. The breaking of the form is thus itself formally contained even as it enables the poet to reach out of bounds. (By contrast, "An Urban Convalescence"—the lead poem in *Water Street*—opens with stanzas that approach but fall short of sonnet form, an octave followed by a five-line stanza.) Here is that quatrain and a half which, at second glance, is the sestet of a sonnet; notice how the exclamation at the end simultaneously concludes one movement and announces the start of the next:

> Twenty-five hundred years this city has stood between
> The passive Orient and our frantic West.
> I see no reason to be depressed;
> There are too many other things I haven't seen,
>
> Like Hagia Sophia. Tea drunk, shaved and dressed . . .
> *Dahin! Dahin!?*

Of the "three / Interpolations" that follow, the last—a paragraph of prose—illustrates well Merrill's characteristically "vertical" expansion of a spot of time along the "horizontal" vector of the poem's narrative graph. No sooner has the verse announced the surfacing of an "infantile / Memory" than the prose, as if in obedience to a summons, steps dutifully forth. The Proustian click has happened on the poet's walk "across the bridge," a movement the poem enacts; we travel across from the troubled "now" of Istanbul to the healing "then" of memory, from "I" to fictive "he," verse to prose, the "mosque of Suleiman the Magnificent" to the wen on a grandmother's wrist, the "hard mauve bubble" that the mosque recalls:

> And now what? Back, I guess, to the modern town.
> Midway across the bridge, an infantile
> Memory promises to uncramp my style.
> I stop in deepening light to jot it down:

On the crest of her wrist, by the black watered silk of the watchband, his grandmother had a wen, a hard mauve bubble up from which bristled three or four white hairs. How often he had lain in her lap and been lulled to a rhythm easily the whole world's then—the yellowish sparkle of a ring marking its outer limit, while in the foreground, silhouetted like the mosque of Suleiman the Magnificent, mass and minarets felt by someone fallen asleep on the deck of his moored caïque, that principal landmark's rise and fall distinguished, from any other, her beloved hand.

As in Proust, the apprehended object has retreated from central stage, has evolved into a simile for an object it imperfectly resembles; as in Proust, the simile's value rests in the quickening of memory, the conjuring up of early sensations. By thus disrupting the narrative to accommodate a glimpse of an anterior one, while insisting that the disruptive element itself be formally circumscribed, Merrill argues for the affirmative powers of form. *What* it affirms seems secondary to the blessed realization *that* it does; it speaks to the imagination's provisional success in either sensing or willing an order to things while maintaining fidelity to the appearance of disorder, disunity, dispersal.

The same strategy is at work in "From the Cupola," which together with "The Thousand and Second Night" provides a frame for *Nights and Days*. Again the poet conducts his train of verse to a prose detour; again the prose is in counterpoint to the verse around it, and here it is overtly a surviving fragment from an abandoned manuscript. The verse portions of "From the Cupola" record the breathless exchanges between Psyche and Cupid; the prose functions as a digression, a "breather" during which the poet drops anchor off the coast of a more prosaic island of activity, where campy kitchen conversations take place. Psyche, it seems, lives with her sisters Alice and Gertrude in the Connecticut equivalent of 27, rue de Fleurus; or rather, they live in the imagination of the imaginary Mr. Clarendon:

> "Oh, Psyche!" her sister burst out at length. "Here you are, surrounded by loving kin, in a house crammed with lovely old

things, and what do you crave but the unfamiliar, the 'transcendental'? I declare, you're turning into the classic New England old maid!"

Once it has furnished a contemporary social context for the mythic personages of the poem, once it has shifted them from one kind of fable to another, the prose rounds itself off with an unexpected rhyme that marks its completion and signals a return to verse: "Piercing her to the brain. // Spelt out in brutal prose, all had been plain." The intrusion is somehow assimilated; the interruption has been, in effect, a scheduled one, in the same way that in Kafka's parable the leopards invading a temple come to be accepted as part of the ritual.

The tug-of-war between poetry and prose is on center stage in *The (Diblos) Notebook*. This attempt at a nouveau roman keeps wanting to slide into poetry, and we expect it to. Consider this representative example:

> How to describe the change? I use my body less. If I swim at all, it is closer to the shore. Now that I know what liquor does to my liver, I drink ~~less~~ more. I don't take people as seriously. I move from place to place. I no longer think of myself as having a home. (Orson: Home is where the mind is.) I read more (alas) & (alas again) I *write*.

By making visible the "invisible" hand of the author, the *Notebook* mediates between alternative texts, shedding skins like a snake and retaining what it discards, albeit in canceled form. The erasure and substitution (e.g., "~~less~~ more") make clear that the events of a novel, any novel, are expedient fictions, products of choice. The rhyme itself is funny because unexpected, perverse: we are, I think, meant to see that the logic of the psyche may fly in the face of all human reason or wisdom; it may conform instead to the logic of a rhyme.

III.

If it is relatively easy to tabulate Merrill's literary debts, that is partially because he himself has kept scrupulous records. A consciously literary artist, for all that he wears his learning lightly, Merrill invites us to read his poems with poetry in mind, to examine parallels and precedents; his respect for tradition leads him to want to experiment with it. Like all authentically "new" poetry, Merrill's invents a past for itself or more than one; he squares the exigencies of formal verse with a contemporary idiom and "novel" material, and while doing so he directs the latter-day reader's attention to poets and writers who might otherwise, regrettably, seem foreign to our time. Merrill's attempts at invigorating what has already started to ossify, his effort to breathe new life into a form or a phrase that has fallen on evil days, not to mention his successful thefts from past masters, are exemplary at a time when we may have more poets, but we certainly have more ignorant poets, than ever before.

I have mentioned the lifelong influence of Marcel Proust; in the trilogy a far more apparent presence is that of W. H. Auden. The apocalyptic epic as a genre allows for huge chunks of personal history, and so it must have seemed especially attractive to Merrill as he entered mid-career—our contemporary euphemism for the middle of life's journey— preparing to come to terms with Auden's eclipsed generation. Here one must be careful to distinguish between the Auden who figures as a character in *Mirabell* and *Scripts* and the Auden who has served Merrill as a literary exemplar, a poetic father. As a familiar spirit, a historical personage filtered through Merrill's myth-making prism, a friend among the newly dead whose beneficent good cheer robs death of its terror if not of its sting, Auden is the wise guy and the wise man in one, no less sagacious for his foppery; it is his genius to convert seemingly contradictory impulses into complementary ones, to embody the spiritual and to sanctify the profane. This dream of Auden is likewise a dream of Merrill himself; both have a side in them for which Congreve's Mirabell furnishes an apt sobriquet. Auden is honored equally in strictly technical ways, for strictly technical reasons. In Auden's smithy Merrill had done his apprenticeship, after all. He learned to practice a strict economy of form and to play with language, to test his ingenuity and its flexibility at once; he had emulated the older poet's stylistic virtuosity and had borrowed some of his tricks. Merrill's right-angle rhymes ("leaves" with "lives," "washes" with "wishes"), for example: they derive from Wilfred Owen but almost certainly by way of Auden's *Paid on Both Sides*. Also on long-term loan from the Auden library are Merrill's unisex rhymes, alternating masculine and feminine endings—"change" paired off with "arrangement," "courier" with "your," "silver" with "chill." The delight Merrill takes in random collisions of verbal particles bespeaks a deep affinity with Auden—and with Nabokov as well. In Merrill's poetry as in *Lolita* and *Pale Fire*, creative pretexts—an anagram here, a spoonerism there—are left like purloined letters in everyone's view, comical clues for the reader as sleuth to uncover.

Merrill has a weakness for the "hexagonal" (that is, "sick-sided") pun, but much of his paranomasia is founded on the conviction that words yield their choicest secrets through playful means, that linguistic "accidents"are meaningful and therefore not really accidents at all, that language's special logic can lead to discoveries that seem "altogether too beautiful not to be true." When, in "The Will," appearing surprised at Ephraim's moral suasion, JM says "you think the Word by definition good," he is roundly reproved: "IF U DO NOT YR WORLD WILL BE UNDONE / & HEAVEN ITSELF TURN TO ONE GRINNING SKULL." Ephraim is, of course, preaching to the zealously converted. From the start the trilogy opposes the immortal life of words against the fact of death: what establishes contact with the dead, and thus resuscitates them, is a board full of letters and numbers; and what else is the Ouija board if not a clear though audacious metaphor for language as the source of death-defying poetry?

The poet's faith in the power of language—"THE REVEALD MONOTHEISM OF TODAY," Mirabell calls it—does in fact inform his puns and wordplay; they are a function as much of his metaphysical or moral imagination as of his aestheticism and verbal hedonism. Take this extraordinary moment near the end of *Mirabell*, this parenthetical aside with power enough to capture the very essence of the volume:

> It's the hour
> When Hell (a syllable identified

> In childhood as the German word for *bright*
> —So that my father's cheerful "Go to Hell,"
> Long unheard, and Vaughan's unbeatable
> "They are all gone into a world of light"
> Come, even now at times, to the same thing)—
> The hour when Hell shall render what it owes.

How much this passage beautifully says about childhood and innocence; how much about the poet's native romanticism, his trust in language as the great reconciler of opposites, his optimism. Notice too how the sci-fi comic book character we'd been hearing about—"Von," in his Star Trek cape—has turned here into the metaphysical poet, Henry Vaughan; and recall that the book aims to synthesize elements of high culture and of low, to bring together two far from ideal sorts of reader, "ONE ON HIS KNEES TO ART / THE OTHER FACEDOWN OVER A COMIC BOOK." Finally, consider the passage as an example of what I have called Merrill's comic sublime: haven't wit and wordplay made an imprecation sound ironically "cheerful" indeed? "Whitebeard on Videotape," the poem separating "The Will" from "The Book of Ephraim" in *Divine Comedies,* concludes with the reminder that "along with being holy, life was hell." But Merrill's seasons actually run counter to those of Rimbaud or Eliot; he has always believed heaven more real than hell. Accordingly he finds *Paradiso* the most persuasive volume in Dante's *Commedia:*

> The resulting masterpiece takes years to write;
> More, since the dogma of its day
> Calls for a Purgatory, for a Hell,
> Both of which Dante thereupon, from footage
> Too dim or private to expose, invents.
> His Heaven, though, as one cannot but sense,
> Tercet by tercet, is pure Show and Tell.

There has always been a metaphysical dimension to Merrill's wit. Like John Donne, Merrill is distinguished by his love of conceit, of the baroque elaboration of a comparison or figure of speech, as in this trilingual pun from "The Book of Ephraim":

> To touch on these unspeakables you want
> The spry nuances of a Bach courante
> Or brook that running slips into a shawl
> Of crystal noise—at last, the waterfall.

The "Bach courante," or dance, metamorphoses into a running brook, or "Bach courante," *Bach* meaning "brook" in German, *courante* as the French for "running": thus, brook and dance act as surrogates for one another at the same time that they both define Merrill's "unrelenting fluency." As Donne likens the legs of a compass to a pair of parting lovers, or identifies the sexual act with the exploration of the Americas, so the metaphysical Merrill invests a special significance in the doing of laundry ("The Mad Scene") or the solving of jigsaw puzzles ("Lost in Translation"). Such activities turn into rituals for the poet and as such serve an additional "metaphysical" purpose: they bear witness, they prompt self-examination, they become ways of disclosing, in brief and on a local level, larger mysteries of the cosmos.

With the conviction that the dramas of daily life participate in grand or mythic patterns, Merrill translates our cardinal winds into human terms—as "Nought," "Eased," "Sought," and "Waste." Again one thinks of Donne and his anatomy of the universe. "I am a little world made cunningly," Donne writes in one of his *Holy Sonnets,* "of elements and an angelic sprite," elements that must brave the assault of the elements:

> Pour new seas in mine eyes, that so I might
> Drown my world with my weeping earnestly,
> Or wash it if it must be drowned no more.
> But oh it must be burnt!

For Merrill, too, reality is elemental. The little world of the self, of earth and air composed, requires the destructive but holy powers of fire and water to intervene periodically. The envisioned angel in the window must endure a trial by water ("A Vision of the Garden"), and so must a mother's messages ("The Friend of the Fourth Decade"), while the houses of poetic tenancy inevitably undergo a fate of flames ("18 West

11th Street") before "OUR TRIALS BY FIRE YIELD TO THE TRIAL BY TEARS." "Log," the keynote poem of *Braving the Elements,* initiates the reader into the ritual blaze; a lyric of great delicacy, it likens itself to a burning log, made "less" by the very flames that cause "dear light along the way to nothingness." Writing, then, would seem to involve kindling the past, sending it up in smoke, and then recomposing it, a new "house" rising phoenixlike out of the ashes and sparks. Thus "18 West 11th Street" concludes with its "original vacancy" recaptured, while "The Broken Home" survives its trial by air to end with "the unstiflement of the entire story," a revealing pun, reinforcing the metaphoric identity shared by narrative and house. In effect the fate of Merrill's houses (lived in, abandoned, exploded, repossessed) is not merely described by such poems but enacted in them.

"The Will" offers a vanishing point for a number of the perspectival lines I have been drawing in this essay. One may fruitfully examine the poem in the context of Merrill's narrative aims; one may wander through the poem collecting evidence of the poet's fidelity to the Socratic axiom ("the unexamined life is not worth living") as modified by a reading of Freud; the poem may teach us how the flowers of poetry bloom from the wreckage of prose. Thematic continuities between "The Will" and earlier poems stare one in the face. At one point, for example, the poet suffers a figurative paralysis that brings to mind the "rigor vitae" of "The Thousand and Second Night"; like that poem, "The Will" is a "healing hieroglyph," a statement of resolution and independence in the Wordsworthian tradition, as well as a rejection of artifice, of the type of art that would paralyze experience. Stylistically, the poet's signature appears in the slant rhymes, the renewed clichés ("O dogwood days"), the way that language impels metaphysical conceit, as the title impels us to understand human volition in the terms of a legal document. From the point of view of form as well, "The Will" erects a bridge between Merrill's past and future selves. It introduces the telegraphic, uppercase line Merrill reserves for his otherworldly voices; in so doing it looks to the future—it is clearly an annunciatory poem, a harbinger of the benevolent "no accident" clause of

Mirabell. As a series of sonnets, a poem composed of sonnets and not a sonnet sequence in the conventional sense, it as clearly seems to extend the past.

The use of sonnets as building blocks, linked yet separate, retaining their individual integrity yet flowing into a whole larger than the sum of its parts, qualifies as one of Merrill's most significant and original contributions to the treasure chest of poetic forms. An inveterate sonneteer, Merrill has sought to adapt the form to the peculiar exigencies of his present, to tamper with the tradition and thus to renew it; as a result, as Kalstone notes, an entire Merrill volume can read "like a sonnet sequence following the curve of a love affair to its close." As early as in "Three Sketches for Europa," Merrill had experimented in the direction of linked sonnets. The impulse is successfully realized in "The Broken Home" and in several poems in *The Fire Screen,* and by the time of "The Will" Merrill could confidently display his mastery of the form. More than anything else, it calls for a rigorous balancing act; the poem must be poised between the wish to "build in sonnets pretty rooms" and the urge to tear down the walls separating one from the other. Much of the poem's power derives from this tension between narrative fluidity and what sportscasters call "a break in the action." The conclusion of an individual sonnet acts at once as a climax and as a transition to the following sonnet in a way that suggests one of time's paradoxical properties: that the moment of completion and the moment of origin are one; that while completion is illusory, the illusion itself is meaningful.

Consider what happens when the first sonnet in "The Will" comes to a close:

Now to pack

This canvas tote-bag. I have wrapped in jeans
With manuscript on either side for wadding
Something I'm carrying to a . . . to a wedding . . .

Then, wondering as always what it means
And what else I'm forgetting,
On my cold way. A car is waiting.

The subtlety of the final rhyme is an exact measure of the extent of compromise in the sonnet's closure. The lines seem deliberately anticlimactic, even prosaic, serviceable for advancing the narrative. But they demand, however subtly, to be read in a second way also, as concluding something. When read with this slight extra emphasis, the terminal phrases of the three lines gain in significance. The quest for "what it means" and the art of "forgetting" turn out to be two of the poem's major concerns; and as for that ominously waiting car, is it what it seems or not? Is it, as a matter of fact, a limousine—or a hearse? The poet has said he is on his way to a wedding, but could this ceremony follow hard upon a funeral? Perhaps he is somehow in Hamlet's predicament—perhaps, in some metaphoric sense, the funeral baked meats will coldly furnish forth the marriage tables. Could this be why the poet, a stanza earlier, hesitated before informing us that a wedding was his destination?

The constant give-and-take between formal means and narrative meanings allows for some startling effects. Sometimes the form gives way—two sonnets overlap, or one simply bisects another. At one point in the poem, the narrative is advanced by a purely formal maneuver: the sestet of the third sonnet in the series likens itself to the flight of a plane, while the space between an equivocal comma's temporary closure and the next sonnet's opening phrases enacts the landing:

> we have effortlessly risen
> Through on occasion to a brilliant
> Ice blue and white sestet
>
> Six lines six miles above, if not rhyme, reason.
> Its winged shadow tiny as an ant
> Keeps up far down, state after sunnier state,
>
> Or grown huge (have we landed?)
> Scatters into human shadows all
> Underfoot skittering through the terminal
> To greet, lulled, blinded,
>
> The mild, moist South. Che puro ciel . . .

At other points it is the narrative that breaks apart, undergoing changes of tense and of point of view, moving rapidly from event to interpretation, stopping for a Ouija session, looking at itself being written. While the story seems to have to do with a wedding, it is in actuality a wedding *gift* that the plot revolves around, and the poem doesn't get to the church on time. The story is suspended, postponed, and never completed—until we realize that what seemed an interruption has become the story itself. Upon inspection, then, "The Will" resembles a diagrammed sentence in Proust; in both cases, the richness resides in ostensibly subordinate elements.

As "The Will" opens, we intercept the poet in "a living room" that keeps at bay "the dead of winter" outside; into the cold he will soon have to go, for this is a poem of spiritual rejuvenation and artistic rebirth, requiring a preliminary death—if only in metaphor. Enter two men and a woman "with a will." The scene eerily reverses the last tableau in "A Tenancy," the end poem of *Water Street*. There "my three friends" had come bearing gifts, welcoming the poet to his career as a host; here, like a dark version of that angelic trio, they are dressed in mourner's black. It is in effect a house-cooling party: what the lease was for "A Tenancy" the last will and testament is for the later poem. The poet prepares us for haunted happenings. Though familiar, the "living room" (with its hint of *lebensraum*) feels more than a little strange, reminding perhaps of Freud's contention that the "uncanny" (*unheimlich*) is the homely in disguise, the demoniacal return of the domesticated ghost. Just as the room is "somehow both David the Wise's and not his," so the will is both the poet's own (he does sign it) and not (it takes him by surprise). At a later moment, the poem will state the paradox more directly. It will decide that the human will can express itself inadvertently, that it necessarily takes time for one's consciousness to catch up with one's self. Now, taking leave of his mysterious visitors, the poet packs his bags; "in jeans / With manuscript on either side for wadding," he wraps the gift he has planned to bestow upon the bridal couple, a sculptured ibis whose "funerary chic" and handsome artifice "could stand for the giver"—for one of his defunct selves, that is, that the poem will leave behind.

After a parenthetical sonnet interrupts the narrative with a deliberate regression into the previous night's premonitory dream, a dream within the envelope of another, the poem makes way for a new theme, that of the "accidentally" self-inflicted wound:

> I'm at an airport, waiting. The scar itches.
> Carving, last month I nearly removed my thumb.
> Where was my mind? Lapses like this become
> Standard practice. Not all of them leave me in stitches.

The pun on "stitches" makes its wry point: there is a connection between laugh and scar, the latter being a sign at once of injury and of healing; the broken skin will mend with laughter as, with the help of high spirits, the poet will gain ample compensation for his losses. "What's done is done, dreamlike"; it has to happen and cannot be prevented. So it is far from an accident that the bag, "gone underwater-weightless," is forgotten on the floor of the taxi taking the poet from airport to city. Nor, given the compulsion to repeat, does it mystify that again "self-inflicted / Desolation a faint horse-laugh jars."

Switching from "I" to "he," Merrill conducts "the prodigal" to his mother's house. It is here that, after joining his mother's friends—elderly "sirens" who "love their sweetly-sung bloodthirsty games"—at bridge, he discovers his loss. As often in Merrill's poetry, incidental details yield metaphoric energy, and so the game and their singing orchestrate this sestet:

> He is sitting at the table, dealing,
> When a first tentative wrong note
> Is quickly taken up ("What is it, darling?")
>
> By the whole orchestra in unison.
> The unbid heart pounds in his throat—
> The bag, the bird—left in the taxi—gone!

In a linkage like that between stanzas 7 and 8 of "Ode to a Nightingale," Merrill makes the last word of the sestet the keynote of the sonnet that follows:

> Gone for good. In the first shock of
> Knowing it he tries
> To play the dummy, dreads to advertise,
> "Drinks water" like a character in Chekhov.

The bag and its contents are "gone for good" in both senses. Initial dismay and wonderment give way to relief at Ephraim's reassuring words, in a flash forward to the Ouija board months later:

> U DID WELL JM TO DISINHERIT
> YR SELF & FRIENDS OF THAT STONE BIRD

Why? Because its malevolent presence causes disaster to strike all who would possess it. What symbolic significance could it have for JM? The fate of its latest victim, the cabdriver's sister, explains "what it means": she is paralyzed. More "burden" than bird, the sculpture represents the sort of art that runs this danger, an art that has calcified, like Lot's wife, all natural force abated. The "old wall-eyed stone-blond / Ibis" is thus very like the "little tumblers finely etched" that we came across in "Charles on Fire." And JM, though tempted by "exquisite / Peek-a-boo plumage," must declare against it, must reject such time-arresting artifice in favor of the art of losing, of man unaccommodated and experience unadorned. He must renounce by an act of will what he had lost by a stroke of luck. *Felix culpa!* The lesson stands as a comic footnote to Kierkegaard's Knight of Faith. He who renounces, him we can save—only in Merrill's poem the renunciation is ex post facto. Since there are no accidents in the "overdetermined" realm of the psyche, the *passive* experience of forgetting can become a spiritual *action* (or an action instinct with spirit). By a mental lapse that somehow expresses his will, JM has—in Ephraim's precise phrase—managed to "DISINHERIT" himself and friends of the ibis and what it represents.

117

Ephraim's reassurance extends to the "missing bag's / Other significant cargo," the manuscript with which it had been packed. This is none other than the "mistaken / Enterprise" to whose loss "The Book of Ephraim" owes its existence: "Ephraim" substitutes for the missing manuscript just as, in *The Importance of Being Earnest,* the "real" Ernest Worthing arrives as the substitute for Miss Prism's lost three-volume novel. Indeed, "The Book of Ephraim" takes its place among those works of modern literature that seem, with greater or lesser irony, to prescribe the burning or abandoning of a manuscript as a necessary liberation. The "GLUM PAGES" of JM's lost novel lacked the "GLORY" they wished to capture because, Ephraim implies, the poet had relied on artifice; he is advised instead to go straight to the source, to "SET MY TEACHINGS DOWN." The connection between manuscript and stone ibis is now complete; they stand for one another. It is here, with his injunction to live and lose, to "LIVE MORE LIVE MOST" and "GIVE UP EVERYTHING EXCEPT THE GHOST," that Ephraim brings to mind Wordsworth's leech-gatherer: this is the timely utterance that heralds the intimations of immortality to come. Lest the point otherwise be lost on readers of *Divine Comedies,* the opening section of "Ephraim" contains this cross-reference to "The Will":

> Blind
> Promptings put at last the whole mistaken
> Enterprise to sleep in darkest Macon
> (Cf. "The Will"), and I alone was left
> To tell my story.

"And I only am escaped alone to tell thee." So, quoting Job, Melville begins the epilogue to *Moby Dick.* "Because one did survive the wreck."

"The poem's logic," Merrill comments in *Scripts,* "calls for the shattering of a glass." The logic of "The Will" calls for something similar, a breaking of form preparatory to, or coincident with, a redemptive epiphany. A bit of Proustian "foreshortening" finds the poet at his desk, suffering from "Paralysis," laboring fruitlessly on "drafts" of his experience, the formless "wastes and drifts / Of time."

> Then a lucky stroke unearths the weird
> Basalt passage of last winter,
> Tunneling black. The match struck as I enter
> Illuminates . . . My word!

The knowing use of a cliché works wonders. As the direct object of "Illuminates," the exclamatory "word" completes a crucial thought; as an interjection, it breaks off the flow of words and brings the quatrain screeching to a halt. The imaginary tunnel with the real light in it has led to the climax of the poem, a flash of seeing that expresses itself as a formal disruption. For at this point the sonnet we thought we were reading stops, suspended after two quatrains, shattered by the advent of *another* sonnet. The latter, set off by parentheses, as though conscious of itself as an interpolation, bears glad tidings, a restorative vision brought about by the illumination of the poet's word:

> [(] Here was a manuscript. Here were
> Five catgut stitches laid in lusterware.
>
> And here in final state, where lost was found,
> The ibis sat. Another underground
>
> Chamber made ready. If this one was not
> Quite the profoundest or the most ornate,
>
> Give it time. The bric-a-brac
> Slumbered in bonds that of themselves would break
>
> One fine day, at any chance unsealing,
> To shining leaf and woken shades of feeling.)

Like a zigzag of stitches, this couplet sonnet enables the poem to recover from its self-inflicted wound. Only after this sonnet has run its course can the one it interrupted complete itself; only then can the poem attain the status of a "healing hieroglyph." For this pattern of interruption and postponed completion, Merrill had in mind a musical precedent. In Mozart's Piano Concerto in E Flat (K. 271) a rondo breaks off for the length of a minuet. But surely it is tempting also to see the interruption as a dramatic instance of Merrill's vessel-cracking art, his willingness to subject the forms he lives by to a ritual blaze. Through such displays of elemental bravery, Merrill achieves at last the exaltation that marks his great trilogy, an affirmation able to withstand the pressure of reality. So, at the end of "The Will," the dirty noise of a helicopter drowns out the vows of lovers and dying men, the sweet voices of doves and finches, but its shadow cannot "eclipse / The sunniness" below, the house no longer haunted (except for cozily familiar spirits), the "living room" illumined from within by words that have been put to a fiery test.

A. R. Ammons

Where Motion and Shape Coincide

"Continuous present is one thing and beginning again and again is another thing. These are both things. And then there is using everything." Had Gertrude Stein set about to characterize the long poems of A. R. Ammons, she could not have proved her prescience better than with these words from "Composition as Explanation." It is as if she were listing the primary ingredients of the recipe with which Ammons has cooked up quite a storm, tossing "everything" into his tempestuous teapot or oversized cauldron. As he writes in "Hibernaculum":

> one thing poetry could be resembled to is
> soup: the high moving into clarity of quintessential
> consommé: then broth, the homogeneous cast of substance's
>
> shadow: then the falling out of diversity into specific
> identity, carrot cube, pea, rice grain: then the chunky
> predominance of beef hunk, long bean, in heavy gravy.

The metaphor serves a purpose beyond its charm and humor. By Ammons's reckoning, the humblest phenomena, closely observed, will be seen to participate in "a united, capable poem, a united, capable mind"; the workings of each disclose the logic of all. Poetry is the supreme hierarchy, madame—or so Ammons would revise Wallace Stevens to read. Ammons's

---

This essay is the synthesis of two articles, one of which appeared in *Parnassus* under the title "Where Motion and Shape Coincide" (1981), the other in *Epoch* under the title "The Turnings Intricate of A. R. Ammons's Verse" (1982).

project is as much prophetic as imaginative in character: he aspires to apprehend "a unity / approach divided"; to give the sense of a turbulent but harmonious whole, "homogeneous" yet thriving on "diversity" and on the "specific identity" of each component, ever in motion whether the soup is stirred or not, and blessed with the capacity for spontaneous change.

It is very much as a dizzying downpour of language that one enjoys "Essay on Poetics" and "Hibernaculum" and the yet more magnificently torrential poem for which "Hibernaculum" seems, in retrospect, to have served as a study, *Sphere: The Form of a Motion* (1974). For these works Ammons contrived a form that would enact the motion of a spiral, twisting and coiling incessantly like a snake, and as apt to shed the skin of its defunct selves in order to begin anew. The poems' relentlessly self-renewing energy gives the effect of a continuous present, a grand pageant of simultaneous "events" (in the sense that, because their shape and motion coincide, beach dunes are "events of sand"). Above all, the long poems are monuments to inclusiveness and possibility as twin ideals. Cheerfully "not a whit manic" about Whitman's influence, Ammons is indisputably large, multitudinous, and democratic, given to the making of lists and to the use of the widest possible focus for his lens: everything from etymological investigations (*true* goes back to *tree*) to weather reports (variations on a theme of snow) to car repair receipts (quoted verbatim) can enter the picture of poetic possibility. As a nominal subject of the poetry, and as a statement of the formal principle it bodies forth, "motion as a summary of time and space" enables the poet to "Pray without Ceasing" in the uplands, and at sea level to "talk fairly tirelessly without going astray or / asunder," while he works to extend the Orphic tradition of praise to particulars of Einstein's cosmos, once thought inimical to the spirit of poetry. With the friendly air of a Sunday stroller, Ammons has dedicated his formal innovations, his poetry in motion, to the task of achieving what Emerson called "an original relation to the universe."

"A poem in becoming generates the laws of its / own becoming," Ammons observes in "Essay on Poetics." The statement occurs within the context of a theory of organic form: "we are not only ourselves—i.e.,/the history of our organism—but also every process that went into / our making." Accordingly, like verbal equivalents of action paintings, Ammons's long poems aim to chronicle the career of their making, and they do so with remarkable knowingness; few poets seem so well-informed about what they're up to as the Ammons of "Essay on Poetics." As if to illustrate "the laws of its / own becoming," the poem interrupts itself to accommodate several self-contained short poems; in the process we meet with various of Ammons's stylistic signatures, tried on for size. Apparently, when Ammons starts to write a poem he has his choice of three weapons. One, derived from William Carlos Williams, relies on short lines, quick jabs and feints. The perfect example is "Reflective":

> I found a
> weed
> that had a
>
> mirror in it
> and that
> mirror
>
> looked in at
> a mirror
> in
>
> me that
> had a
> weed in it

Such poems as the frequently anthologized "Corsons Inlet" feature a more rambling gait, uneven lines with jagged edges that suggest a grammar of space; the poet constantly shifts his margins in an effort to set up antiphonal patterns apposite for "a walk over the dunes" beside "the inlet's cutting edge." The measure that predominates in "Essay on Poetics," making room for the others, is a long line curving dramatically at its close in a serpentine gesture. This last, I would argue, is a distinguishing trait of Ammons at his best—in short poems like "The City Limits," "Triphammer Bridge," "Cut the Grass," and "The Unifying Principle," as well as in *Sphere* and "Hibernaculum," each of which consists of a series of three-line stanzas. This is the stanza of "Ode to the West Wind" and "The Triumph of Life," and indeed, in his handling of it, it almost seems as though Ammons—equally enamored of the wind—had undertaken to translate Shelley across an ocean and a century.

In these poems, Ammons's "hard" enjambments, winding syntax, and Shelleyan stamina, all work to produce a bend-and-swerve motion; the reader participates in the poem as a skier on a slalom slope. The effect is rather like that of *terza rima* without the *rima*. Every trick up the poet's sleeve impels the reader to turn and turn about, whirling like a dervish from line to long line, stanza to stanza. The sense is variously drawn out from one verse into another, as Milton prescribed, in these lines from "The Unifying Principle":

> what then can lift the people
> and only when they choose to rise or what can make
> them want to rise, though business prevents: the
>
> unifying principle will be a
> phrase shared, an old cedar long known, general
> wind-shapes in a usual sand: those objects single,
>
> single enough to be uninterfering, multiple by
> the piling on of shared sight, touch, saying:
> when it's found the people live the small wraths of ease.

Notice how the two "what" clauses stretch across lines; to complete the thought, the reader must turn his head. By enjambing both the definite and indefinite articles in subsequent lines, Ammons issues an even more forcible reminder that *versus,* the Latin root of "verse," literally means "turning" or "turning toward." The repetition of "single" at the end of the poem's penultimate stanza and at the start of the finale adds insistence and reinforces the sense of continuity, continuation, extension; and both "general" and "multiple by," set off between commas on their left and blank space on their right, beckon the reader to spin around to the following line. Only with "saying" in the next-to-last verse do end-of-line and end-of-thought coincide; only at the very end is there the sense of an ending, of resolution and rest, and even here a fine semantic explosion ("small wraths of ease") goes off in counterpoint to the syntactical resolution toward which the lines' downward pull has guided us.

Characteristically, it is through the language of landscape that Ammons discloses the principles of his prosody. I refer to "A Note on Prosody," which Ammons published in *Poetry* in June 1963; he is discussing the verse line:

> The center of gravity is an imaginary point existing between the two points of beginning and end, so that a downward pull is created that gives a certain downward rush to the movement, something like a waterfall glancing in turn off opposite sides of the canyon, something like the right and left turns of a river.

Again with an appeal to landscape Ammons accounts, in "Essay on Poetics," for the dialectic between his lyric "briefings" and his epic (or mock-epic) extensions of the self:

> I would call the lyric high and hard, a rocky loft, the slow,
>
> snowline melt of individual crystalline drops, three or four to
> the lyric: requires precision and nerve, is almost always badly
> accomplished, but when not mean, minor: then there is the
> rush,
>
> rattle and flash of brooks, pyrotechnics that turn water white.

In one sense the suasion (to use a word the poet favors) that led in the direction of the longer poems betokens a shift from the "minor" key of "individual crystalline drops" to the grand, symphonic boom of the sea, a perpetual motion machine:

>   genius, and
>
> the greatest poetry, is the sea, settled, contained before the
>   first
> current stirs but implying in its every motion adjustments
> throughout the measure: one recognizes an ocean even from
>   a dune and
>
> the very first actions of contact with an ocean say ocean over
>   and
> over: read a few lines along the periphery of any of the truly
> great and the knowledge delineates an open shore:

what is to be gained from the immortal person except the
    experience
of ocean.

The cause of celebration becomes the cause of lament, how-
ever, when the terms of discussion are drawn from the topo-
graphical paradigm that holds an evident attraction for this
poet. Ammons has always loved a neighborly chat with a
mountain—in *A Coast of Trees,* "Continuing" takes the form of
such a dialogue—and for this predilection I can think of sev-
eral compelling reasons. The shape of an average mountain,
to one who sets store by the shapes of things, cannot fail to
fuel some abiding philosophical interests: in its pyramidal as-
pect, a mountain signifies hierarchy; peak corresponds to "the
one," base to "the many." Moreover, mountains figure as em-
blems of religious experience; they loom large as stern figures
of authority—excellent to question or talk back to—though it
is usually they that have the last word, as in "Classic":

>and the mountain that
>was around,
>
>scraggly with brush &
>rock
>said
>I see you're scribbling again:
>
>accustomed to mountains,
>their cumbersome intrusions,
>I said
>
>well, yes, but in a fashion very
>like the water here
>uncapturable and vanishing:
>
>but that
>said the mountain does not
>excuse the stance
>or diction

To move from uplands to sea level is to describe a downward
arc; "it's surprising to me / that my image of the orders of
greatness comes in terms of / descent," Ammons muses.

That mountains should give rise to a myth of decline is indeed a subtle irony, but the logic is unassailable. Ammons associates the lyric impulse with the "summit" of a mountain; to embrace the epic world of "differences"—"enriching, though / unassimilable as a whole / into art"—requires that the poet slide to the prosaic base, to a place "comfortable on the lowerarchy." Something like Harold Bloom's parable of the poet as "spent seer" emerges: with the wind as guide, the wind that has "given up everything to eternal being but / direction," the poet has ascended the heights of soul-making where, in the "changeless prospect," he cannot find "an image for *longing*" but suddenly draws a blank in nature; he has no choice now but to come back down, having like Moses communed with the Lord, whose tablets he must shatter upon his return to the riotous tribe. The wonder is that, as Bloom argues, the smashing of vessels occurs not as an imaginative defeat but as a necessary prelude to the achievement of restitution, the gathering of dispersed light.

Unlike his lyrics, Ammons's long poems have encountered resistance from critics who discern in them a falling off in intensity from the controlled outbursts found over and over in his *Collected Poems* (1972)—and now again in the fiercely elegiac poems of *A Coast of Trees* (1981). It seems to me remarkable that poems such as "Hibernaculum" and *Sphere,* which give about as much word-for-word pleasure as one could ask for, should want defending. Not merely do they complement the lyrics but they round them into a completed vision. Without denying "the bitterest thing I can think of that seems like / reality," and without surrendering to it, they assert the priorities of the creative imagination, the "radiance" that never "winces from its storms of generosity," however provoking the circumstances. The particular quandary that has nourished Ammons from the start is at once resolved and renewed in these lengthy meditations on motion, as if increase of appetite had grown by what it fed on. Wedding Williams's love of minute particulars with Stevens's "metaphysicals . . . sprawling in majors of the August heat," Ammons finds the mechanism

> by which many, kept
> discrete as many, expresses itself into the
> manageable rafters of salience, lofts to comprehension . . .

The mechanism is the poem itself, an ordered but not too orderly cosmos. Within its flexible borders all things are seen, by an assertion of Romantic will, as destined to end up in "the form of a motion," a phrase the poet has liberated from the language of the faculty meeting. All things exist in patterns of correspondence, having a design in common. Mountain peak "equals" vertex of isosceles triangle "equals" mound of Venus; if nothing else, lust links subject and object. From *Sphere:*

> if one can get far enough this way where imagination
> and flesh strive together in shocking splendors, one can
> forget that sensibility is sometimes dissociated and come . . .

"Fluted trashcan" and "fluted Roman column" likewise enjoy separate but equal status since, Ammons writes in "Hibernaculum," "matter is a mere substance design takes / its shape in."

The formal choices Ammons makes—choices of design and shape—are decisive to his meaning. Form he conceives as waterfall, not container: he favors a cascade of words rather than a tidy English garden of them; the *sine qua non* of his prosody is a "downward rush," like that exhibited vividly in *Tape for the Turn of the Year* (1965), Ammons's most "vertical" poem. In another sense, form provides the hidden unity that can suffer the many to cohabit peaceably on its vast expanse. One distinctive quirk of form deserves special notice in this connection: I refer to what several critics have punningly called Ammons's "colonization" of the universe. Ammons has invested the humble colon with poetic potency; he has made it his own, as Byron and Emily Dickinson may be said to share a patent on the dash. No first reader of Ammons's poetry can fail to register surprise at encountering colons where commas, periods, or semicolons usually go. To some extent the colons in *Sphere* and in the other long poems act like the word "so" in Ammons's early "Ezra" poems: like shrugs of the shoulder, implying consequentiality but leaving the exact causality unclear. Frequently they seem determined to establish linkage between seemingly unrelated phenomena, as between essence and fashion, center and periphery, the "radiant" and the "lowly"; the sublime and the quotidian link hands by dint of these elliptical transitions. And yet the transitions differ from what Elizabeth Bishop described when she wrote of "everything only connected by 'and' and 'and.' " Both writers wish to give new meaning to E. M. Forster's "only connect," but where Bishop's "and" does the work of an inspired ampersand, Ammons's colons act now as equal signs, now as miniature arrows pointing in opposite directions. Acts of closure that double as re-beginnings, they advance the tape without erasing it.

Consider the multiple functions entrusted to the colons in the following section of "Hibernaculum":

> work's never done: the difficult work of dying
> remains, remains, and remains: a brain lobe squdging
> against the skull, a soggy kidney, a little vessel
>
> smartly plugged: wrestling with one—or those—until
> the far-feared quietus comes bulby, floating, glimmer-
>   wobbling
> to pop: so much more mechanical, physical than
>
> spiritual-seeming grief: than survivors' nights filled
> without touch or word, than any dignity true for a state
> of being: I won't work today: love, be my leisure:

The first colon indicates that an explanation will follow; the second introduces specific, concrete examples in illustration of the abstract explanation; splicing together the run-on thoughts, the next three permit the meditation to spill over the bounds of ordinary syntactical limitations—they eliminate the usual need for verbs; and the final two precede lyrical leaps forward, taking the place of periods. The unity of the section is clear; the movement from "work's never done" to "I won't work today" has, in effect, been annotated in the lines. But the last two clauses are kept from appearing conclusive by the colons around them and by the absence of capital letters. Think how different the effect would be were the lines printed this way:

> I won't work today.
> Love, be my leisure.

By insisting that all utterances renew or extend those that precede them, the colons reduce the pause between one and the next and in so doing they imply that each is a mere fragment of some larger, cohesive structure. A unifying principle rolls through them all.

Once he had rejected, early on, "the box-like structure of rhymed, measured verse," Ammons knew he would have to come up with a suitable replacement; he would have no choice but to invent a form and motion of his own. It is a testament of his skill that in heeding this imperative Ammons managed to breeze along as though he were exercising an aesthetic prerogative. His poetry became a prosodic adventure; in making his experiments Ammons conveyed the impression that he had thrown caution to the winds and was improvising his way to a solution. (Hence the curious affinity one senses between his work and that of jazz musicians.) *To find the true cadence,* as Allen Ginsberg is overheard to say in a John Hollander poem, was not the whole of Ammons's enterprise, but it was certainly a vital aspect of it.

Ammons began with the assumption that verse emphasis should shift from the line as a discrete entity to the line as a measure of continuity, the line weighted at both ends. The effort to add stress to the lefthand margin of the verse stands behind the triumphantly thin *Tape for the Turn of the Year.* This poem goes on for 205 pages, but that is an extremely misleading figure. Not only its length but its width has been fixed in advance: the poet has decided to compose his poem on a roll of adding machine tape, a decision that, while seeming arbitrary (with all the virtues this semblance entails), is actually a sign of cold calculation, a controlled experiment designed to give the poet maximum room for spontaneity within a severely constricted space.

The poem is fully aware of itself as a shape and motion. Coming out of the typewriter, the typed tape goes into a wastebasket, a perfect choice of receptacle considering the poet's

ironically self-deprecatory streak. As enough of it lands in the
basket, the possibility of serpentine motion occurs to Ammons:

> if I had a flute: wdn't
> it be fine
> to see this long thin
> poem
> rise out of the waste-
>   basket:
> the charmed erection,
> stiffening, uncoiling?
>
> anyways, that wastebasket
> is coiled full: wonder if
> I should stomp
>   in it?
>
> in & out: weaving in &
>   out: a
> tapestry, looking for all
> the world
> as if it were alive:

The tape will bear its burden of significance as well as would a
last duchess in oil on canvas hanging on the wall. Ammons's as-
sumption is that his relation to the tape can stand for his rela-
tion to all other things, just as a Freudian analyst assumes that
by being impersonal he may come to stand in the analysand's
mind for anyone and everyone. By being about themselves,
both *Tape* and later *Sphere* are thus about all things. If *Tape* is
not nearly as sophisticated a success as *Sphere,* it is because more
of the former's motions remain in the process of composition;
in the latter the motion inheres in the lines, or between them.

To achieve the measure of *Sphere,* Ammons "constructed"
his version of stanza form, and he did so with characteristic
self-consciousness. Upon the "downward pull" he had devel-
oped earlier, he began now to impose a lateral movement,
what he calls "grid seepage" in "Extremes and Moderations":

> constructing the stanza is not in my case exceedingly
> difficult, variably invariable, permitting maximum change
> within maximum stability, the flow-breaking four-liner, lattice

> of the satisfactory fall, grid seepage, currents distracted
> to side flow, multiple laterals that at some extreme spill
> a shelf, ease back, hit the jolt of the central impulse:

Again, as in *Tape,* the charm of the arrangement is that it is "variably invariable, permitting maximum change / within maximum stability." Regularity of stanza and extended line length have permitted the poet to add "English" in the ping-pong sense of a reverse spin. The result is that the line endings function as turning points in a way that recalls Milton's manipulation of the righthand margin in *Paradise Lost.*

Nowhere does Ammons manage his "multiple laterals" more successfully than in *Sphere,* which eschews "the flow-breaking four-liners" of "Extremes and Moderations" in favor of the poet's distinctive brand of *terza libre.* In his folksily classical way, Ammons likes to start a long poem with some sort of statement about its measure. True to form, the opening section of *Sphere* speaks of "opposite motions away and toward // along a common line." The enjambment is crucial. Hanging at the edge of its line, "toward" points back as well as forward. Each line will, if it lives up to the poet's intention, wind *away* and *toward* simultaneously; each will slither into a spiral or helix, will join with its neighbors to make "a common line." The theme is perpetual motion. It is talked up enough during the poem, but even if it weren't, the point—"a flowing point," to use Plato's definition of a line—would have been made by the prosody, the way Ammons gets his lines to curve on both ends. Ammons's "colonization" enhances the effect, since of all punctuation marks the colon looks both ways before crossing over to the far side of the street. An example, from *Sphere:*

> can we make a home of motion: there is a field
> of sheep, vanishing: something terminal may be arriving to
> that house, but we are leaving: mortgage payments, water
>   rent,
>
> phone bills, medical insurance, steep steps imprisoning an old
> man: but we are fueled and provisioned: motion is our place:
> history lists and you know by the difficulty of getting around
>
> at an angle all day that something is too much or amiss:

Ammons's prosodic choices ensure that, when quoting from *Sphere*, one is likely to call up what Wordsworth called "the turnings intricate of verse" rather than individual lines. Every statement comes accompanied by a before and an after, and consequently the lines that commit themselves to memory bring their line breaks along with them, temporal suspensions of meaning that contribute to the meaning.

Having set his motions going, Ammons sees himself holding on for dear life, as on a roller coaster ride, "in the bosom of reconciling but progressing / motions." Or he sits in the car of a Ferris wheel, the car spinning around itself as the wheel it is part of spins around its axis. Appropriately, *Sphere* closes by making explicit this amusement park metaphor. The excited rush of the words attests to the union of form and motion:

> we're gliding: we
>
> *are* gliding: ask the astronomer, if you don't believe it: but
> motion as a summary of time and space is gliding us: for a
>   while,
> we may ride such forces: then, we must get off: but now this
>
> beats any amusement park by the shore: our Ferris wheel,
>   what a
> wheel: our roller coaster, what mathematics of stoop and
>   climb: sew
> my name on my cap: we're clear: we're ourselves: we're sailing.

Why the summer-camp gesture, the order to "sew my name on my cap"? Because, in the whirl, it is likely to fly off; finders keepers, but at least the cap will retain the identity of the uneasy head that now, briefly, wears it. As such the cap points metaphorically to the poem itself, which will escape from the poet's personal gravitational field instantly upon completion. Whether or not he abandoned it, it abandons him, retaining his name only, the merest metonymy of an existence, the part that survived the whole. The poem speeds away, as though it were its own most reliable source of energy and motion.

With its expression of a native Romanticism, its self-sustaining power of affirmation, "The City Limits" may well be Ammons's single most celebrated poem. Composed at roughly the same time—maybe the same day—"Triphammer Bridge" seems to me an equally memorable performance. "Triphammer Bridge" is a poem occasioned by a place, and yet it is not of that place; the transaction between the merely real and the grandly imagined is there in a nutshell. Or in a word: "Triphammer Bridge" takes a word and gives us, in the *New Yorker* sense, its "profile." The poem follows:

> I wonder what to mean by *sanctuary,* if a real or
> apprehended place, as of a bell rung in a gold
> surround, or as of silver roads along the beaches
>
> of clouds seas don't break or black mountains
> overspill; jail: ice here's shapelier than anything,
> on the eaves massive, jawed along gorge ledges, solid
>
> in the plastic blue boat fall left water in: if I
> think the bitterest thing I can think of that seems like
> reality, slickened back, hard, shocked by rip-high wind:
>
> *sanctuary, sanctuary,* I say it over and over and the
> word's sound is the one place to dwell: that's it, just
> the sound, and the imagination of the sound—a place.

As a meditation on words and names, and on their relation to "real" places, "Triphammer Bridge" reminds of Wordsworth's response to the perceived discrepancy between "Mont Blanc"—as a name, as a bundle of expectations and imaginings—and the actual Mont Blanc. This is from the 1850 edition of *The Prelude,* Book 6:

>   That very day,
> From a bare ridge we also first beheld
> Unveiled the summit of Mont Blanc, and grieved
> To have a soulless image on the eye
> That had usurped upon a living thought
> That never more could be. The wondrous Vale
> Of Chamouny stretched far below, and soon
> With its dumb cataracts and streams of ice,
> A motionless array of mighty waves,

> Five rivers broad and vast, made rich amends,
> And reconciled us to realities.

For Wordsworth, the actual place, however grand, comes as a disappointment, "a soulless image" that consigns to oblivion his anticipatory imaginings; it takes a new act of imagination, one that "reconcile(s) us to realities," to compensate for the loss. Ammons, too, wishes for such a reconciliation, but in his case the disjunction between word and place stretches into a widening chasm separating man from nature, across which a new, conceptual bridge must be built.

Ammons's poem "Reflective" had optimistically proclaimed an identity between man and nature, perceiver and perceived, but the pendulum swings the other way, and in poems of his maturity Ammons openly doubts this easy wisdom. In the prefatory poem to *Sphere: The Form of a Motion,* Ammons puts the matter plainly: in the natural world he can find no adequate correlative for human nature:

> for the word *tree* I have been shown a tree
> and for the word *rock* I have been shown a rock,
> for stream, for cloud, for star
> this place has provided firm implication and answering
>   but where here is the image for longing:

The alienation he feels—"I am / as foreign here as if I had landed, a visitor"—is inexorable; but it is also a necessary preparatory step toward achieving the visionary power that makes "rich amends" for the failure of nature to meet the aspirations embodied in the mystery of words.

The relation of the title "Triphammer Bridge" to the text it heads is disjunctive in a way that suggests the schism between name and place, speech and nature I have described. The poem begins by cross-examining a word—*sanctuary*—and immediately, by way of strategic enjambment, an epistemological problem is versified:

>   if a real or
>
> apprehended place . . .

We must pause, flickeringly, over "or" long enough to remember that the word means both "alternatively" and "equally." Are "real" and "apprehended" synonyms or antonyms? The question sets up the possibility that there is a reality beyond apprehension, a metaphysical reality available only to the imagination. Prosodic devices throughout the poem are charged with like significance. Take the break between the first and second stanzas as an indicator of the poem's grammar of space. When first we encounter "silver roads along the beaches" we think of them as alternatives in nature to the sanctuary of art or church ("a bell rung in a gold / surround"). But the "overspill" of the line into the next stanza—

> silver roads along the beaches
>
> of clouds seas don't break or black mountains
> overspill

—completes the image by taking us away from the shore, where we had thought we were, and moving us to the sky; the "beaches" are figurative, we now see, part of a witty way of talking about every cloud's silver lining. (The lining itself reinforces the sense of "roads"—of, indeed, linings.) Further, the serpentine gesture of the lining makes possible an extension of the original image, a compounding of the metaphor: seas don't break *these* beaches: no, they are naturally supernatural, removed to an ethereal place, far from the sphere of our sorrow.

As candidates for "sanctuary," as more-or-less objective correlatives for this particular "longing," we have had first art, then nature. Now arrives a third possibility, itself perhaps an attribute of any place of refuge or asylum, whether sacred or not: jail; and the placement of the word, lodged tightly between semicolon and colon, isolated from the flow of discourse, is an object lesson in syntax as sense: the word "jail" is, in effect, jailed, immobile and fixed in its line. Here we encounter the first of the poem's all-purpose colons: it smooths over an elliptical leap, permits closure to blend into extension, signifies the activity of a species of poetic logic with laws of its own: and we are "here," "along gorge ledges," standing on one of Cornell University's famous bridges, surveying the wintry scene below. The causality is left deliberately unclear as, by dint of a colon, we move back from description to argument, from the here-and-now to the hypothetical there-and-then; we enter a conditional clause resting on the poet's ability to call forth "the bitterest thing I can think of that seems like / reality." The dilemma has now been dialectically spun out: "reality" at its bitterest shall prevail over such tangible "sanctuaries" as that word can denote. It remains for the poet to turn to the word stripped of all correlatives, the word as pure possibility; and the turn is made in and by the verse itself. The colon concluding this, the poem's third stanza, marks the turning point, dramatically announcing the poem's conclusion. But the colon also leaves crucially ambiguous whether "then" is implied or whether, on the contrary, the "if" has trailed off into the abyss. In other words, the emphatic pause at stanza's end doubles the meaning: we are at liberty to regard what follows as a resolution to the dilemma or as, instead, an imaginative leap beyond a dilemma meant to be formulated but not solved. Notice how the repetitions in the final stanza (*sanctuary* twice, "over and over," "sound" mentioned thrice, "place" twice) create an incantatory effect:

> *sanctuary, sanctuary,* I say it over and over and the
> word's sound is the one place to dwell: that's it, just
> the sound, and the imagination of the sound—a place.

This is, if you like, a last-ditch romanticism, or one could call it a realistic romanticism (as opposed to a romanticized realism). It is a lonely business, but for one who resolutely keeps his eyes open to all that argues against beauty and truth, what beside this final resort to the word is left? The only *sanctuary* to which he can repair comes italicized on the page; language, the very measure of discrepancy between man and nature, must become the agent by which the discrepancy is overcome. The test of language's limits turns thus from lament into praise; language, larger than nature—the sound of the word, larger than its sense—provides the imagination with what it needs to build a temple out of sublime emptiness and space.

Were evidence needed to counteract the charge that Ammons is too abstract, that he doesn't plant enough people in his poetry, the prosecuting attorney might be pacified by *A Coast of Trees*, some of whose most moving poems are populated—not only by the backyard elm, the local brook, the lofty "saliences" of the terrain, and like presences—but by the infant brother who died when Ammons was a child, by the elderly in "homes" but not at home, and by other denizens of "the bleak land of foreverness," burger eaters magnetized by the twin golden arches on yellow brick roads. "Parting" and "Sweetened Change," for example, are no less kindly and warmhearted for their terrifying vision of ultimate aloneness. An aged husband wheels his sickly wife

> through the hospital doors; soon the quick
> man is out again, squeals away to parking
> spaces alotted longer stalls of time:
> he jogs back by and back through the doors
> he goes: one mate gives out and the other
> buzzes fast to sing he's not alone and idle.
>
> ("Sweetened Change")

A unique moment of lucidity permits the victim of a stroke almost to recognize her spouse of fifty years:

> her mind
> flashed clear through, she was
> sure of it, she had seen
> that one before: her husband
>
> longed to say goodbye or else
> hello, but the room stiffened
> as if two lovers had just caught
> on sight, every move rigid
> misfire in that perilous fire.
>
> ("Parting")

That, for Ammons, is one half of the truth; the other is that "being here to be here / with others is for others," as he writes, somewhat anxiously, in "Poverty." But the knowledge brings ample compensation in its train:

alone, I'm not alone:
a standoffishness and reasonableness
in things finds
me or I find that
in them: sand, falls,
furrow, bluff—
things one, speaking things
not words, would
have found to say.

("Strolls")

The world consents to our poetic experience of it; its "things" have been spoken into existence. It is, of course, the God of Genesis who enjoys this "original relation to the universe" that Ammons holds up as an unattainable ideal. He would seem to subscribe unabashedly to Coleridge's conception of the primary imagination as "a repetition in the finite mind of the eternal act of creation in the infinite I AM." Therein lies the problem: repetition implies lateness, and the discrepancy between the primal word and its most recent echo measures the extent of the poet's alienation from the natural world. "I looked into space and into the sun," Ammons writes in one of his great moments, "and nothing answered my word *longing*." It is this consciousness of the imagination's constraints and limits that tempers the sweetness of the lonely urge to celebrate, always strong in Ammons. But precisely because it is problematic, the rift between nature and human nature acts as a sort of stimulant to this exemplar of what Quentin Anderson calls "the imperial self."

In the tone of an Old Testament prophet, Ammons starts *A Coast of Trees* with a lyric statement of the problem of naming, the inadequacy of language for the task Adam mythically performed:

if the name nearest the name
names least or names
only a verge before the void takes naming in,
how are we to find holiness,
our engines of declaration put aside,
helplessness our first offer and sacrifice . . .

("Coast of Trees")

The question gets, in lieu of either a question mark or a definitive answer, the resolve to "know a unity / approach divided," to trust "to the cleared particular." Ammons puts enormous pressure on his capacity for such trust, his ability to suspend the disbelief that gnaws away in his mind. Like William Carlos Williams, Ammons goes out on fact-finding missions, looking for the raw materials of a renewed belief. But where the author of *Paterson* prized the concrete particular for its concreteness, Ammons would grasp—if you will—the zen of the thing "emptied full." Harold Bloom has a word for this puzzling trope: *kenosis.* It puts in several appearances in *A Coast of Trees.*

The ways Ammons departs from Williams's example are instructive. While the two poets have certain prosodic habits in common, and while both bet heavily on the American idiom, Ammons breaks fundamentally with Williams on the latter's central dogma, that there can be "no ideas but in things." Here is the final word on that subject, from the "Essay on Poetics":

> the symbol carries exactly the syrup of many distillations and
> hard endurance, soft inquiry and turning: the symbol apple
>   and the
> real apple are different apples, though resembled: "no ideas
>   but in
>
> things" can then be read into alternatives—"no things but in
>   ideas,"
> "no ideas but in ideas," and "no things but in things": one
>   thing
> always to keep in mind is that there are a number of possibilities:

If, following Williams's lead, Ammons writes a poetry of reportage, he differs in giving equal time to the metaphysical news, broadcasting landscapes made into metaphors, not morals, as the poet sees (and sees through) them. These are crucial distinctions. Much will also have been ascertained about the differences between an English and an American sensibility once we compare Auden's moralized landscapes (in the *Bucolics,* for example) with the landscapes and country matters that Ammons favors although (or because) they exist seemingly without reference to human passions, love, and grief. Where Auden preferred a "region / Of short distances and definite places" to the "reckless" sea, Ammons opts for "a region without definite boundaries" ("Terrain"); where Auden, distrustful of the high and mighty and dangerous mountain, sought the reassurance of a limestone landscape, Ammons depicts himself as an inveterate mountain climber; where Auden opposed the artist's mirror to life's sea, Ammons would wish *his* mirror to have the sea's choppy surface and unrelenting motion. Ammons adopts the scientist's neutrality in the presence of his landscapes; it is their sublime otherness that fascinates him. Significantly, one of the elegies in *A Coast of Trees* has the refrain, "this is just a place."

Nature's neglect of us is, one feels Ammons would aver, benign, because it implies an aesthetic rather than an ethical universe. The elements refuse to "mean" anything, yet they cohere; they form "patterns and routes," and apprehension of these casual (as opposed to causal) designs comes as the sublime afterglow to a bout with terror and awe. With "majesty and integrity" nature can be counted on, finally, to calm if it cannot quite placate the unappeasable heart. Accordingly, the most transcendent image in *A Coast of Trees* exemplifies a type of "natural supernaturalism," to use M. H. Abrams's useful term: it comes in an Easter ode that makes no reference to Christianity, and it heralds an entirely secularized resurrection. "Easter Morning," whose crisis of mourning and mortality marks the vital center of the book, concludes with the image of "two great birds, / maybe eagles," flying in circles. As if endowed with the Tiresian ability to interpret the secret messages of birds, Ammons watches them perform

> a dance sacred as the sap in
> the trees, permanent in its descriptions
> as the ripples round the brook's
> ripplestones: fresh as this particular
> flood of burn breaking across us now
> from the sun.

The divine adjectives ("sacred" and "permanent" and "fresh") attach themselves to natural particulars. The point is made by enjambment partially: the "particular" hanging at the edge of space three lines before the conclusion does duty as a noun before taking its place as a modifier. And partially by trope: notice that the similes all emerge from the same rural picture, the identical scene, as that of the things they illustrate. Nature refers only to herself, not to any wished-for presence off-stage. And if the emphatic, somewhat abrupt ending makes it difficult to ignore the old sun/son pun, the metaphysicals sprawl, if at all, in majors of the physical morning.

Students of the sublime may wish to relate the workings of this ambitious, sure-to-be-anthologized poem with those of Stevens's "Sunday Morning." By his title alone Ammons takes the risk of making such a comparative reading inevitable. Some broad strokes link the two poems. Most visibly, the swooping eagles at the end of "Easter Morning" recall Stevens's "casual flocks of pigeons" which "make / Ambiguous undulations as they sink / Downward to darkness, on extended wings." Both poems revive a Romantic formula; they make the sort of appeal to the sensually real that Helen Vendler associates with Keats's ode "To Autumn." But the value of any such comparative reading would derive not from what "Easter Morning" shares with its antecedent but from how it veers off into a space of its own. Ammons's poem is personal, autobiographical, intimate, idiomatic, as by temperament Stevens never was or wanted to be. As an elegy, "Easter Morning" leads ineluctably from the death of another to the realization that time and change mean death for the self. And it is as such that the poem would seem to indicate a new phase in Ammons's career: he pictures himself now as "an old man having / gotten by on what was left."

Impelled by a Wordsworthian visit "to my home country" (North Carolina), "Easter Morning" begins as a meditation on the death of a younger brother, "a life that did not become, / that turned aside and stopped" in infancy. The memory of that death aches like a miscarriage. To see the event "by / the light of a different necessity" promises some relief "but the grave will not heal" and the grief widens to include the friends and relatives who populated the poet's childhood—and that childhood itself—irrevocably "gone." "The grave will not heal": this, the poem's dominant chord, chimes throughout *A Coast of Trees,* as though it were a carol of death. Death is conceived variously as the still point in a turning world ("Where"), as an ontological issue ("In Memoriam: Mae Noblitt"), as an "immediate threat" ("Swells"), as the fatigue that announces imaginative loss in "Distractions"—

> sometimes
> a whole green sunset
> will wash dark
> as if it could go
> right by without me

—and as the lonely cry that cleaves the graveyard air in "Easter Morning":

> I stand on the stump
> of a child, whether myself
> or my little brother who dies, and
> yell as far as I can, I cannot leave this place, for
> for me it is the dearest and the worst,
> it is life nearest to life which is
> life lost.

Of all contemporary poets, Ammons employs the most idiosyncratic vocabulary, and strewn like markers throughout the volume are the *multiplicities* and *radiances* and *motion* that serve as counterpoise to this weary weight of mortality. The last two lines of the last poem in the book gesture wonderfully to the whole:

> in debris we make a holding as
> insubstantial and permanent as mirage.
>
> ("Persistences")

A Coast of Trees is a spare volume. Like *Briefings* and *Uplands,* it omits the inventories, statistics, elephant jokes, folksy ruminations, and assorted time-killers with which the poet liberally spices his longer poems. This is the stuff that drives sober critics to take a powder. I rather miss it, however, and—in a digression that will, I hope, find the true direction out—I want to put in a good word for the noble eccentricity responsible for *Tape for the Turn of the Year* and *Sphere* and *The Snow Poems* (1977). As Auden put it, you can count on a poet to read a poem as "a verbal contraption," to keep an eye out for what makes it tick; as Eliot might have put it, the poet in the act of reading prepares for the larcenies of composition. From this point of view, the point of view that prizes technical innovation and audacity, one must give a high valuation to Ammons's most extreme performances. Take *Sphere.* Through "the turnings intricate of verse" it renders the rotations and revolutions of an ordinary planet; its logic is that of the metonymy, a single common characteristic—the speed of gravitational pull, for example—sufficing to connect everything. The only thing like it is William Gass's *On Being Blue,* in whose ravishing prose blue laws and dahlias and blazers and Mondays all have their place—and in whose "blues" we find confirmation of the truth of *Sphere*'s opening proposition, "The sexual basis of all things rare is really apparent." Like Gass's philosophical revery, *Sphere* has high, orgasmic moments—"ecstatic as mating, the transforming's pleasing." The poem's "low" moments seem equally vital, however, not only because they are "true to life" but because it would be impossible to imagine the lyric flights without also imagining an authenticating, quotidian context for them to lift off from. All points along the periphery are potential centers, Ammons is saying, and it is precisely their potentiality, their curve of possibility, the whole doppler shift of their existence that the poet praises in *Sphere.* Generosity is a critical aspect of the radiance he continues to aspire to in *A Coast of Trees,* albeit in terse accents edged with sorrow. The force of lamentation can meet but not vanquish the power of praise, the impulse of objects as they approach to "praise themselves seen in / my praising sight" ("Vehicle"). The tug between elegy and praise defines, I think, the special quality of Ammons's latest volume. And if it lacks the ecstasy and creative abandon of *Sphere* or *The Snow Poems,* the lack is also its own poignant compensation.

One of poetry's great walkers, who composes while walking and whose poems keep to a peripatetic pace, Ammons continues on his unappeasable, peregrine way to explore the states of mind as landscape, of landscape as mind, that in his aloneness he experiences. In his poems he makes palpable his willed apprehension of *abundances*—"an abundant tranquility," "the abundance of clarity." And it is *clarity*, in its oldest sense of "brilliance, glory, and divine lustre," that we find in satisfying abundance in all of Ammons's work. It is a pity that, for the new collection's cover, the publisher used a photograph of a bank of trees, since, in the terms proposed in "Essay on Poetics," Ammons's poetry fronts the ocean, not a mere river:

> read a few lines along the periphery of any of the truly great and the knowledge delineates an open shore:

> what is to be gained from the immortal person except the experience
> of ocean.

John Hollander

*The Sound and Sense of the
Sleight-of-Hand Man*

Two voices are there, of wit and despair, from the start. Both
are indefatigable; neither will rest until it finds a hearing. In
the dialectic between the two is the Jewish literary imagination,
and at his best John Hollander fuses the impulse so that his
excess of joy weeps, his excess of sorrow laughs. Reversing
Pope's terms, Hollander asserts that "the sense must seem an
echo to the sound," and since an echo is a secondary event there
is usually an air of sadness about it; sadness, at any rate, can
function as a catalyst in the conversion of cleverness into wit,
and wit in turn sharpens language into "a direct sensuous ap-
prehension of thought." The phrase is from Eliot's essay on the
metaphysical poets, and if Hollander can claim a unique place
in contemporary letters, it is due in large part to his success at
integrating erudition with sensibility, as Eliot commended.

Hollander can, it often seems, transmute ideas into sensa-
tions, observations into mental landscapes. What enters his
work from outside, as echo or shadow, ends as something
made over, made his own, a part of a new whole. In his first
volume, *A Crackling of Thorns* (1957), a moment praised by
Auden for its immunity to translation sounds the characteris-

---

This essay appeared in *Parnassus* in 1984 as a review of John Hol-
lander's *Spectral Emanations: New and Selected Poems, In Place, Blue
Wine and Other Poems, Rhyme's Reason: A Guide to English Verse, The
Figure of Echo: A Mode of Allusion in Milton and After,* and *Powers of
Thirteen.*

tic note of melancholy—an echo made aware of its lateness, "transumed" into levity:

> Europe, Europe is over, but they lie here still,
> While the wind, increasing,
> Sands teeth, sands eyes, sands taste, sands everything.
>
> ("Late August on the Lido")

In a later poem, an inversion of Keats produces the desired effect: the poet and college cronies have assembled at the West End bar in Columbia territory, "half in / Death with easeful love." More lately still, in one of the poems in *Blue Wine*, a painted moon

> Sets and leaves dark night with a
> Valediction forbidding
> Morning or the like, and which
> The faithful darkness may try
> To observe, for all we know,
> Its failure being our light.
>
> ("Pictures in a Gallery")

Such a gesture, down to the object lesson in enjambment, is nothing if not literary, at least at its base, even when as here the lines modulate into a version of paradox that leaves behind their immediate source in John Donne. Literary has become a dirty word in some literary circles these days, but it oughtn't to be: is our generation so hooked on "deep" imagery that it cannot savor the sophisticated wordplay of "Mount Blank" or "A Season in Hellas" or "Crocus Solus," to cite just three ingenious Hollander titles? One would like to think otherwise. For a bias against the literary, as against the sleight-of-hand man's way with words, would amount in this case to a bias against ambition: Hollander's repertoire of strategems and tropes goes hand in hand with an intellectual curiosity that seems limitless in scope. With his assured dexterity, he has managed to squeeze more and more of the universe into a ball; and his mythmaking is itself informed with the weight of a people's heritage. It may even be argued that Hollander's poems affirm their Jewish identity not at the expense of his literary imagination but as a result of his having placed it at the vital center of his cosmos.

Two more voices are there, then: the voice of Jewish moral seriousness and that of the heir "transumptive" of English poetic history. These work well together even when nothing on the surface suggests a linkage. Hollander has, virtually as a moral obligation, honored poetry as a craft and discipline (in *Rhyme's Reason*), done some brilliantly original work on poetic allusion (in *The Figure of Echo*), and given us our best shaped verse since Apollinaire (in *Types of Shape*, 1968, examples from which appear in *Spectral Emanations*). In some of his poems Hollander is, like Stevens's "rose rabbi," a scholar of love. Many others give explicit treatment to a Jewish theme or motif. Hollander has, in fact, a range of Jewish accents to choose from. The Hebraic lamentation of "The Ninth of Ab" gives way to gallows humor with a Jewish nose for the noose in "On the Calendar"; the talmudic commentator in "Blue Wine" had previously been the joyous kabbalist of "The Ziz" and, before that, Allen Ginsberg's city boy sidekick in "Helicon." Hollander has superbly rendered several of Moishe Leib Halpern's Yiddish poems; "The Bird" is unforgettable. He has also, in "New York," contrived to canter in Augustan hoofsteps while delivering a monologue such as one associates with Bickford's cafeteria in days gone by. And as the rhetorician and Jewish tale-teller meet in Hollander's night mirror, so the Miltonic and Mosaic modes and moods merge in the difficult title poem of *Spectral Emanations*, which aspires to kindle a feast of dedication, sustaining the consecrated oil on the bright menorah of poetic invention.

Spectral Emanations is really two books in one: it contains a gathering of new poems (superseded in turn by *Blue Wine*), and to these it adds selections from all of the poet's earlier collections, excepting the unexcerptable *Reflections on Espionage* (1976). *Spectral Emanations* thus allows a retrospective look at the growth of this poet's mind, a tailor-made opportunity for revaluation. And perhaps the first fact to be noted, annotated, pondered, is Hollander's virtuosity, evident from the start—and his periodic attempts to pursue visionary projects that require him to subordinate his powers of craft to the possibilities of trope. Again one has the sense of a duality within dualities, a fork in the road that this peripatetic poet visits more than once. Hollander describes the crossroads in his essay on Ben Jonson in *Vision and Resonance* (1975):

> Modern poets can take one of two directions, it seems, in moving toward a characteristic use of form, in seeking to "learn a style from a despair" of belated arrival in a world where forms are not given, where style is not canonical. One of these is that of American Modernism, following the Emersonian injunction to "mount to Paradise / By the stairway of surprise"—in short, to seize early enough upon a poetic tessitura of one's own, to frame a mode of singing, as it were, that would make any other formal style impossible. . . . The other tradition is best exemplified by Auden, and in this he was Ben Jonson's heir in our age. His grasp of the competing necessities of the public and private realms was mirrored not only in his poetic morals but in his stylistic practice; using a vast array of forms, styles, systems, differentiating between private messages, songs, sermons, inscriptions, pronouncements, and so forth, he made of his technical brilliance more than merely a matter of his own delight. In craft began, for him as well as for his predecessor Jonson, responsibilities.

Hollander has explicitly obeyed "the Emersonian injunction" in such long poems as "Spectral Emanations" and "The Head of the Bed," in which elements of Judaic legend—"the Recovery of the Sacred Candlestick" in the one case, "a filthy myth of Lilith" in the other—provide the vehicle for the poet's tenor, with effects that go beyond the operatic.

Hollander has come to attach the greatest importance to his visionary voyages into the dark regions of self and soul. Not incidentally, it is this side of the poet that most interests his friend and colleague Harold Bloom, whose analysis of the *Angst* caused by "belated arrival" applies with a vengeance to Hollander's poetry. To Bloom, Hollander remains "the very witty neoclassical lyricist and verse essayist . . . but . . . only occasionally, and with the work of his left hand." Bloom might argue that with *Rhyme's Reason*, as with such command performances as "Upon Apthorp House" or "New York," Hollander satisfies an irrepressible urge toward the shimmering surfaces of "stylistic practice"; by absorbing the urge, these works make it possible for the poet to devote other occasions, undistracted, to acts of "organized imagining," in Bloom's exact phrase. In the past, critics have taken Hollander to task for his allegedly "disembodied virtuosity" (Robert Alter), for indulging his "terrifying knowledgeability" (Donald Davie), and for employing "complication for complication's sake" (Helen Vendler), but the evident complication and erudition and technical skill of such a poem as "Spectral Emanations," while terrifying in some ways, do body forth a subject. "Spectral Emanations," as Bloom persuasively argues, is a quest romance, a parable of the poet's progress; with its system of correspondences, it aspires to achieve what Yeats called "unity of culture." Tropes are trumps: a polymathic range of references furnishes the figures through which the poet can commune with his imagination, casting his nerves in polychromatic patterns on a screen, with the anomalous twist that the dream-texts come equipped with their own interpretative apparatus.

Much of Hollander's work, ever since *Visions from the Ramble* (1965), becomes newly available when considered within a high romantic context; Hollander himself has endorsed the line of reasoning Bloom proposes. Still, Bloom's right-handed compliment may lead to misunderstandings, based as it is on the tenable but not necessarily valid assumption that the romantically sublime is superior in kind to the classically restrained. In his scrupulous examination of successive Hollander collections, Richard Howard takes a not unrelated stand but puts a significantly different emphasis on it. Howard praises *Visions from the Ramble* for its departures from the impregnable fortress of intellect—or, more exactly, for the intellectual leverage that can bear an autobiographical burden, the poet's "entire confrontation with himself"; *The Night Mirror* (1971) is in its turn celebrated as a "glyph of self-disclosure." One senses in Howard's commentary, as in Bloom's, an admonition and a piece of advice. It is as though, according to either view, Hollander's prodigious gifts and broad range of references carry with them the danger that he may misdirect his efforts. It might almost be averred that any critic of Hollander must choose between Howard's way and Bloom's: does Hollander go wrong when he fails to toe one or the other line? Ought he to turn his energies to frankly autobiographical enterprises or, contrarily, to what Bloom calls "a kind of bardic ordeal . . . in search of a late sublimity linking form and subject"? Yet, because a peace treaty between the rival positions should not be ruled out, one is inclined to suspend judgment. And perhaps one ought to complicate matters further by putting the case for Hollander's "other tradition," whose Dioscuri are Jonson and Auden. Though Hollander himself might value the less what comes as second nature to him, surely there is something to be said in favor of a poetry that can invest rhetorical flourishes with moral responsibility—that can make "stylistic practice" a matter of "poetic morals," as *Rhyme's Reason* does by exemplifying and thereby renewing the forms and conventions of English verse. To what else does this marvelous manual testify if not to happy stewardship of the "talent which is death to hide"? This is pedagogy at its best:

> Even as when some object familiar to us all—
> A street, a spoon, a river, a show, a star, a toothache—
> Is brought to our attention, called up from our memory
> To light up the darkened surface of something we've barely
>   known of
> —So did the epic simile sing of a silent past.

Auden would have loved it.

It would be impossible, and scarcely desirable, to consider Hollander without reference to his "other tradition"—and indeed to the idea of tradition itself, the sense of the past as a heavy weight that, when set down, haunts with its absence, giving rise to the feeling that something is missing. One way to read *The Figure of Echo* and, to a less pronounced degree, *Rhyme's Reason* involves thinking of them as parts of a serial study of poetic influence, the "anxiety" more or less displaced by scholarly zeal in the former and by the playfully didactic impulse in the latter. And one way to read Hollander's recent poems, from "Spectral Emanations" and "Blue Wine" to the recently completed *Powers of Thirteen*, is to discern in them the poet's deliberate effort to reinvent his influences, to fuse one with the other and to subordinate both to a style of wit learned from despair, a mode of speech filtered through a tunnel of silence. "When styles one had to find could be / The ultimate morality, / I worked progressions on the lute," Hollander writes in "Upon Apthorp House," acknowledging an early commitment to Ben Jonson's "poetic morals" but putting it in the past tense. "Now I must learn to play the mute."

In the beginning, Hollander's reading of tradition led him to cast the primal poet as a maker not a seer, as Adam not Orpheus. The tendency persists, if not always in a major key. With a breezy exuberance reminiscent of Auden, Hollander performs "Adam's Task" in the delightful poem of that title:

> Thou, pambler; thou, rivarn; thou, greater
> Wherret, and thou, lesser one;
> Thou, sproal; thou, zant; thou, lily-eater.
> Naming's over. Day is done.

Hollander's debt to Auden, as "Ben Jonson's heir in our age," can scarcely be overestimated. However often he has lately turned to Stevens for poetic guidance, it was through his distinctive assimilation of Auden's influence that Hollander originally defined himself; his very ambivalence on the subject confirms its importance. Consider the ease with which "Under Aquarius," written in commemoration of Auden's sixty-fifth birthday, slips into the cadences of "In Praise of Limestone":

> Languid and unregimental,
> Hand in hand but, alas, thereby thus somehow in step,
> Young people drift in the square, the evening's readying early
> Still, and the quiet shade daubing the pavements with dim
> Colors of doubt, and of colder shadows awaiting their
> moment.

Omitted from *Spectral Emanations,* this fine poem argues a degree of poetic intimacy that has its threatening side, as Hollander notes by way of a typically rueful echo, a sober "alas." Auden's "band of rivals" climb "arm in arm, but never, thank God, in step"; by following their "unregimental" example, however, Hollander's latecomers cannot but be "in step." As long ago as the time of "Upon Apthorp House," Hollander recognized the problem, likening *his* "W. H." to Shakespeare's:

> Take care, Old Enterprise! One tries
> The ancient models on for size
> And leaves them off when he can know
> They're more than something to outgrow.
> I've learned that time will not be tricked,
> So thanks, old habits I have kicked!
> And onelie begetters, please go pack,
> Old W. H., get off my back!

The Audenesque technique would seem to belie the manifest content of these lines. Like Yeats in "The Tower," Hollander feels he must bid his muse go pack, but he is careful to say *à demain* and not *adieu;* he can't quite kick the Auden habit—luckily for us, since Auden's influence has frequently given Hollander a needed shot in the arm. The rhythms of Auden's "Caliban to the Audience" are apparent in Hollander's prose sequence *In Place;* "Upon Apthorp House" itself has much the same relation to Marvell's "Upon Appleton House" that Auden's "Letter to Lord Byron" has to *Don Juan. Reflections on Espionage* is only the most dramatic example of an influence that in the end has proved more an inspiration than an inhibition. If that poem's machinery comes from *The Double Cross System* by John Masterman, its spirit is identifiably that of *The Orators* and other of Auden's early "spy" poems (e.g., "The Secret Agent"); from Auden, too, comes the conception of the poet as a double man, in need of a "cover" if only—only!—to make a living. Significantly, the death of Steampump—Auden's code-name in *Reflections on Espionage*—serves Hollander as his point of departure and as one of his poem's governing conditions:

> Steampump is gone. He died quietly in his
> Hotel room and his sleep. His cover people

Attended to everything. What had to
Be burned was burned. He taught me, as you surely
Know, all that I know . . .

One might fruitfully compare the image of Auden that survives in Hollander's poetry with WHA, the familiar spirit that advises James Merrill in *The Changing Light at Sandover;* the latter similarly aims to honor this dominant influence and, in the process, to master it.

Above all, Hollander admires Auden for his pride of craft and his "grasp of the competing necessities of the public and private realms." In the echo chamber of Hollander's poetry, these "competing necessities" translate into opposing choruses. Hollander's public verse, his occasional poems and his virtuoso *tours de force,* honor Auden and before him Jonson, while his more private, "bardic," and esoteric speculations follow the lead of Milton's "darkness made visible" and Stevens's "supreme fictions." (It is revealing that Milton, not Jonson, dominates the discussion in *The Figure of Echo.* Had the book been written a dozen years ago, it would have been a different story.) One explanation for Hollander's prolific output is his need to accommodate the diverse voices that have beckoned him; he has wished not only to give vent to each in its turn, but also, and increasingly of late, to attempt to join the dualities inherent in his makeup, willingly admitting impediment but clinging to the hope that a new synthesis will emerge. Thus it is a Protestant text (a suggestive passage in Hawthorne's *The Marble Faun*) that mediates the search for the Judaic menorah of "Spectral Emanations"; the poem links spectroscopy and spectral self-disclosure, poetry and prose, the American sublime and the Jewish imagination. The public world retreats but does not vanish—it is less a subject in its own right than a metaphor for the poet's inner self. In the first station of the spectrum, for example, the story of the poet as Jonah plays itself out against the allegorical backdrop of the Yom Kippur War. It is to Hollander's purpose that the story of Jonah, a parable of repentance, is one of the portions of the Torah that is read in the temple on Yom Kippur, the day of atonement:

Along the wide canal
Vehement, high flashings
Of sunlight reflect up
From rock, from bunker, from
Metal plate. In the mild
Shade of his waiting place—
Shade a gourd might afford—
J sits embracing his
Automatic weapon,
Crowned by a sloppy cap,
Inhaling the fire of
White air from the parched east.

Rather than turn down our thumbs reflexively at such a display of applied erudition, we might better lament that the "workshop" generation is insufficiently equipped to contend with poetry of this order on its own demanding terms.

II.

Since Eliot, no poet besides Hollander has so relentlessly woven quotations into the fabric of his original texts. One effect of such a procedure is to raise anew the question of what originality entails. "The fore-going generations beheld God and nature face to face; we, through their eyes," Emerson wrote. "Why should not we also enjoy an original relation to the universe?" Given the imitative nature of language, however, what would constitute literary originality? Adam's task having once been performed, is it not patently impossible to make an intelligible statement "in one's own words"? (Harry Mathews plays a fine trick on his students when he asks them to do just that.) Leave it to Hollander's Doctor Reinkopf, a man of pure mind, to pose the problem in Platonic terms in *Powers of Thirteen*:

> "*Every soul is unique, and, thereby, original:*
> *It is only when it employs the body to make*
> *Something of something else, or utter something, that it*
> *Falls into the nature of being imitative.*"

The testy Doctor insists on a rigid division between soul and body, dance and walk, poetry and prose, originality and imitation. But the poet knows better. Language does not live by denotation alone; where else do the material and spiritual realms intersect if not in the Word? With its surplus of meanings, language is as much an agent of creative imagination as it is an instrument of representation. Ambling along in measured footsteps, we can therefore count on "our soles and our wingtips" to circumvent the problem of "an original way of walking" or lift us beyond it, as Hollander demonstrates in these lines:

> *Walk* holds *talk* and *work* by their hands,
> Between, yet beyond, them both, perplexing the Doctor.
> The body's stride and trudge aside, our strolling involves
> Our soles and our wingtips equally beating against
> The pavements of the pure air and the clouded sidewalks;
> Whether gliding through the rainy town on errands of
> Light, or idling in some brightened mews at midnight, or
> Making the city's great *paseo* late on a fine
> Afternoon as shadows beckon to the light of shops.

Making "errands of / Light" out of light errands is a minor masterstroke.

Like Eliot before him, Hollander would behold God and nature book to book, from a seat in a Borgesian library of Babel, after the deluge of cultural history. For Eliot's "visions and revisions," Hollander serves up "the future / Repast"; where *The Waste Land* splices together Marvell, Spenser, the Psalms, and Mrs. Porter, "Mount Blank" arranges an easy commerce between Shelley, Petrarch, *Exodus,* and the "ludicrous Snifflehorn." Hollander seems intent, Paul Zweig has observed, to "make it old." But he does so not out of a reactionary impulse, nor merely in order to make a virtue out of his necessarily "belated arrival," but in an effort to reclaim his original sources, originality being a condition of priority as much as of novelty. A true echo, Hollander points out, cannot but distort the sound that preceded it, and in the distortion is originality enough; to echo a past is to originate a future. For Hollander's echolalia, as much as for his habit of smuggling into his poems his exegetical tactics of his prose, a second explanation also proposes itself. Jews are people of the Word; consequently, exegesis becomes a sacred act. In an essay on Gershom Scholem, Robert Alter states the case: "Scholem cites Aquinas's characterization of mysticism as *cognitio dei experimentalis,* the experiential knowledge of god. Elsewhere, in his masterful essay on revelation and tradition, he emphasizes the mediated nature for rabbinic Judaism of every experience after the initial revelation. As a result, exegesis becomes the characteristically Jewish means to knowledge and perhaps even the characteristically Jewish mode of religious experience." Accordingly, Hollander's "Blue Wine" and "The Ziz" present themselves as *midrashim,* or rabbinic explanations; "Pictures in a Gallery," with its commentary on imaginary paintings, represents a secular version of this tendency to elevate a means of knowledge into a mode of religious experience, "a mode of singing . . . that would make any other formal style impossible."

Hollander's intertextuality, the way his poems illuminate one another and are illumined in turn by his critical writing, ensures that separate treatment of any of his volumes will branch out eventually to touch upon the others. To take late things first, as echoes do, we might frame a discussion with *The Figure of Echo,* knowing that the many forms allusion can assume—from repetition to deliberate misquotation to erasure—all find a home in Hollander's verse. *The Figure of Echo* reads rather like a poem that happens to cloak itself in the language of critical discourse: just as Hollander's verse poems perform acts of interpretation, so his prose, defying easy categorization, has come to avail itself of some of the liberties of poetry.

The book begins with "Echo Acoustical." Under this heading, Hollander presents scientific explanations and mythic reverberations (thunder apprehended as an echo of lightning, for example), pausing to ponder some singular properties of the ineluctable modality of the audible. By nature, echo is a "trope of silence," Hollander argues. The thought under-

scores "Last Echo," one of the songs in the "Lyrical Interval"
at the center of *Blue Wine:*

> Echo has the last word,
> But she loses the rest,
> Giving in to silence
> After too little time.
> And, after all, what is
> A last word, then? After
> All the truth has been told—
> No more than a cold rhyme.

(Notice, in lines three and four, the characteristic play on an
antecedent poem—in this instance "Ode on a Grecian Urn"
with its "silence and slow time.") Hollander's esoterica is a
delight, and the category of "Echo Acoustical" includes such
gems as "echoes that would answer in Spanish what was cried
out in French," "portable echo chambers," and "frozen ech-
oes, or the voices of mariners flung up from shipboard in
wintry northern seas, and released again in summer thawing."
For textbook illustrations of these creative sorts of echo, we
need only turn to Hollander's verse. Consider rhyme as a
linguistic echo chamber in "The Old Guitar," whose music
resounds "wildly, like the roaring wind's melody, / Only an
echo of its malady." Or listen to the trilingual, delayed reac-
tion echo in "Crocus Solus," where the poet adopts the trans-
formational grammar Raymond Roussel put to use in *Locus
Solus.* From "A sigh? No more" we travel to *"vivace assai . . . ô
Mort"* and end with "A sign? O, more. . . ."

The second chapter of *The Figure of Echo,* "Echo Allegori-
cal," contains among other speculations some that might trig-
ger off a comparative discussion of James Merrill's "Syrinx"
and John Ashbery's "Syringa," two highly distinctive render-
ings of mythic original song. "Syrinx" names the nymph who,
pursued by Pan ("the great god Pain," in Merrill's poem),
turned into a reed; Ashbery's poem has to do with the myth of
Orpheus, but its title alone proposes a closer basis for compari-
son. A passage Hollander quotes from Francis Bacon moves
me to put the issue on the agenda:

The world itself can have no loves or any want (being content with itself) unless it be of *discourse*. Such is the nymph Echo, a thing not substantial but only a voice; or if it be more of the exact and delicate kind, *Syringa*,—when the words and voices are regulated and modulated by numbers, whether poetic or oratorical.

While he cites beneficent versions of Echo the goddess, Hollander's own poetry is manifestly Judaic in its conception of echo as "a secondary, or derivative, voice of the holy spirit" with "at best a contingent authority." It is worth keeping in mind that *bat kol,* meaning "daughter of a voice," is the Hebrew idiom for "echo." Hence the pathos of "Cohen on the Telephone," where we come across "Ben Cole, the son of your voice," who has changed his name from Cohen. "An assimilated echo," Hollander wryly notes.

"Echo Schematic," subject of the third chapter of *The Figure of Echo,* is exemplified in *Rhyme's Reason*—

> Echo will have it that each line's last word
> (ECHO:)   *Erred.*
> Echo will chop down words like "fantasize"
> (ECHO:)   *To size.*
> Out of what stuff is Echo's wit then spun?
> (ECHO:)   *Pun.*
> Can English have a full, Italian echo?
> (ECHO:)   *Ecco!*

—and, more complexly, in *Powers of Thirteen:*

> That great, domed chamber, celebrated for its full choir
> Of echoes: high among its shadowed vaults they cower
> Until called out. What do echoes do when they reply?
> *Lie, lie, lie* about what we cried out, about their own
> Helplessness in the face of silence. What do they do
> To the clear call that they make reverberate? *Berate,*
> *Berate* it for its faults, its frangible syllables.

But only with "Echo Metaphorical" and "Echo Metonymic" do we reach the figure of speech that takes center stage in Hollander's poems. Simply put, it is a pun charged with meaning;

the meaning derives from a subversive allusion to a prior text. The accents of Milton's Satan are clearly audible in both of the following:

> . . . to howl a loud howl like, "Down
> Be thou my Up."

> Despite the bleakness of most rural sights,
> Choose Adirondack over Brooklyn Heights,
> Better in solitude than fear to dwell,
> To yawn in heaven, than explode in hell.

In the hierarchy Hollander proposes in *The Figure of Echo,* a quotation that takes liberties with its source—an echo in the true sense—is superior in kind to a faithful citation. Echoes distort; and the manner and degree of distortion, its subtlety and profundity, form the basis for distinguishing a fruitful trope from a bad pun. Hollander's poems approach the world as though it were a text commanding interpretation or mistranslation—"a rod of text held out by / A god of meaning."

The most sophisticated form of mistranslation is Hollander's "Echo Metaleptic," the trope of transumption. With his exposition of this term and his delineation of its usage Hollander has done the critical community a considerable service. It is a fascinating trope. It proceeds, Hollander tells us, from "an interpretive or revisionary power which raises the echo even louder than the original text"—another way of saying that it signals, and authorizes, an act of appropriation; it eschews borrowing in favor of theft. (Harold Bloom would say it reverses priorities. Thus, according to Bloom, Wallace Stevens seems to have been influenced by John Ashbery.) By linguistic sleight-of-hand, the trope manages a complete transformation of the quoted material. Indeed, by substitution of a like-sounding word or by subtle erasure, "Echo Metaleptic" acts very much like an inspired typo. Hollander's canonical example is from Virgil's first eclogue: "Shall I, beholding what was my empire, marvel at a few ears of grain?"—where *ears* stands for *years*. Similarly, *swords* chips off into *words*, leaving us with "the clashed edges of two words that kill" in Stevens's "Le Monocle de Mon Oncle." Titles are notorious places for metaleptic reversals to lurk in. Hollander's "A Season in Hellas" makes the lyric that follows seem, precisely, pre-Rimbaldian; on the facing page of *Spectral Emanations,* "Mount Blank" supersedes Shelley's "Mont Blanc" with the universal blank of Emerson's "Nature."

It would be useful to compare Hollander on this score with Ashbery, whose pantoum "Variation on a Noel" leaves "Variation on a Novel" somewhere behind. Hollander's titles imply an effort to reconstitute and repossess the past by determined acts of will. Ashbery's thefts are equally deliberate but are predicated on the seemingly perverse wish to ignore the past even in the act of including it. Ashbery has mentioned that, writing a poem, he begins with the title rather than arriving at one as an afterthought. Twice in *Self-Portrait in a Convex Mirror* he begins with quotations: "As One Put Drunk into the Packet-Boat" is a line from Andrew Marvell's "Tom May's Death"; "As You Came from the Holy Land" comes from a poem attributed to Sir Walter Ralegh. By contrast, Hollander's sources are apt to conceal themselves out in the open; if "Mount Blank" subverts its predecessor, it must depend for its effects on the reader's awareness of the original. Ashbery's modifications of tradition with individual talent would seem to rest on no such Eliotic assumption. His quotations paradoxically call little or no attention to their sources; they serve as openings, and their destination is unprecedented space. The quoted phrase is liberated from its initial context; the poet *presents* it, in several senses. Yet, as Hollander writes in *The Figure of Echo,* "in order to understand the title [of a poem], its relation to the work, and thereby something about the work itself, the fragment of quoted material must be traced to its source"—and yes, something about Ashbery's poems *does* impel the reader to go back to their launching pad. It is as though the relation between Ashbery's "packet-boat" and Marvell's is meant "to be proposed but never formulated," as Ashbery put it in another context; it must remain mysterious, a matter for the mirrors of speculation to reflect on.

III.

I should like to conclude with some comments on *In Place* and *Powers of Thirteen,* the former because, obscurely published, it has been unfortunately neglected; the latter, though not yet officially published as I write, because its brilliance is such as to warrant sending out the appropriate early warning signal loud and clear.

As prose poems, the works that constitute *In Place* are unusual. A representative example, short enough to be quoted in full, goes by the Stevensian title of "Figures of Speech. Figures of Thought. Figures of Earth and Water."

> Once upon a time, the old, wild synecdoche of landslides was frighteningly transumed when a mountain—Mt. Black—rolled downward like one of its own boulders, over the whole peaceless land. In metonymy meanwhile, beyond the other mountains, a mad sea was flowing somewhere, like a river.

The nearest thing to an antecedent form for this poem is Kafka's "On Parables." The world is apprehended in the one case as a rhetorical strategem, in the other as a parable with an enigmatic punchline.

As in Auden's "Caliban to the Audience," the dominant mode of *In Place* seems to be late James made elegant; smooth if purely rhetorical transitions substitute for the master's hems, haws, and evasive patches of dialogue. I am struck by the presence of what Ashbery once called "the great 'as if.' " It makes appearances in a number of poems, including "The Sense of Place," "In Place of Body," and "A Week in the Country"; it is at the heart of "The Old Pier-Glass." One could chart out "The Old Pier-Glass" as a progression from "as if" to "more as if" to "what if" to "would have had" to "would be": the conditionals surround an absence, as in a frame:

> It was as if, he thought, someone had censored the whole of a well-meaning but naively loquacious wartime letter, leaving about its cut-out center only a frame to be sent on nevertheless, with needless earnestness, to its addressee.

The phrase "so that" creates a similar effect in "Keepsakes," "Not Something for Nothing," and, especially, "Patches of Light / Like Shadows of Something." In the last named, the pattern leads from the suspended causality of the opening ("—So that we have, after all, to be grateful that our light lies broken in pieces") through a series of suppositions ("were we to have to live in the generality of it") and conditional statements ("Perhaps if everything were to be reconstituted along with it") to a very equivocal "as it is": "the very breaking-up of the radiance that might have for ever remained a deep ground was what will always cause us to have embraced these discrete fragments—turning on and off, fading, ending in a border of darkness—as with the arms of our heart." Audacious though it is, this final simile must play second fiddle to the verbal pyrotechnics that precede it: the extraordinary juggling of tenses, the insistent "it," make us read the poem as the very epitome of a contingency clause.

The point, and it's a Jamesian point, is the construction of palpable metaphors out of airy nothings; the imagination is centered on the word. Grammar is generative, conjuring its own reality into being; reality is contingent on language, instead of the other way around. (An exponent of deconstruction with any interest in contemporary poetry might find in Hollander's work a metaphoric enactment of certain precepts associated with the theory.) As though to dramatize the perceived disjunction between word and world, "The Old Pier-Glass" is a free-floating metaphor, where A = B but B is never identified. Something like this occurs at that moment in "The Beast in the Jungle" when James lets drop the idiomatic "sounding of their depths" and proceeds to renew the cliché: "It was as if these depths, constantly bridged over by a structure that was firm enough in spite of its lightness and of its occasional oscillation in the somewhat vertiginous air, invited on occasion, in the interest of their nerves, a dropping of the plummet and a measurement of the abyss." Out of nothing, something comes, and we can trace its shape even if we remain uncertain as to its meaning. "Patches of Light," meanwhile, presents itself as the consequence of some unknown cause, the "therefore" of an argument whose premises cannot be ascertained. Again I think of James's John Marcher, for whom May Bartram's face was "a reminder, yet not quite a remembrance": "It affected him as the sequel of something of which he had lost the beginning."

Like *Reflections on Espionage, In Place* seems to scatter clues liberally about, as though to facilitate decoding. These poems all concern aspects of writing; tropes are trumps. "The Way We Walk Now," which begins the sequence, is "about" the writing of prose poems; the vehicle is so apt—Valéry famously identified prose with walking, poetry with dancing—that the tenor need not be named straight out. In this way the poems assert their independence from a "key" even as they appear to lend the codebreaker a helping hand—and this is their final strength, an abstract lyricism:

> . . . But when true beauty does finally come crashing at us through the stretched paper of the picturesque, we can wonder how we had for so long been able to remain distracted from its absence.

That is the whole of "End of a Chapter," another sequel to a lost beginning.

Powers of Thirteen is a far more ambitious sequence, holding 169 poems, or thirteen squared; each contains thirteen lines, and each line contains thirteen syllables. In the manner of Harry Mathews's *Trial Impressions,* numbers head the individual poems while for good measure italicized titles appear below them and to the right. The titles themselves convey a sense of the book's range of moods ("Taking It Easy," "Being Puzzled," "Speaking Plainly"), styles ("Literal Account," "Dreams and Jokes," "Promissory Note," "Eclogue"), and areas of inquiry ("Body and Soul," "An Apology for Poetry," "Public Landmarks," "Highway, 1949"). In these *sonnets manqués* or "maker's dozens," Hollander has framed an original mode of singing "in a world where forms are not given, where style is not canonical." The sequence achieves its most privileged moments not at the expense of poetic craft but precisely by its agency; the poems' form provides the author with both the means and the motive for metaphor. In "Letter," for example, every line begins with *M*, the thirteenth (and middle) letter of the alphabet. What results is an explosion of alliterative association, a "mess of amazing amusements"—pun on maze, pun on muse—and "mid-forest musics." In the process the poem explores the nature of "the middle," which it comes to define as the place where "both ends meet." It goes without saying, perhaps, that "Letter" is located near the heart of the sequence and that "meet" both begins and ends the poem.

The "you" to whom most of *Powers of Thirteen* is addressed stands for any number of muses, from Calliope and Melpomene to "Laurie, Stella, Delia, Celia, Bea and the others," from "the bemused / Daughters of memory" to language itself as the necessary medium for all musings. (At one point a working title for the sequence was "Taking You at Your Word.") Hollander has cheerfully appropriated Ashbery's habit of liberating the pronoun from a fixed point of reference. This "indeterminacy," far from nihilistic, generates a multiplicity of meanings, and that is its virtue. Again and again in *Powers of Thirteen* Hollander salutes "the power of 'might' that makes us write"— the conditionals of language that give poets their right of way. The book is, first and foremost, a celebration of linguistic possibility and verbal metamorphoses. As "a perpetual calendar," it marks occasions (May Day, the Fourth of July, Labor Day), meditates on the seasons, dwells on the theme of erotic love, studies public monuments, mixes memory and desire; in short, it performs many of the services of the traditional sonnet sequence, the poet having found a formula for subverting and thereby renewing that most venerable of extended forms. But as Hollander has remarked, "unless poetry is parabolic about itself, it cannot be about anything else," and it is as a parable of its own making—a series of "quests for the nature of the quest"—that *Powers of Thirteen* establishes itself as Hollander's finest long work to date.

As usual with Hollander, the reader will need a scorecard to get the most out of the action. Hollander has appended two pages of notes to the sequence; there could as easily be six-and-a-half times as many. It pays, for example, to have in mind the famous first poem of Sidney's *Astrophel and Stella* ("Loving in truth, and fain in verse my love to show") when we read Hollander's "The Pretext" ("Lying in love and feigning far worse") or when we confront the poet's "truant pen" in "Your Command." Still, the esoteric mythmaking that made "Spectral Emanations" a difficult pleasure is absent here. From a subsequence of thirteen poems about the charms and perils of that magical integer, consider this meditation on names and numbers, beginnings and ends:

> *J*ust the right number of letters—half the alphabet;
> *O*r the number of rows on this monument we both
> *H*ave to share in the building of. We start out each course
> *N*ow, of dressed stone, with something of me, ending where
>   you
> *H*andle the last block and leave something of you within
> *O*r outside it. So we work and move toward a countdown,
> *L*oving what we have done, what we have left to do. A
> *L*ong day's working makes us look up where we started from
> *A*nd slowly to read down to the end, down to a base,
> *N*ot out, to some distant border, the terminal bland
> *D*estructions at their ends that lines of time undergo.
> *E*ndings as of blocks of text, unlit by the late sun
> *R*eally underlie our lives when all is said and done.

Italicized, the initial letters of the lines spell out their message for all to see, but the closing letters also form an acrostic: "The unnamed one." In its complexity, wit, and sheer ingenuity, the gesture is perfectly representative of the sleight-of-hand man in action.

The Pleasures of John Ashbery's Poetry

. . . The flowers don't talk to Ida now.
They speak only the language of flowers,
Saying things like, How hard I tried to get there.
It must mean I'm not here yet. But you,
You seem so formal, so serious. You can't read poetry,
Not the way they taught us back in school. . . .
                    —John Ashbery, "Never Seek to Tell Thy Love"

"I don't entirely understand it, but what I understand I love, and what I don't understand I love almost better," Randall Jarrell once wrote about one of Marianne Moore's poems.

Many readers feel the same way about the poetry of John Ashbery, and indeed Jarrell's statement points to some of the paradoxes at the heart of Ashbery's achievement. An Ashbery poem has an extraordinary immediacy, but you can't "entirely understand it." Its pleasures are accessible, but its meanings are so elusive that the poetry itself sometimes seems to be its first and last subject. It accommodates any number of interpretations, but at the same time it resists conventional critical analysis, and it nearly always defeats any attempt to paraphrase it.

All of this is true, and none of it deters the faithful. Ever since Ashbery's 1975 collection *Self-Portrait in a Convex Mirror* made a clean sweep of the nation's major literary awards, this allegedly hermetic poet has won a genuine and genuinely avid audience for his work. The critical naysayers are now in a minority, though there remain some who routinely charge that Ashbery is either a deliberate obscurantist or a "profes-

New York Times Magazine, December 16, 1984.

sional mindblower," whose work is abstruse, self-involved, and coy. Yet he is widely considered America's most significant contemporary poet, and that recognition extends internationally. In England, where many notable American poets are indifferently received, Ashbery's books are taken very seriously indeed. And in the United States, where the poetry public has splintered into so many rival factions, regional loyalties, and clashing impulses, Ashbery might well be the only poet about whom there exists a consensus of acclaim.

The poet himself puts his popularity into wry perspective: "To be a famous American poet is not the same as being famous." The poet's distinctively flat, nasal twang doesn't exactly divulge that he was born in Rochester fifty-seven years ago. Ashbery is tall and slender, casually but nattily dressed, clean-shaven. His silver-rim eyeglasses match his silver hair, and when he laughs at one of his ironic turns of phrase, the prominent gap between his two front teeth seems to underscore the irony.

"I think I'm famous among people who may never have read a line of my poetry," he says. "I've heard myself described as 'the most successful American poet,' but 'successful poet' seems a contradiction in terms—like 'negative capability.' Poetry seems to involve failure—a celebration of a failed state of affairs." Ashbery admits that he once despaired of finding a readership; that, ever since, he has written to please himself, and that this seems to have been a shrewd strategy after all. "Very often people don't listen to you when you speak to them. It's only when you talk to yourself that they prick up their ears."

Someone approaching Ashbery's work for the first time would be wise not to look for a didactic message in it—let alone for the chain reaction of personal revelations that regularly sets off sparks in the work of Robert Lowell or John Berryman. Ashbery's poetry is explosive in a different manner altogether. About the only thing one can confidently expect of an Ashbery poem is the constant sense that the unexpected is upon us. The leaps are dazzling; the individual lines, stunningly precise in themselves, cohere in ways that can only startle, making us laugh at times and at other times leaving us feeling that we don't know quite what hit us.

Ashbery's poetry is so richly textured, so replete with allusions and red herrings and complicated rhetorical gestures, that a critic with any degree of ingenuity can easily appeal to his lines as the support system for a pet critical theory. But for many of us, any key or code to the poems—however ingeniously put forth—might well work to diminish rather than enhance our delight. Which may simply be another way of saying that Ashbery's poetry often induces in its readers the state of mystified alertness that only the most intense of esthetic experiences can afford.

At a time when collections of poetry tend to gather dust at out-of-the-way bookstores, Ashbery's books do extremely well. Extremely well for a poet of Ashbery's stature means an average annual income of $12,000 in royalties and honorariums for poetry readings, a sum that is buttressed by his other professional activities. *Self-Portrait in a Convex Mirror* has sold nearly 36,000 copies in combined hardcover and paperback sales; *A Wave,* which came out last May, virtually sold out its first printing of 5,000 copies within five months. But these figures, impressive though they are, tell only part of the story. To get a true notion of Ashbery's impact, one would have to enumerate the bonanza of critical articles that have been devoted to him; consider the diverse array of younger poets who list Ashbery as an influence or an inspiration; add the crowded audiences from his active schedule of poetry readings, and factor in the creative-writing seminars, coast to coast, in which Ashbery's poetry almost amounts to a rite of initiation.

Ashbery's literary reputation should properly be a source of astonishment in any case, because he has never deviated from the commitment to an experimental ideal that characterized his very first book of poems, *Some Trees,* chosen by W. H. Auden for the Yale Younger Poets series in 1956. Ashbery's poems, then and now, do waken an anxiety in some readers. What, they wonder, does it all mean? "Last night, at a poetry reading I gave at Seton Hall University in New Jersey, I said, 'I believe in communicating, but I don't believe in communicating something the reader already knows,'" Ashbery tells a visitor to his Chelsea apartment in New York City. "A man in the audience said, 'Yes, but what is it then that you *do* want to communicate?' I was rather at a loss to reply. I guess the answer is that I don't really know until I'm actually in the process of writing, and after that happens, I forget what it was. But my aim is not to puzzle and terrorize readers but to give them something new to think about."

Ashbery speaks slowly, carefully, with the air of a man who is eager to clear up misunderstandings but is almost resigned to their taking place. "I think that in the process of writing all kinds of unexpected things happen that shift the poet away from his plan, and that these accidents are really what we mean when we talk about poetry," he says, lighting an unfiltered Gitane. "The pleasure one gets from reading poetry comes from something else than the idea or story in a poem, which is just a kind of armature for the poet to drape with many-colored rags. These are what one really enjoys but can't admit it, since there *is* this underlying urge to analyze and make sense of everything. But what is 'making sense,' anyway?"

Or, as Ashbery writes in the brilliant title poem of *A Wave*, his latest volume of poetry and quite possibly his strongest to date:

> . . . And the issue
> Of making sense becomes such a far-off one. Isn't this
>   "sense"—
> This little of my life that I can see—that answers me
> Like a dog, and wags its tail, though excitement and fidelity
>   are
> About all that ever gets expressed? What did I ever do
> To want to wander over into something else, an explanation
> Of how I behaved, for instance, when knowing can have this
> Sublime rind of excitement, like the shore of a lake in the
>   desert
> Blazing with the sunset? . . .

Merely to list some of Ashbery's characteristic procedures will convey an idea of what makes his poetry so unusual and so compelling. Begin with his titles, for Ashbery does—he invariably chooses a title before writing the poem that it heads. "I feel it's a kind of opening into a potential poem, a door that suddenly pops open and leads into an unknown space," he says. Like Wallace Stevens, whom he cites as a precedent, Ashbery favors picturesque titles that bear a quizzical relation to the lines that follow. If his poems were paintings, these titles would amount to an invisible extra color.

Look at examples from *A Wave*. Alliteration goes wild in "Around the Rough and Rugged Rocks the Ragged Rascal Rudely Ran." Paradox turns into punch line in "I See, Said the Blind Man, As He Put Down His Hammer and Saw." Critical reactions are anticipated, and perhaps disarmed, by "Purists Will Object" and by "But What Is the Reader to Make of This?" "Try Me! I'm Different!" and "Ditto, Kiddo" revel in Ashbery's affection for colloquialisms, clichés, and "plain American which cats and dogs can read," to quote Marianne Moore. Ashbery would sooner celebrate the language of the tribe than purify it. "It's sacred for me, just because it's the way we all talk," he says, adding with maddening logic: "We must know what we're doing or we wouldn't talk as we do."

Perhaps it is a striving for universality that lies behind his audacious disregard for an exactness of reference. Writes Douglas Crase, one of the best in an emerging generation of poets upon whom Ashbery has had a profound influence: "Ashbery is insouciant about place; he is prodigal with pronouns, profligate with tenses and extravagant with evasion and hyperbole. Who, what, where, why and when—they are spun off like freed electrons."

In Ashbery's poetry, "I" can turn into "you," "he" into "we" without warning—as though the pronouns all represented aspects of a universal consciousness and functioned like the variables in an ever-changing equation. This has its humorous side, too, of course. Quipped fellow poet Kenneth Koch, when he and Ashbery were colleagues on the *Harvard Advocate* in the late 1940s: the paradigmatic Ashbery line is, "It wants to go to bed with us."

Not that Ashbery eschews logic in his poetry. It's just that the logic he leans on resembles that of an unedited dream—or a musical composition. "What I like about music is its ability of being convincing, of carrying an argument through successfully to the finish, though the terms of this argument remain unknown quantities," Ashbery wrote twenty years ago, and the statement applies as strongly today. Cheerfully calling himself "a frustrated composer," Ashbery speaks of polyphony and polytonality as "privileges which I envy composers for having" and which he tries to incorporate in his poems not only through his patented proliferation of pronouns but through "a choir or cluster of voices" that speak as if between invisible quotation marks. Just when the "argument" seems headed toward resolution, a new voice will interrupt; a concrete image will appear where further elaboration seemed called for. "This mirrors my own attempts to acquire knowledge," says Ashbery. "At the very moment when abstract thinking seems about to produce a result, something concrete steps in and takes its place." The result very often reads like a "visible soundtrack" of a mind in motion, a mind that can be quite mindless a split second before, or after, it hits upon an insight or a truth.

Ashbery is nowhere near as doctrinaire as the French Surrealists were about the significance of the dreaming mind to the creative process. "I feel there are other mental states as interesting as dreams, or as uninteresting," says Ashbery, "but in order to present a complete picture of one's experience, what goes on in one's head, one needs to use lots of them."

It's the structure or grammar of a dream, the part that defies interpretation, that especially endears itself to Ashbery. "The logic of a dream has a persuasiveness that logic doesn't have," he declares. "Suppose in a dream you found yourself in two different places at the same time. If somebody argued that you weren't, you wouldn't believe him, you would believe the dream situation, which would seem right to you for reasons you are unable to guess."

Does he attach any special significance to tarot cards, astrology, or other forms of divination? No, because "the occult is not mysterious enough." Nevertheless, these have provided the poet with some incidental imagery in the past, and they appeal to him, one suspects, for the same reason that dreams do: they're a means of stirring up the unconscious in pursuit of "the real reality, beyond truer imaginings"—a phrase, like so many in Ashbery's poetry, that stops one in one's tracks. In dreams begin paradoxes:

> . . . I never think about it
> Unless I think about it all the time
> And therefore don't know except in dreams
> How I behave, what I mean to myself. . . .

Ashbery has never made it easy for critics to predict the course his work will take. Each of the fifty poems in *Shadow Train* (1981), his last collection before *A Wave*, consisted of sixteen lines broken into four equal stanzas. Ashbery gravitated to this form, he reports, in reaction against the "fearful asymmetry" of the sonnet. Yet "At North Farm," the lead poem in *A Wave,* is recognizably a sonnet—though an unrhymed and inverted one; its fourteen lines are divided into two stanzas, which behave very much like the octet and sestet of a traditional sonnet. Ashbery thanks his interviewer for pointing this out to him. "I was doing this completely unconsciously," he says. "I wasn't counting the lines. The poem ended when it ended, as usual. So I guess it *is* a good thing we have critics around to tell us what we're doing."

Playing the critic, to oblige his guest, Ashbery allows that the two stanzas enforce a set of contrasts. The messenger in the first stanza "is coming across deserts, but once he arrives he'll be in a place where there are a lot of people. He may not find the right person to deliver the message to."

The second stanza takes us away from the city and back to the farm, where "we" reside, "we" being passive observers of the drama involving "you." "The idea is, I think, that the plenty alluded to has an unnatural origin, some magical reason for being there, since it didn't grow there, which would be borne out by the act of leaving a dish out for the goblin to ensure that the plenty would continue." What about the paradoxical "sometimes and always" in the last line? "Just as feelings can be mixed, so 'sometimes and always' can coexist," says Ashbery.

The title "At North Farm" derives from the *Kalevala,* a

Finnish folk epic. "It's a place referred to frequently in that poem, with the epithet 'gloomy and prosperous north farm,' " Ashbery says. "It's situated somewhere near hell." The critic Helen Vendler, reviewing *A Wave* for the *New York Review of Books* last June, interpreted the poem's "gloomy and prosperous" locale—a barren place whose granaries are bursting—as a metaphor for middle age. According to Vendler, the traveler in the poem is "the Angel of Death" and "Ashbery's propitiatory dish of milk for the goblin" is a folk remedy to keep death at bay.

But Ashbery, who had a close brush with death as the result of a spinal infection in 1982, prefers to think of "At North Farm" as a love poem. It "was written before I became ill and had no inkling that I would become ill," he says. He identifies the "someone" in the first line not as an emissary from heaven or hell but as "a lover, perhaps of a somewhat ominous kind that would remind one of mortality." But Ashbery is reluctant to press his own interpretation. "I remarked to a friend, after I read Helen's review, that I had thought these poems were really dealing with love rather than death," he says. "But sometimes it's difficult to tell the difference between them."

Ashbery recently moved into a larger apartment in the highrise building he has lived in for the last dozen years, and signs of the move are everywhere. Books remain boxed, but Ashbery's old living room has reassembled itself. At its center is a low glass table that makes the room look more spacious than it actually is. A wall-to-wall window faces the Hudson River, treating the poet to "pollution-pink sunsets" on a daily basis. On an adjacent wall hangs a painting of an artist's worktable by Jane Freilicher, a longtime friend. An art critic for much of his professional life, Ashbery currently serves in that capacity for *Newsweek*, and he himself has been the subject of portraits by such painters as Fairfield Porter, Alex Katz, Larry Rivers, and, most recently, Francesco Clemente, the Italian neo-Expressionist.

It was during a ten-year stay in France—where he'd gone as a Fulbright fellow in 1955—that Ashbery "backed into a career as an art critic." To support his poetry and other literary activities, he wrote hundreds of reviews for the Paris edition of the *Herald Tribune* between 1960 and 1965.

The task of writing a weekly article, "rain or shine, exhibitions or no exhibitions," convinced Ashbery that "I could sit down the same way with a poem and type if I wanted to." This remains his *modus operandi:* Ashbery approaches his typewriter once a week or so to write poetry, confident that he will tap his unconscious in the very act of tapping the keys. With a journalist's discipline, he imposes a deadline on himself when he undertakes to write a long poem.

"I began *A Wave* around New Year of 1983 and finished the first draft at the end of February, my cut-off date," he says. "That's probably what caused the poem to end. I mean, the fact that I realized I was now within a day or two of the limit I had set myself caused me to produce an ending."

Besides deadlines, poetry and journalism have something else in common for Ashbery. "A newspaper article does have a form," he explains. "Nobody is going to tell you what it is. It's something you have to find out for yourself, and the same thing is true of poems."

Ashbery insists that music rather than painting has been the more immediate stimulus for his poetry. He writes while listening to an all-classical FM station; he is receptive to other kinds of music as well, and, in fact, his poem "The Songs We Know Best," with its hilarious couplets—"Too often when you thought you'd be showered with confetti / What they flung at you was a plate of hot spaghetti"—was written to the rhythms of the pop lyric "Reunited and it feels so good." An important breakthrough in Ashbery's poetic development occurred when he attended a concert of John Cage's music in the early 1950s. "In the case of Cage, the idea that chance can be the determining element in a work of art was very exciting," Ashbery says. "It wasn't only the actual music that I found exhilarating, but the possibilities that this way of composing seemed to open up, not just for musicians but for artists in general."

The parallels between Ashbery and a composer like Elliott Carter—whose musical setting of Ashbery's poem "Syringa" invites the comparison—have been explored in a perceptive essay by the critic Lawrence Kramer. "It is not that the poems have no meaning, or hide their meanings," Kramer maintains. "It is that they, like Carter's compositions, consist of a plurality of meanings woven into one fabric." Other critics contend, with perhaps equal justification, that Ashbery's poetic practices approximate a literary equivalent of Abstract Expressionism. An Ashbery poem, they point out, is very nearly as opaque and self-referential as a canvas by Jackson Pollock or Willem de Kooning; it chronicles its own development, serving as a metaphor for the mind of its maker.

Certainly Ashbery's art criticism helps illuminate some of the fundamental principles that govern his own poetry. From 1965 until 1972, Ashbery worked as executive editor of the New York-based magazine *Art News,* in which he published major essays on de Kooning, Saul Steinberg, Joseph Cornell, and avant-garde art in general. One such article saluted the gambler's instinct that experimental art seems to require. Ashbery drew a surprising analogy to religion. "Most reckless things are beautiful in some way," he argued, "and recklessness is what makes experimental art beautiful, just as religions are beautiful because of the strong possibility that they are founded on nothing. We would all believe in God if we knew He existed, but would this be much fun?"

More recently, in an appreciation of the American expatriate artist R. B. Kitaj, Ashbery virtually defined the common ground between painter and poet. After *The Waste Land,* Ashbery wrote that "the randomness and discontinuity of modern experience" could no longer be ignored. "Art with any serious aspirations toward realism still has to take into account the fact that reality escapes laws of perspective and logic, and does not naturally take the form of a sonnet or a sonata."

But for all his affinities with modern artists, Ashbery's most celebrated poem takes its title and its point of departure not from a work of abstract art, but from a sixteenth-century painting by the Italian Mannerist Parmigianino. It's hard to look at the several convex mirrors in Ashbery's apartment without thinking of his magnificent "Self-Portrait in a Convex Mirror." "That was the first time I ever took a painting as the subject for a poem," Ashbery recalls. "And I did it only after I left *Art News* and supposed that I wouldn't be involved with writing about art anymore. It was as though I had been consciously avoiding this particular input while I was in the business of being an art editor, as though I shouldn't be writing about what is so close to my daily business."

During the winter of 1973 in Provincetown, Massachusetts, Ashbery happened upon a small bookstore on an obscure back street and bought a book of Parmigianino reproductions. Soon he found himself using the painting as the pretext for poetry, the motive for metaphor. "The funny thing is, when I went to find that bookstore it had completely disappeared. There was no trace of its ever having been there. It was like De Quincey looking in vain for the store where he first bought opium. Being kind of susceptible to all kinds of mystical, superstitious ideas, I felt that this bookstore had just materialized for a few moments to allow me to buy this book, and then vanished." Seen in the light of a crucial passage near the end of the poem, this eerie anecdote seems almost a parable about poetic inspiration:

> . . . the "it was all a dream"
> Syndrome, though the "all" tells tersely
> Enough how it wasn't. Its existence
> Was real, though troubled, and the ache
> Of this waking dream can never drown out
> The diagram still sketched on the wind,
> Chosen, meant for me and materialized
> In the disguising radiance of my room. . . .

Since 1974, Ashbery has directed the graduate poetry-writing program at Brooklyn College. The assignments he gives to his students differ dramatically from the usual agenda in creative-writing workshops. One Ashbery assignment is to write in a constricting form like the sestina, whose intricate rules can prove curiously liberating. The students are also asked to translate a poem from a language they don't understand—without the help of a dictionary; to solve a rebus; and to transform "a poem that's in the public domain" into a poem of their own.

Robert Frost defined poetry as "what gets lost in translation." For Ashbery, it sometimes seems, poetry is closer to an inspired form of *mis*translation.

Ashbery's students speak of him—and his exotic methods of composition—with unabashed enthusiasm. "He was marvelously laid-back in class," recalls Star Black, who was well advanced in her career as a photographer when she enrolled in the Brooklyn College writing program in 1980. "He wanted us to subvert—and expand—our minds. He also wanted to undermine the cranky standards we had for judging poetry. One time he asked us to write a deliberately amateurish poem. I found that, much to my amazement, my poem really worked. I wrote one of my better poems trying to write a bad poem."

John Yau, a former student whose book of poems *Corpse and Mirror* was selected by Ashbery for the National Poetry Series in 1983, singles out the mistranslation assignment. "Dealing with a page of Egyptian hieroglyphics forced you to make other connections, to manipulate your syntax so that it did things that declarative sentences can't do," says Yau. "Ashbery taught us that a poem could follow a logic of its own. It didn't have to fulfill a traditional expectation. Most poetry in America is anecdotal, a form of storytelling, and he made you go beyond that. He encouraged you to try to go beyond the mainstream of what's acceptable."

Although his academic credentials include a Master of Arts degree in English literature from Columbia University, Ashbery is a self-taught instructor—he was close to fifty when he taught his first class—and this may help to account for his unique pedagogical style. "What startled me most about Ashbery's teaching was his seemingly offhand manner," says Elizabeth Brunowski, a student in the program. She is a clinical psychologist and is completing a book about Nijinsky. She says she entered the program largely because of a published interview in which Ashbery made frequent reference to Nijinsky. Ashbery's commentary on the great dancer's diary—on "the quality of language of someone going into a psychotic state"— impressed her enormously. "His psychological insights were nothing short of brilliant," says Miss Brunowski.

For the last several years, Ashbery has taught only during the fall semesters, a decision dictated by the life-threatening illness he suddenly came down with in the spring of 1982. A common staphylococcus infection in an uncommon place—the spine—required that he be rushed to the hospital for major surgery. The operation was a success, but for months thereafter Ashbery needed a mechanical walker to get around, and he continues to suffer from an assortment of permanent, if slight, disabilities.

On the subject of his health, Ashbery assumes "the stoic pose, tinged with irony and self-mockery," that he describes in one of his poems. "I can't run, and I get tired if I walk a long time or stand a long time," he says. "These seem a small price to pay for being alive, so I'm not really unhappy about them." How has the death's-door experience affected his poetry? "I don't know that it has," is the somewhat surprising reply. "Many of life's major disasters and calamities don't seem to have made much of an impression on me."

The illness and its aftermath have scarcely deterred the poet from leading his customarily active social life, though he admits to having become "more of a stay-at-home in the past few years." His is a familiar presence at literary events and celebrations in New York. He has an extremely wide range of friends and acquaintances, many of long standing, and though he is besieged by visitors he erects few barriers between himself and the outside world. At an impromptu postdinner party in Ashbery's apartment, guests might find themselves listening to recordings of the Firesign Theater comedy group, as Ashbery guffaws delightedly. Or he might play the works of little-known nineteenth-century and early modern composers on his stereo. Ashbery, who once referred to himself in a poem as an "insatiable researcher of learned trivia," has a phenomenal memory that enables him to recite recondite lines off the top of his head—or to speak about flowers or cooking, two of his passions, with expertise:

> . . . And then the results are brilliant:
> Someone is summoned to a name, and soon
> A roomful of people becomes dense and contoured

And words come out of the wall
To batter the rhythm of generation following on
    generation. . . .

Sipping a cup of coffee in his living room, Ashbery explains
that the assignments he prepares for his poetry classes "work
for the purpose of distracting the students to the point at
which they're able to write the poem they were planning to
write anyway, without worrying about it, because they imagine
they're solving some problem." Asked whether he assigns
these or similar tasks to himself, Ashbery at first demurs but
then obligingly pulls out a new poem called "Forgotten Song,"
which begins by juxtaposing two lines from folk ballads—"O
Mary, go and call the cattle home / For I'm sick in my heart
and fain would lie down"—and branches off from there.
Other recent works, too, come to mind as examples of Ash-
bery's fondness for fairy tales and once-popular ballads in the
public domain. "Description of a Masque," a prose poem in *A
Wave,* features Little Jack Horner ("a tall and roguish-looking
young man wearing a trench coat and expensive blue jeans")
as well as Simple Simon and the Pie Man (two vaudevilleans, it
appears) among its nursery-rhyme heroes.
    Ashbery readily acknowledges folklore as an influence—or
at least as a fund of poetic material. The distinction is an
important one to Ashbery. "I don't see influence the way liter-
ary critics see it," he says. When pressed, he mentions Auden
and Stevens, "hybrid" French Surrealists like Pierre Reverdy
and Max Jacob, German Romantic poets like Hölderlin and
Novalis. "But I don't sit down to write a poem and think, well,
since I've been influenced by Wallace Stevens, I will now write
a poem that's influenced by Wallace Stevens."
    Virtually everything, on the other hand, can serve Ashbery
as a source of material or as the occasion for a poem. It might
be a comic strip that sets him off—he has published a sestina
about Popeye as well as a poem titled "Daffy Duck in Holly-
wood," whose range of references includes Speedy Gonzales,
the Princesse de Clèves, and Milton's Satan in *Paradise Lost.*
Should the telephone ring during the hour or so a week that

Ashbery reserves for the writing of poetry, he'll welcome the interruption—and allow it to modify the poem in progress. Nothing is excluded or suppressed: Ashbery can leap in an instant from Sydney Carton to a wrong number to an affirmation of love, and make it seem the most natural thing in the world.

"When I began writing poetry, I was a compulsive reader of all the contemporary poetry of that time," Ashbery says. "Now I look for ideas for poetry elsewhere—in other kinds of writing, movies, daily life in New York City." Ashbery considers "the New York School" of poetry—in which he, Koch, James Schuyler, and the late Frank O'Hara are commonly thought of as charter members—a misleading tag. "I never really thought of myself as being a sort of spokesperson for New York," he tells his guest. "But I was wondering, when you were asking me about the simultaneity of high culture and low in my poems, whether that might be a result of living in New York City, where everything is mashed together that way. I look out my window and see what seems to be a Gothic church tower and a big building that says ABIE'S BABY on it right next door." The latter is an "office furniture supermarket"; the former is the spire of the General Theological Seminary, where South African Bishop Desmond M. Tutu, lately awarded the Nobel Peace Prize, is currently a visiting professor. "It must be a state that I find it profitable to reflect on," muses Ashbery. "The simultaneity of conflicting states of being"—something that New York City specializes in.

These days, Ashbery divides his time between his Manhattan apartment and an eclectic American Victorian house in the Hudson Valley, a convenient train ride away. He shares his Hudson Valley digs with David Kermani, his companion for more than a decade, who works as a rug and art dealer in nearby Albany. The pair spend weekends together, until Monday classes compel Ashbery to return to the city.

Ashbery writes in either place, though his professional obligations—at *Newsweek* and at Brooklyn College—limit the time he has available. "Being both a lazy and ambitious person, I want to get some work done and also get it over with so I can get back to being lazy," says Ashbery. "I'm not sure that I'd write much more poetry than I do. But I'd like very much to try other kinds of writing, such as fiction, that I don't have the time for. I have ideas for some short stories."

Conspicuously absent from Ashbery's poetry are the autobiographical tales and details of his life. You wouldn't know from reading his verse that Ashbery grew up on a farm in Sodus, New York, during the Great Depression—"Actually, I had a sort of Victorian childhood," he says—or that he was extremely close to his maternal grandfather, a prominent physicist at the University of Rochester.

His poems won't tell you that the bookish lad became a radio "quiz kid" and later attended Deerfield Academy, "an uncomfortably conservative, WASP, jock school," where he gradually gave up painting for poetry—and where another boy pirated two of his early efforts and published them in *Poetry* magazine under the pseudonym "Joel Michael Symington."

Ashbery attributes his reticence to a feeling that "the circumstances of my own life are of no compelling interest to me." It isn't really a question of privacy; on the contrary, it's a predilection for writing poems about "paradigms of common experience," poems that invent their own experiences rather than simply record events in the life of the poet. "My own autobiography has never interested me very much," Ashbery once told an interviewer. "Whenever I try to think about it, I seem to draw a complete blank.

"There is the title of a Japanese film by Ozu: 'I was born, but . . .' That's how I feel about it."

> . . . Heck, it's anybody's story,
> A sentimental journey—"gonna take a sentimental journey,"
> And we do, but you wake up under the table of a dream:
> You are that dream, and it is the seventh layer of you.
> We haven't moved an inch, and everything has changed. . . .

III

The Life of Words

Money and Poetry

Money is a kind of poetry.

—Wallace Stevens

Get the Money.

—Ted Berrigan

The starving artist in his cold water garret is an example of a stereotype that is not only stale and flat but unprofitable as well. It is frequently used to idealize both the artist and his penurious condition, thus compounding one error with another. That garret, for one thing, turned into a six-figure SoHo loft a decade ago; and its inhabitant is more likely to be shrewd than naive about his practical affairs. There's no equivalent in poetry of the big money art market, where fantastic sums of cash are routinely exchanged for the possession of paintings by modern masters. Van Gogh's *Irises* fetched $53.9 million at Sotheby's in 1987; Picasso's *Acrobat and Young Harlequin* found a willing Japanese buyer at $38.45 million in 1988, mere weeks after *False Start* by Jasper Johns set a record for the highest price ever paid for a work by a living artist, $17.05 million. From the point of view of the art critic (as opposed to the social historian), the really interesting question has to do with the effect of these figures on the art that is now being produced—and the emergence of a new generation of art stars whose skill at self-marketing can make a little talent go a long way. What is the relation of monetary value to aesthetic worth? Does the aura of the contemporary art object inhere in it as an artifact or as an event? The relation of art to the mechanisms of hype on the one side and the fevers of financial speculation on the other side—the whole question of

From *Epoch* (Fall 1989).

value in art—could be the central theoretical problem facing art criticism today.

A poem is not a commodity, at least not in the sense that a painting is; and the truths of the book business, which is the commercial venue of poetry, are very different and far less bullish than those governing the salon-and-gallery scene. In America, no poet was ever made rich by his poetry, and there's no reason to expect this situation to change. Nevertheless, the garret image and the sentimental baggage that comes with it are as bogus for poets as for painters. The reason is simple. The serious writer can't afford to be a saintly, unworldly fool. Probably that was always the case; surely it's true today. To succeed as an artist of any kind, in any genre, you are obliged to be more resourceful, not less, at balancing your books; where the stakes in financial terms are low, economic survival becomes a closer calculation.

Poets in particular take for granted that their mode of making a living may either be unrelated to their artistic work or related in a problematic way; most have done different things at different times to make ends meet. The chances are that your local poet-in-residence may be a secret expert at—or at least has some experience of—numerous financial gambits: applying for grants, deducting a home office on income tax returns, getting "matching funds" for poetry readings, and so forth. The sums tend to be minuscule by the standards of other professions and therefore scheme must be combined with scheme. All the politics and the paperwork involved, the bureaucratic busywork, the treadmill of hustle—it's all part of what Wallace Stevens called "the pressure of reality," against which the imagination must press back. Money represents the stubborn, intractable material world. It is the a priori proposition of a syllogism: first comes grub, then comes morality, and to get the bread you need the dough. Money, in short, is real.

Money remains real despite the junk bonds and the leveraged buyouts; it is part of the pressure of reality even though, as often as not, it's invisible, a line of figures in a computer printout, something backed not by the gold standard but by "faith"—you credit it or you don't—which puts it on a metaphysical footing akin to that of a monotheistic deity. A conception of reality (or of cognate terms such as realism) that doesn't take money into account is, or should be, highly suspect. Yet there's also a disturbing aura of unreality about money, and it's this large, unfocused unease, rather than any more localized panic, that is arguably the prime residue of the colossal five-hundred-point stock market crash on October 19, 1987. The sense of unreality surrounding the means of exchange is not unique to this era; think of the inflation in Germany in the 1920s when you needed to be a millionaire to pay for a cup of coffee. What *is* unique to our era is not only the unprecedented glamour of money, the careerist fetishism of the moment, but also the extent to which this phenomenon dominates the airwaves and feeds the cultural appetite of the masses, who can't seem to get enough of programs like "Dallas," "Dynasty," and "Lifestyles of the Rich and Famous."

Money, often taboo, is almost equally often a clandestine item on the agenda in conversations between writers—especially those involved in the creative writing industry—in the United States today. Despite or because of that fact, however, money as a subject has by and large gone unexplored, or been ignored or evaded, among recent novelists and poets. There are significant exceptions, of course: novelists as different from one another as Louis Auchincloss and William Gaddis make the progress of wealth a central concern in their writing. But much highly celebrated fiction takes little note of financial exigencies, ways, and means, and many lyric poems seem almost by definition to exclude from their purview the world of making a living. Nor is it as though writers, in their practical and social lives, are indifferent to money, and the need to make it, and the thought of what it can buy. Money may in fact be the one subject we all talk about constantly—but rarely in prose or verse.

The idea of a poets' symposium on money followed from these reflections. I wrote to twenty poets—representatives of an array of literary styles, geographic locales, and professional identities—in the hope that fifteen would respond and that the responses would clash here and overlap there and generally prove stimulating in a group display. Since I didn't want to lead my witnesses, I was fearful of saying very much in my letter to contributors soliciting their participation. I limited myself to tossing out "two potential epigraphs" for the symposium: "Money is a kind of poetry" (Wallace Stevens) and "Get the money!" (Ted Berrigan, quoting Damon Runyan).*

Both epigraphs have antecedents. Horace wrote, "Money, make money; by honest means if you can; if not, by any means make money." Ben Jonson adopts the sentiment in *Every Man in His Humour:* "Get money; still get money, boy; / No matter by what means." The English Renaissance poet Barnabe Googe in probably his most famous poem propounds a rationale for the principle. Here in full is "Of Money":

> Give money me, take friendship whoso list,
> For friends are gone come once adversity,
> When money yet remaineth safe in chest,
> That quickly can thee bring from misery;
> Fair face show friends when riches do abound;
> Come time of proof, farewell, they must away;
> Believe me well, they are not to be found
> If God but send thee once a lowering day.
> Gold never starts aside, but in distress,
> Finds ways enough to ease thine heaviness.

I like the way that "God" in the eighth line modulates into "Gold" in the ninth.

Stevens's view of money as "a kind of poetry" reverses the commonsense wisdom of Robert Graves ("If there is no money in poetry, there is also no poetry in money") but is itself subject to ironic or wistful reversal. No one ever confused the poet's coin with that of the king's realm. As Thomas Randolph wrote in "A Parley with His Empty Purse," "Hexameter's no sterling, and I feare / What the brain coins goes scarce for current there." But though the resemblance between money and poetry stops far short of identity, the process of mind that links the two is itself a fine example of poetic logic. I am indebted to Douglas Crase for tracking down the source of Stevens's aphorism in Ralph Waldo Emerson's essay "Nominalist and Realist": "Money, which represents the prose of life, and which is hardly

---

*Responses from fifteen poets were printed with this essay in *Epoch.*

spoken of in parlors without an apology, is, in its effects and laws, as beautiful as roses." Before anyone rebuts Emerson by quoting the price of a dozen red roses in Manhattan, let me point out that Fitzgerald ("The rich are different from you and me") was more profound if less worldly-wise than Hemingway ("Yes, they have more money") in their famous exchange. The Hemingway side of our brains scoffs at the analogy between money and poetry, for we are accustomed to placing these terms in opposition. Yet the analogy is neither willful nor perverse and indeed the very terms *poetry* and *money* become more potent as allegorical agents if we sketch out the correspondences between them. In conversation Archie Ammons proposed this pithy paraphrase of Stevens's line: "The quickest way to negotiate from a wish to its fulfillment is through money, and the same is true of poetry in the realm of language. The dynamics of the psyche and of the economy are parallel." Put another spin on it, and money resembles human language as an instrument of desire. Money, how we spend it or hoard it, expresses what we want and therefore who we are. Which prompts perhaps the rueful rejoinder that there are as many failures of the imagination in the use of wealth as in poetry.

The great majority of American poets today are employed in academe. Those with tenure enjoy a respectable income and long-term security; those without lead a nomadic life. But whether it is a short- or long-term financial fix, academic employment is scarcely a panacea. On the contrary, the need to "get the money" has brought about a situation many feel uncomfortable with but few feel they can buck. A graduate degree in the writing of poetry is a curious proposition. What else can one do with the MFA but enter the work force of aspiring creative writing instructors? And while there is much to be said in favor of creative writing as a field of study, it would be regrettable if one consequence were the proliferation of literary clerks—as though the spirit of poetry could flourish within a bureaucratic structure. (Maybe it can.) In any event, the segregation of creative writers within the standard English department bears witness to the marginal status of poetry within the larger society. No one can be too happy about that.

The other day I was thinking of the two remarkable times in movie history when a character folds a wad of bills into a newspaper, and the newspaper is lost, and how different the films are otherwise except for the association of money and panic. Into a newspaper Janet Leigh folds the embezzled bank notes in *Psycho* just before she enters the shower in the Bates Motel, and is knifed to death. The movie promptly forgets all about Ms. Leigh's felony, since her punishment so far exceeds her crime. The money is lost and will never be recovered. It has become irrelevant, made so by her death. What looked like the plot of the movie—the story of a desperate woman in love and on the lam—has been replaced by pure Horror Show; the realm of the melodramatic and neurotic has given way to the infinitely more exciting realm of psychotic terror. Goodbye Janet Leigh, hello Anthony Perkins. The other great instance of money placed in a folded newspaper occurs in *It's a Wonderful Life* when Jimmy Stewart's affable but somewhat dim-witted uncle, distracted in conversation, leaves the newspaper behind, and it's picked up by the Scrooge-like villain, thus precipitating the grave financial crisis that ends happily when it snows dollars in the Jimmy Stewart household on Christmas Day. In either case I like the image of the money in the newspaper—the way the two things are mutually involved, our means of exchange and our means of public communication, our wallets and our words.

Time is money and money talks and talk is cheap but writers are supposed to put their money where their mouths are. In my experience there are very few subjects about which poets feel more strongly than they do about money. Money for them, for us, is all too easily understood as an antithetical constant. Money means necessity as poetry means luxury; money is bread and poetry is cake; but more, money equals matter as poetry equals spirit; money walks to the bank, poetry dances on a stage. Poetry is Ariel or Puck, incorporeal, invisible, but money, as Norman O. Brown analyzes it in *Life against Death,* is crap. "If money were not excrement, it would be valueless," Brown argues, and I remember seeing a production of *Timon of Athens* in which the rich man surrounded by his money is like a child in a sandbox playing with his shit.

These dichotomies allow for all manner of dialectical development, including the alchemical transformation of "filthy lucre" into an aesthetic experience. Scott Fitzgerald captured better than anyone else the romance of wealth, which is a young man's romance. In *The Great Gatsby,* when Gatsby tells Nick Carraway that Daisy's "voice is full of money," the line is like an epiphany to Nick. He suddenly understands: "It was full of money—that was the inexhaustible charm that rose and fell in it, the jingle of it, the cymbals' song of it. . . . High in a white palace the king's daughter, the golden girl." George Bernard Shaw was neither as rhapsodic nor as romantic but he did manifest a comparable ardor on the subject of money. In *Major Barbara,* poverty is a crime and money is (I am quoting from Shaw's preface) "the most important thing in the world," representing "health, strength, honor, generosity and beauty as conspicuously and undeniably as the want of it represents illness, weakness, disgrace, meanness and ugliness." In short, "money is the counter that enables life to be distributed socially: it *is* life as truly as sovereigns and bank notes are money." Money is energy.

"Money reproaches me," Philip Larkin writes in his poem "Money," for it represents the potential for pleasure that the poet refuses to tap. Larkin has a couplet in that poem whose sardonic rhyme sums up the logic of a monetary transaction: "I am all you never had of goods and sex. / You could get them still by writing a few cheques." He grants that money "has something to do with life," though he is more diffident than Shaw in proclaiming them identical. For Larkin money is all the paths not chosen, the days unseized. He can hear the money singing: "It is intensely sad," he concludes, leaving it deliberately unclear whether the "it" in the last sentence refers to money, the music it makes, or the experience to which he has likened it: the experience of gazing "from long french windows at a provincial town, / The slums, the canal, the churches ornate and mad / In the evening sun."

Poetry and the Golden Age

"A friend who teaches at a prestigious midwestern university told me I am the only person she knows who reads literary quarterlies in which his own work doesn't appear." We expect the statement to be the prelude to a complaint: poets are the only audience poetry has, yet even they, terminally self-absorbed, aren't paying attention, so is it any wonder that no one else is? We may even expect an accusation to follow; the discourse on this subject is often charged with a reproach, or fueled by a resentment. What we overlook is that it really should be a source of wonderment and pride that so much poetry, some of it spectacularly good, is being published despite the unfavorable conditions with which we are all so familiar. True, much that is published is as perishable as a crate of tomatoes; much is indeed downright awful; the need to make discriminations is a pressing one, always. But this is a problem for criticism and would not be, other things being equal, the poet's immediate concern. As to the unread or little-read literary magazines, before we reach conclusions about our allegedly narcissistic writers, shouldn't we pause, first, over the good fortune that has given us so many interesting publications that no one—not even a team of readers—can keep up with them all? We sometimes forget how large our country is, how many European nations would fit into our land area. Our poetry is as various as our population, and as plentiful; that should surely be cited in its favor before the speaker pronounces on the moribund state of contemporary verse.

AWP Chronicle (May 1989). Written in response to Joseph Epstein's essay "Who Killed Poetry?" in *Commentary* (August 1988).

Many dismissals of contemporary poetry seem to rely on a blame-the-victim logic. If curriculum committees decided to eliminate canonical texts from the syllabus, surely Joseph Epstein wouldn't conclude that there must be something wrong with those books. Yet he rests his case against poetry on the absence of a sizable audience. "Contemporary poetry in the United States flourishes in a vacuum," he writes. It is possible to assent to this thesis—*flourishes* is the right word—without reaching Mr. Epstein's dire conclusions. So far as I can see, he makes reference to but two poems in the course of his indictment: one about "a strip of land in Hawaii," the other a "cookie and milk" update of Proust's magical madeleine. (Mr. Epstein didn't exactly read the poems; he heard them at a poetry reading.) Whatever the merits of the poems in question, it is a curious fact that in an article of considerable length—eight full double-column magazine pages—the writer offers so little evidence of reading even a portion of the vast body of poetry he dismisses.

I would not have initiated the annual *Best American Poetry* series—nor would I have been able to sell a trade publisher on the idea—if I didn't believe that American poetry is remarkably vital and that the lack of a sizable audience is a condition that we can ameliorate. That there *is* such a lack is undeniable; Mr. Epstein adduces a number of causes, and makes a number of valid observations. One vexing problem, as I see it, is that poets today must labor in—to advert to Mr. Epstein's term—a *vacuum* of critical response. With but few valued exceptions, professors of literature, from whose ranks critics of poetry used to emerge, seem content to ignore contemporary writing. Many brainy assistant professors and graduate students prefer the autotelic world of critical theory: criticism without an object outside of itself. I wish we could get these potential readers to see what they're missing. Critical theorists tend to regard the making of evaluative aesthetic judgments as either beside the point or as downright pernicious. Given this dismal state of academic affairs, it seems to me that poets may have little choice but to serve as our own critics—at least to the extent of trying to create the taste by which our works will be enjoyed.

It's hard to predict what will be read a century hence—we live in our time, not after it, and that is fortunate, because history tends to perpetuate the half-dozen great poets of an age while consigning other worthies to the edge of oblivion. Our age isn't all that different except for the problem of the audience, though even in this area is won't do to idealize the past; there never really was a golden age.

The Vision Thing

It has sometimes been said that contemporary poetry, however technically brilliant, lacks statement or vision. Please comment.

Perhaps there is some unwritten rule of lit-crit discourse that presumes an invisible but highly questionable link between the pulse of poetry on the one side and the agents of presidential power on the other. Seven or eight years ago, when the New Formalism was new, I remember seeing it smeared as "Reaganetics." And now all of contemporary poetry is accused of being Bush League—another victim of that "vision thing."

It seems absurd to expect the poets of our time to speak with one voice or adhere to a monolithic view of the cosmos. Look for a single governing vision among American poets and you will look in vain. You will find not one vision but many—and that is as it should be. If what you mean by *vision* is a distinctive way of seeing things as they are or an imagined apprehension of things as they could be—if the term embraces the senses of observation and aspiration, prophecy and fantasy, the vatic utterance and the penetrating gaze that tears off the false appearance of things—you'll find a plethora of examples in the works of contemporary poets. Think of James Merrill reporting on the celestial afterlife, or A. R. Ammons eyeing the radiance around the lowly ticks and beggars of being. The centerpiece of Donald Hall's *The One Day* is a prophetic vision in the bonecrunching manner of an Old Testament seer. "The First Hour of the Night," Frank Bidart's new long poem, is a nightmare of Western philosophy, a vision in

---

Published in *Mississippi Review* (1991) as part of a symposium on the state of contemporary poetry. Contributors were asked to comment on the proposition printed as an epigraph above.

which the great figures of Raphael's School of Athens come to life and make history. Read Jorie Graham's "Fusion," or Norman Dubie's "Of Politics, & Art," or Mark Strand's "Orpheus Alone," and then tell me that contemporary poetry lacks vision. Or read Rodney Jones or Thylias Moss or Allen Grossman or . . .

It could be said that the poets have given us their visions, not told us about them. Fair enough: it is not the poet's obligation to clarify, in prose and by way of a critical exegesis, the heart of his or her mystery. From poets we value what comments about their work they wish to make—these are often fascinating and invariably helpful in ways that the writers themselves may not fully realize or intend. But interpretation is what critics are supposed to do. If people think that contemporary poetry is short on substance, on meaning, on vision, or on a public self, maybe the critics have not done their work.

The presumed crisis in poetry is quite possibly a crisis in poetry criticism. Too many academic critics operate on a theoretical plane, and some of those who deign to address contemporary poetry seem to think that the world is divided in two, with the New Formalism on the one end and Language poetry on the other. If that is how you divide the world, you may well conclude that poetry has a vision problem—when the problem is really with your division. In Japan recently I was asked to comment about the New Formalism and the Language poets. I responded by trying to distinguish the talent of individuals from the mediocrity of schools. But it occurred to me that from one point of view, the two movements were aspects of the same phenomenon. Supposedly polar opposites, both have in common an emphatic formalist tendency, which in lesser practitioners can be indulged at the expense of content. The two movements also have a polemical tendency in common. It could even be argued that both were invented to give the professors something to talk about at the MLA Convention.

W. H. Auden famously remarked that a young poet who liked tinkering with words had a better chance of getting somewhere than a young poet who wrote because he or she had something to say. I think that's true. But something further needs to be said. If verse without some kind of formal restraint is like playing tennis without a net, poetry that is short on statement conjures up an image out of the movie *Blow-Up:* tennis without the ball.

Poets Who Work for a Living

It used to be that poets earned their living the same way other people did. Wallace Stevens spent most of his adult life in the employ of the Hartford Accident and Indemnity Company. William Carlos Williams practiced medicine in New Jersey. T. S. Eliot worked in a London bank, Marianne Moore at a branch of the New York Public Library. All that changed, for better or for worse, with the advent of the creative-writing industry. Nowadays poets tend to support themselves by teaching their craft. In the last decade alone more than a hundred degree-granting programs in creative writing have sprung up on campuses across America. Ted Solotaroff, the respected Harper and Row editor, calls it "the one genuine revolutionary development in American letters during the second half of the century."

But, as Solotaroff is quick to add, it hasn't been an unmixed blessing. Among the occupational hazards is a publish-or-perish mentality that leads to all too many perishable poems, tailored to conform to a currently fashionable model. A second problem is insularity. Cut off from the world beyond the campus, workshop poets may find themselves with little enough to write about. Then, too, the whole idea of getting credentials in poetry is more than a little suspect. Treating poetry as an income-producing profession, says poet A. R. Ammons, "is like putting chains on butterfly wings."

Creative writing is here to stay—as the hoopla surrounding the recent fiftieth-anniversary celebration of the University of Iowa's Writers' Workshop clearly proved. But the good

Newsweek, September 22, 1986.

news is that, without much fanfare, a growing number of poets seem determined to buck the trend of this new academic orthodoxy. They are not failed academics or Sunday poets idly pursuing their passion but impressive versemakers who happen to double as businessmen and lawyers, journalists and farmers. A heterogeneous lot, they have come to the conclusion—as one of their number, poet-businessman Dana Gioia, puts it—that academe today "is like Detroit in the 1970s: it's not the place to be."

High on anyone's list of poets who have resisted the blandishments of the academy is Douglas Crase, forty-two, who dropped out of Michigan Law School in 1970 to write gubernatorial campaign speeches for Senator Sander Levin. "When Kent State happened, I wrote a speech for Sandy critical of the use of the Ohio National Guard. He never gave it, and I walked out soon after." Surfacing in Rochester, New York, Crase discovered his poetic vocation while providing himself with an airtight cover: he wrote speeches and scripted industrials for Eastman Kodak's top management. In 1981 Crase published *The Revisionist,* his acclaimed first book of poems. A pair of prestigious grants—the Guggenheim and the Whiting—have since bought him time away from the computer terminal in his Chelsea apartment in New York City.

"I sometimes wonder," he says, pointing to a closet full of filing cabinets and boxes teeming with Kodak reports, "what if every third one of them were a poem?" But Crase doesn't regret his Kodak experience. "You'd have to include the disembodied Kodak narrator in any list of my influences," he wryly says—and means it. His poems favor "the 'civil meter' of American English, the meter we hear in the propositions offered by businessmen, politicians, engineers." What *The Revisionist* revises—or re-visions—is Walt Whitman's vision of America: "As you are dispersed, / Return and inhabit me. In every jurisdiction / And every area I promise I've already arrived."

Diane Ackerman, thirty-seven, is a poet who aspires to be a professional adventurer—or, as the title of her latest poetry collection has it, *Lady Faustus.* She has done a spot of teaching—most recently at Washington University in St. Louis—but disqualifies herself by temperament from the academic life. "I'm a sensation addict," she says. "My curiosity tends to lead with its chin." Ackerman has taken up scuba diving, worked as a cowhand on a New Mexico ranch ("But underneath the jeans I always wore frillies and perfume. It wasn't that I wanted to stop being a woman"), and learned how to fly a plane, an experience she turns into rhapsodic prose in her book *On Extended Wings*. *Parade* magazine is publishing installments of *A Poet's America,* which records her impressions of historical sites and natural wonders from Ellis Island to the Grand Canyon.

Fueled by her self-imposed assignments, Ackerman's poems are notable for their unusual range of subject matter: "Patrick Ewing Takes a Foul Shot," "Cave Diving in the Tropics," "Space Shuttle." Earlier this year she made the first cut in the journalists-in-space program and was disappointed to get no further. "There's an extraordinary buzzing blooming fidgeting universe out there, and I don't want to miss it," she says. "I don't want to get to the end of my life and find that I lived just the length of it. I want to have lived the width of it as well. I'd love it if somebody phoned me up and said, 'We'd like to send you to the Antarctic. Can you be packed up and ready to go by 3 P.M. tomorrow?' I'd say, 'Yes.' "

Do poetry and the law make strange bed-fellows? Lawrence Joseph thinks not. In 1970, with the University of Michigan's Hopwood Award for poetry in hand, Joseph embarked for Cambridge University to study English literature. When he came back he was more committed than ever to his poetry— and to the belief that it would have a better chance of flourishing if he kept it separate from his daily occupation. Keeping a low poetry profile, he went to law school, clerked for the chief justice of the Michigan Supreme Court, and did time as an associate at New York's Shearman and Sterling law firm. The angry, urban poems collected in *Shouting at No One* (1983) were written at the same time as articles on such subjects as "Causation in Workers' Compensation Mental Disability Cases." "I wanted to create a poetic idiom that would reflect my interest in questions of distributive justice," he says.

In his rooftop apartment at the base of the Brooklyn Bridge in lower Manhattan, Joseph, thirty-eight, now an associate professor of law at Hofstra University, draws a surprising analogy between his two professions. "The relation of principle to fact, abstraction to detail, is similar in legal writing and in poetry," he says. "Fact is to legal language what imagery is to poetry." A criminal trial becomes a religious metaphor in "Do What You Can," one of Joseph's best poems. "I wonder if they know," he writes, "that after the sentence of 20 to 30 years comes down, / when the accused begs, 'Lord, I can't do that kind of time,' / the judge, looking down, will smile and say, / 'Then do what you can.' "

A disillusioning experience in a Harvard graduate program in comparative literature prompted Dana Gioia to switch to Stanford Business School in 1975, and he hasn't looked back since. On New Year's Day, 1986, Gioia resolved to complete three works long in progress—a translation of Eugenio Montale's "Motets," a memoir about Elizabeth Bishop (which the *New Yorker* is publishing), and one about John Cheever. All three tasks were accomplished by the time *Daily Horoscope,* Gioia's first poetry collection, hit the bookstores last spring. Not bad at all when you consider that during this time Gioia was also putting in long hours as a mergers-and-acquisitions specialist at General Foods. "I spend most of my time looking over budget sheets to make sure they scan metrically," he jokes.

Gioia, thirty-five, wears his corporate uniform at GF's headquarters in Rye Brook, New York, a daunting postmodernist structure dominated by a domed atrium. His office is adorned with mementos of the successful Kool-Aid campaign he ran a few years ago. An unabashedly formal poet, Gioia distills the poetry of the suburbs (where "careers advance like armies") in his fine poem "In Cheever Country." "The corporation is a reasonably good place for a poet to be," he says. "It's nobody's business that I write poetry, and knowing that is very liberating." In December 1984 *Esquire* magazine named Gioia one of 272 "men and women under forty who are changing America." One change he'd like to make: "I want to explode the notion that poetry and business are incompatible."

Finally, there is the poet as rancher. Kathleen Norris followed her graduation from Bennington College by working as a program secretary for the Academy of American Poets in New York City. In 1974 came the major move: she and her husband, the poet David Dwyer, headed for Lemmon, South Dakota. There they took over a feed and cattle ranch that Norris inherited from her grandparents. The official name is Leaves of Grass, Inc. "When we first moved out here, some of the people thought the name referred to marijuana," she laughs. In addition to their farm work, Dwyer has built two cable-TV systems, while Norris moonlights at the public library to help pay for her poetry habit. *The Middle of the World,* her recent collection, takes its title from the vastness of the prairie sky. "I guess what I do sounds unusual for a poet," Norris says. "To me, it seems ordinary. It's my life."

Ambassadors of the Word

Translators are the invisible men of literature. Overlooked and underpaid, they "require the self-effacing disposition of saints," in the words of writer and translator Alastair Reid. Without them, most readers would have to do without the Bible and the *Iliad,* Dante and Tolstoy, Freud and Kafka. Yet for every hundred readers who were captivated by Umberto Eco's *The Name of the Rose*—to cite just one recent best-selling literary knockout—are there even five who recognize their debt to William Weaver, the book's translator? Probably not, and for a very simple reason: the better the translator has done his job, the less we are aware of his work. The ideal translation resembles a window through which we can behold the original text.

Though little known to the public, a handful of translators is recognized by their peers as the elite in the English language. Heading the list are Weaver translating from Italian, Richard Howard from French, Gregory Rabassa from Spanish and Portuguese, and Ralph Manheim from German and French. By nature, they and their like are a rare breed. They can't be in it for the glory (there isn't much) or the money (no one's going to get rich at the going rate of $50 per thousand words); it must be the love of literature and a sense of loyalty to at least two languages. "A person with very frugal tastes and a paid-up house could live on translation," says Rabassa, sixty-four, the foremost translator of Latin American fiction. "Other than that, no." Penury is only one of the pitfalls. One irony of the translator's lot is that the only reader qualified to

Newsweek, November 3, 1986.

judge a translation is the very reader for whom that translation is unnecessary. What Reid calls "the translation police" are ever ready to pounce—as they should—on the dolt who renders "the Comédie Française" as "French Comedy" or mangles a noble line of German verse into something as awkward as this: "Am I within myself not in what's greatest?" You'll find that in Edward Snow's otherwise fluid version of Rilke's "Girl's Lament."

While lapses like these do occur, standards of translation have gone way up in recent years. By and large, American readers of foreign fiction are now spared the sort of stilted diction that was common a generation ago. Rabassa cites "the old American xenophobia" as a continuing problem, though even that is changing. "I think Americans especially are a little more interested in the outside world than they used to be," says Manheim, without whose labor whole acres of Günter Grass would be lost to us. Weaver is heartened by the huge popular success of Eco's erudite medieval mystery, as well he might be— with the proceeds from his translation of *The Name of the Rose*, he added a study to his house in the Tuscan hills south of Florence. Weaver calls it, naturally, "the Eco chamber."

And indeed, the craft of literary translation has become a far more rewarding enterprise of late. Thanks in part to the efforts of PEN, the international organization of writers, an experienced translator can now count on getting a share of a book's royalties in addition to a flat fee. PEN has also campaigned to increase the translator's visibility—with mixed results so far. Howard, who has collaborated with the French language on well over 150 books, reports he still gets "vexed" when his works are quoted without acknowledgment. But then he sounds the translator's characteristic note of ambivalence. "If the translation isn't noticed, that might suggest that it has an excellence of its own," he says. "Maybe being overlooked is a compliment."

There are adages that attest to the hazards on the translator's course. Poetry, Robert Frost taught us, is precisely what gets lost in translation. "It's an approximate art, a question of fertile mistakes," concedes Howard, whose complete English edition of Baudelaire's *Flowers of Evil* goes a long way toward proving Frost wrong. According to another old saw, translations resemble mistresses—they can never be both faithful and beautiful. Tell that to Gabriel García Márquez, the Colombian author of *One Hundred Years of Solitude.* García Márquez has said he prefers Rabassa's English translation of his masterwork to the Spanish original.

A punning Italian proverb has it that translators are traitors—*traduttore, traditore.* The "terror of betrayal," Howard says, is the greater when translator and author are friends. Still, knowing the author is a definite advantage, translators agree. When Weaver was Englishing *The Name of the Rose,* he traveled periodically to Bologna to confer with Eco. "I would leave with a sack of books on heresies, or whatever," Weaver says happily. "He was my lending library, my bibliography." Rabassa's friendship with the late Argentine author Julio Cortázar emboldened him to take liberties with the English title of one of Cortázar's novels. Rabassa titled it *A Manual for Manuel,* a pun that doesn't exist in Spanish. "I did that with Julio's approval," Rabassa grins. Howard's friendship with Roland Barthes allowed for similar consultation sessions. "I still find myself asking questions of Roland, though he's dead," says Howard. "I would call him to ask him what he meant by quoting Hobbes when I couldn't find the citation in English. And now I leap for the phone, but he's no longer there."

Sporting a monocle and neatly trimmed beard to offset his bald pate, Howard, fifty-seven, welcomes a visitor to his book-lined Greenwich Village apartment. A distinguished poet and critic himself, Howard points to his background in lexicography—he wrote dictionaries in the mid-1950s, after graduating from Columbia University and a stint in France—as the bond that links his diverse literary activities: "I've always been a word kid, delighted that there are alternative possibilities for the words we use." Howard has a hard time choosing favorites from his long list of translations, which encompasses a who's who of modern French literature. "I love all of them," he says simply, and that accounts for the genesis of his translating career three decades ago: "There were books that I loved and my friends couldn't read them."

When did he learn French? "In a car between Cleveland and Miami, with a Viennese aunt, when I was five." However much of an exaggeration this may be, it's the same answer he gave to a nonplused Charles de Gaulle at a luncheon honoring Howard's translation of the second and third volumes of de Gaulle's memoirs. "He didn't know whether to be shocked or pleased that *his* translator had learned French in five days," Howard says.

Like Howard, Rabassa has medals aplenty to show for his services to world literature. On the lapel of his tweed jacket he wears a diminutive green and yellow medallion: the Order of San Carlos, the Colombian government's equivalent of a knighthood. Rabassa has worked hard to bring home the booming world of Latin American fiction, from the magic realism of García Márquez to the baroque prose of the late Cuban writer José Lezama Lima. He has spent more than a year on a much-heralded novel by Brazilian author Jorge Amado, which Bantam has acquired for $250,000, an unprecedented sum for a foreign novel in hard cover. "I have five pages to go," says Rabassa, who holds that "it's more creative to translate a book as you read it than to read it first," because "you never know what's going to happen next." Another of his maxims is that the best writers are often the easiest to translate. García Márquez and Cervantes are two cases in point. "I think it's because in both cases they say the exact word for the right thing at the right moment in Spanish." Among the ethical dilemmas of his craft that concern Rabassa is what he dubs "the silk-purse business": "If you're faced with a sow's ear, should you reproduce that or make it into a silk purse?"

For his translation of Nobel laureate Elias Canetti's memoir *The Play of the Eyes*, Manheim was charged—or credited—with performing just such a silk-purse operation. One reviewer argued that Manheim so improved Canetti's "complex and occasionally circuitous German" that the "English version makes smoother reading without . . . any loss in accuracy." Manheim, seventy-nine, must be used by now to such exclamations of wonderment. A recipient of the MacArthur Foundation's maximum fellowship (an annual stipend of $60,000 for life), Manheim began his translating career in New York City, where he grew up, during the 1930s. He "happened to know" German and French, the languages he has served ever since the dark days when he earned $5 for each thousand words of *Mein Kampf*. Manheim usually works alone, but for *Mein Kampf* he employed a secretary: "I could not live alone in a room with Hitler." Today Manheim "officially" lives in Paris, though he is spending the year in Cambridge, England, after summering in Aldeburgh. He is currently translating a new novel by Grass, whose books he lists among his biggest challenges. "Everything is translatable," he says. "The question is whether it can be translated well."

The soft-spoken Weaver, sixty-three, isn't sure he agrees. He considers the Renaissance poet Ariosto, for one, to be untranslatable. But recent Italian literature, from Eco's multilingual stunts to Italo Calvino's deliberately archaic *Invisible Cities*, has presented no insuperable difficulties for Weaver. A native of Washington, D.C., he graduated from Princeton in 1945 after serving as an ambulance driver in Italy during World War II. This first taste of Italy proved addictive. After a decade of shuttling between his native and adopted lands, Weaver settled in Italy in the mid-1950s: "I realized that otherwise I would be speaking bad Italian all my life." To keep his English fighting trim, he travels frequently to the United States, brushing up on the vernacular by reading "trashy American literature." He has also written a biography of the Italian actress Eleonora Duse, and he reviews opera and murder mysteries for newspapers such as the *Financial Times*. In his electric typewriter is a page from his work in progress: a memoir about Rome in the 1940s.

Weaver, Manheim, Rabassa, and Howard have some distinguished company. William Arrowsmith has done inspired renderings of Italian poets Cesare Pavese and Eugenio Montale. Richard Wilbur brings a poet's lyric resources to bear on the verse dramas of Racine and Molière. The late Sir Charles Johnston, a British career diplomat, managed to find the time to produce a widely praised verse translation of Pushkin's masterpiece *Eugene Onegin*. Donald Keene, America's leading interpreter of Japanese literature, has become an institution at Columbia University, where he teaches. The university has named its new center for Japanese culture after Keene.

A few years ago it became fashionable to talk of a "global village" created by advanced communications, but the biblical Tower of Babel remains a better metaphor for our linguistic condition. Rabassa offers a charming illustration. "A rooster sounds the same in Mexico and in New York," he says. "But when you read about roosters crowing in a book, in the United States he says 'cock-a-doodle-do' and in Mexico he says 'ki-ki-ri-ki.' So we've even made the roosters crow differently." Critic George Steiner devoted his book *After Babel* to the implications of "the magnificently prodigal, redundant multiplicity of mutually incomprehensible human tongues." Steiner reached a grand conclusion: that in order to understand one another, we automatically translate thoughts into words and words into other words, even when we're speaking the same lingo. "Inside or between languages," Steiner asserts, "human communication equals translation." If that is so, it would be fair to call our premier translators the unacknowledged ambassadors of the word, cultural emissaries who cross linguistic frontiers with ease and almost convince us that the book we're reading was actually written in English.

Synecdoches of the Subconscious

Among practitioners of the arts of poetry and criticism, the extent of Harold Bloom's influence—and there can exist no term more apposite for Professor Bloom than "influence"—may, by a curious and revealing process, be calculated in part by the amount of opposition and controversy he cheerfully arouses. An admirer of the dialectics of criticism that Bloom has developed might apply to the voice of dissent, especially if it come from the ranks of the poets Bloom is writing about, a psychoanalytic translation of that old academic warhorse, the intentional fallacy. According to this ingenious stratagem, writers would be seen not only as usually unreliable discussants of their work but as always misleading, the more intensely so the "stronger" the poet. If Bloom sometimes seems maddeningly irrefutable, it is because he has thus, by the very terms of his discourse, made adequate preparation to turn the tables on any of his critics. It would not be incorrect, merely insufficient, to say that Bloom's posture admits of no contradiction; actually, as in psychoanalysis, attempts at contradiction, such as the loud objections currently in the air, can be welcomed with open arms as confirmations of the diagnosis.

Not the least of the attractions of Bloom's system is this internal logic of self-justification, this ability to swallow and digest the poisonous with the wholesome. Whatever its merits in rendering the world more intelligible to us, Bloom's system works brilliantly on its own terms—or, as he himself would say, as a "trope." (One delights in imagining a rival critic,

Review of *Figures of Capable Imagination* by Harold Bloom, published in the *Times Literary Supplement* (London), March 11, 1977.

equally eager to construct a coherent structure out of mythologies of himself, similarly endowed with magnificent learning, only partial rather to Eliot than to Stevens, who would, by praising, dismiss Bloom's lifework as a successful "conceit." No doubt this imagining itself would strike Bloom as a pretty proof of the preeminence of his mental constructs.)

First and foremost, then, Bloom is a successful critic precisely to the extent that he is a real, live, talked-about issue and that his own terms have dominated much of the talk. To be sure, the school of common sense will have nothing to do with him. He is routinely reviled as a hubristic heretic in the throes of a master obsession. It is surely tempting to regard Bloom as one would a one-issue political candidate: besides his opposition to the Vietnam War, what had Eugene McCarthy to offer in 1968? But like the Vietnam War, the issue that has flowered in Bloom is of an extraordinary complexity, so much so that the insights that have fallen, like so many petals in an accidental wind, are of a surprisingly various character.

Figures of Capable Imagination gathers together the occasional essays in appreciation, introductions to books, magazine articles, and the like, written by Bloom during the period in which he composed his quartet of theoretical studies in poetic "misprision." As a work of practical criticism, *Figures* would seem to provide an excellent test for determining whether the Oedipal complex affords as persuasive a reading of the literary mind and the texts that stand for it as it does of the clinically considered human personality. The leap from mind in the abstract to specific texts Bloom makes with ease: since all art operates by synecdoche, the text being the expressive part that gestures to the whole of the mind, the "figures" of the title may properly be taken to refer both to writers and to the rhetorical figures by which they reveal (and conceal) themselves to (and from) us.

So far so good. Yet it is a peculiarity of this book that the more powerful readings occur in spite of the contraptions of the system and that the immense intrinsic appeal of the system has terribly little to do with the reading of an actual text. Nowhere is Bloom more confessedly, but no less tiresomely, solipsistic than where he asks us to see the repressed Ruskin emerging triumphant in the last paragraph of Walter Pater's essay on "Style" or to regard "Lycidas" as the wrathful progenitor of the "Immortality Ode," which then begot "Adonais" and the "Ode to The West Wind," which in turn begot all of Thomas Hardy and much of Wallace Stevens.

No, the importance of Bloom lies elsewhere—in, for example, the timely championing of the contemporary poets John Ashbery and A. R. Ammons, in support of whom the grand scholastic authority of the Yale University English department was invoked, at that sensitive point in their lives known as midcareer when such support is indispensable. This was a masterful stroke on Bloom's part, a singularly shrewd judgment all the more impressive when one considers that scholarly disability from grasping the present is notorious (and might even be lamely excused by an overzealous exponent of Bloom's belief in the necessary "belatedness" of all literary activity since the High Romantic era). And although the Anglo-American prejudice against ideology (on the grounds that it is all too often a rationalization either for a neurosis or for an unexamined assumption) is doubtless justified in the main, still the very by-products of Bloom's ideology serve to make us more tolerant of his excesses.

The resurrection of the fallen study of rhetoric; the supernally clever identification of tropes with defense mechanisms (the hyperbole of repression, the metaphor of sublimation); the Freudian "misreading" of Eliot's "Tradition and the Individual Talent"—it may not help us to hypothesize that the specter of Milton retained his heavyweight crown in the ring with the living Wordsworth, but it is unquestionable that Bloom exists unabashedly "in the shadow of" Sigmund Freud; finally, the synthesizing of such excitingly eclectic sources as the Kabbalah, French structuralism, the great body of English literature, and Freud: that these efforts be undertaken is itself cause for celebration, and the products thereof cannot but be preferable to the verbiage of academics so fearful of saying something barbarous that they say nothing at all in so many words.

It would be unfortunate if the reader of this piece be left with an impression of Bloom as but a jolly old eccentric, a nostalgic Talmudist awash in a sea of literary quarterlies; on the contrary, Bloom needs to be argued with, by the analysts of writing as much as by our conveniently forgotten humanists.

That the author of *The Visionary Company* is better on Walter Pater than on John Ashbery can hardly astonish, and to a large extent the reviewer would content himself with the mere fact of Bloom's good taste, were there not something almost pernicious in isolating Ashbery, as Bloom does, from all the influences implicit in his work as inspirations rather than inhibitions—from the French *symbolistes*, New York painters, certain esoteric literary stylists, the early Auden, and Ashbery's unjustly neglected collaborators, Kenneth Koch and the late Frank O'Hara. (Given Bloom's interest in curiosities of etymology, it may not be entirely impertinent to mention here that Freud means "joy" in German.) To see Ashbery as, simply, "the most legitimate of the sons of Stevens" is reductive enough; further to wonder whether any modern American poet can be "un-Emersonian, rather than, at best, anti-Emersonian" irritates but is saved by a self-caricaturing element from being truly offensive; but to insist that Ashbery's work describes the parabolic arc of Bloom's obsession is to argue foolishly for the interchangeability of great art.

Meditating on the establishment in America of "the imperial self" that would obliterate the world of changes and differences, what would Quentin Anderson make of a critic who twists the evidence, certain that it is in some "transcendental" sense irrelevant, to fit a subjective thesis that makes a virtue of such falsification? An example: "After so many leavings out," Bloom writes of the conclusion of Ashbery's remarkable long poem "The Skaters," "the natural particulars are seen as being wonderfully sufficient:

> The apples are all getting tinted
> In the cool light of autumn.
>
> The constellations are rising
> In perfect order: Taurus, Leo, Gemini."

But of course this "perfect order" is actually a violation of the Zodiac, as any amateur astrologer knows. Far from indicating the satisfaction in "natural particulars" that Bloom would like to find, the end of Ashbery's poem, seen as in itself it really is, presents a characteristically calm and opaque surface, an ironic because arbitrary reconciliation of contradictory impulses.

Wishing to "destroy the false distinction between reading and writing," Bloom fascinates and outrages with his boldness and cunning, and one is moved to protest not because of the annoying but valuable jargon ("metaleptic reversal or transumption . . . is . . . technically the metonymy of a metonymy") but because of the insidious professorial instinct to substitute for primal poetry the prose of abstruse secondariness. To appropriate from Bloom's system, what this amounts to is a reaction formation occasioned by a missed poetic ambition: it is what is potentially dangerous and counterproductive in recent critical trends, backed as they are with the powerful resources of the academy. A metaphysician struggling to stay comfortable in the too snug garb of the literary critic, Harold Bloom would by no means endanger his already significant and substantial achievements if, in the name of the impatient future, he cast a kindly but "revisionary" gaze at the theories he expostulates now with such gusto and, yes, strength.

Under the Influence of Harold Bloom

Harold Bloom looks a lot like Zero Mostel and sounds rather like a sorrowful dandy, a combination of an Old Testament prophet and Oscar Wilde. An indefatigable monologist in a rumpled suit, he reclines in his favorite armchair at the New Haven suite of offices he calls his "factory" for producing literary criticism. The term is apt: Bloom, a professor at Yale University, is editing and writing introductions for five series of critical anthologies comprising no less than eight hundred separate volumes. His subject—the whole of literature. His model—Samuel Johnson's "Lives of the Poets." The task might daunt a lesser mortal but leaves Bloom unfazed and rather excited. This is, after all, a man who blithely claims he can read and absorb up to a thousand pages an hour. A man whose memory is legendary: "I think I have by heart every line of poetry that I like that I've ever read," he says, offering to illustrate with swatches of *The Faerie Queene* and *Paradise Lost.*

At fifty-six, Bloom, the 1985 winner of a MacArthur "genius" grant, is arguably the best-known literary critic in America, probably the most controversial, and undoubtedly as idiosyncratic as they come—a description with which he would not quarrel. "My dear," he says with a deep sigh, "what matters in literature in the end is surely the idiosyncratic, the individual, the flavor or the color of a particular human suffering." Bloom's particular suffering takes the form of "terri-

Newsweek, August 18, 1986.

ble insomnia," which is just as well given the scale and scope of his current ambition.

Backing the critical project is Chelsea House, a New York publishing firm that now maintains a New Haven branch merely to keep up with Bloom's labors and ardors. The projected eight-hundred-odd volumes are grouped under such headings as Modern Critical Views (essays by various writers on individual authors), Modern Critical Interpretations (on individual works), and The Critical Cosmos (on periods or genres). Dozens of books have already appeared, and Bloom's introductions, he estimates, will eventually furnish enough material to fill 25 to 30 volumes by themselves.

It's a publishing venture almost without precedent both in its scope and in the fact that it is guided by a single critical intelligence. In a good week Bloom composes as many as three introductions, averaging twelve pages each—without taking time off from his teaching duties at Yale. In May, the month of final exams, he polished off Forster, Orwell, Arnold, and Pound, plus *Wuthering Heights; Henry IV,* part one; *Pride and Prejudice,* and *Contemporary American Poets.* "I get a chance to reread everybody, and I'm a nonstop reader anyway," Bloom says matter of factly. "I've been doing nothing but read for fifty years now." Adds Chelsea House's Patricia Baldwin, who directs the New Haven team's sixteen full-time staffers and numerous free-lance researchers, "Harold can write an introduction faster than our staffers can turn out jacket copy."

How does he manage to do it all? "The phantasmagoria of it is a challenge," Bloom concedes, owning up to occasional exhaustion. "It makes me feel like Milton's Satan. You know, the authors are God, and what keeps me going is this feeling that it's a kind of hopeless struggle with them." Bloom's scandalously rapid reading rate helps, of course, and his memory serves as his touchstone: "I've always made it a principle that if I cannot remember it, I won't quote it." Yale colleagues confirm his astonishing powers of verbatim recall. "When I was a student," he says, "I would get a bit drunk and recite Hart Crane's *The Bridge* frontwards, then backwards, quite like a tape recorder running wild."

Bloom's career as a critic divides into three distinct phases, culminating in the Chelsea House project. From 1955, when he began teaching undergraduates at Yale, until the late 1960s, Bloom fancied himself "a romantic revivalist, combating what used to be called the New Criticism," in such books as *The Visionary Company.* No critic did more than Bloom to rescue the reputations of Shelley and Emerson, among other out-of-favor exemplars of the romantic imagination. Then came the quintet of books, starting with *The Anxiety of Influence* in 1973, that made him a bête noire in some critical circles. Spinning elaborate analogies between rhetorical tropes and psychological defense mechanisms, Bloom brought Freud's theory of the Oedipal complex (that "masterpiece of emotional ambivalence") to bear on the study of literary influence.

According to Bloom's reasoning, every great poem is haunted by a predecessor and by a sense of its own "belatedness." The successful poet gains his originality only by "creatively misreading"—and hence vanquishing—his literary father. The frantic obsessiveness with which Bloom argued his case brought on a fierce critical backlash. "Bloom had an idea," scoffed British critic Christopher Ricks when *Poetry and Repression* came out in 1976. "Now the idea has him." Such was the fallout over *The Anxiety of Influence* that Bloom and the Yale English department parted company twelve years ago. (He now constitutes Yale's one-man department of humanities.) It's the fate of true originality to seem truly outlandish at first, and Bloom, though admittedly tired of controversy, revels in his notoriety. "I am the pariah of the profession," he says, half in jest and half in pride.

It's easy to see why Bloom's theory of influence antagonized the academic establishment. By de-idealizing literary influence, depicting it not as benign but as a ferocious rite of initiation that poetic sons must endure, Bloom exposed a vital nerve—and the depths of the dismay he caused tell us that he was on to something big. True, Bloom's ruggedly assertive prose occasionally verged on a kind of madly inspired self-parody, as in this priceless sentence: "The word *meaning* goes back to a root that signifies 'opinion' or 'intention,' and is closely related to the word *moaning*." Librarians allergic to the abstruse needn't worry, however; Bloom's Chelsea House introductions honor clarity as a virtue—and go easy on his esoteric vocabulary.

As befits a lifelong student of what Freud termed the "family romance," Bloom chats about contemporary poets as if they were his relatives; John Ashbery becomes "Uncle Ashbery" and John Hollander "Uncle Hollander." This is more than just another idiosyncrasy. It argues a passionate personal involvement with literature and its makers, and it's this that most clearly distinguishes Bloom from the legion of literary theorists ensconced in academe today. The Chelsea House project is a fitting monument to Bloom's critical ideal. In the finest critics, he says, "one hears the full cry of the human. They tell one why it matters to read. They do not give one mere linguistic problematics. I have never believed that the critic is the rival of the poet, but I do believe that criticism is a genre of literature or it does not exist."

Freshman English

I used to teach for a living. In addition to teaching courses in litera-
ture and creative writing, I usually taught at least one section of
freshman composition each semester. As one semester came to a close,
my students asked me to write a model essay for them—to show them
how it was done. When I tried to meet this reasonable request, I found
to my chagrin that my writing had been influenced in rather surpris-
ing ways by my charges. In the time-honored academic tradition, I had
"learned more from my students than they had learned from me," as
the following essay surely proves.

The books we have read this semester have many things in
common, but the most important one is catastrophe. In some
cases, it's the gods' fault, like Oedipus; in other cases, it's
humans who are to blame, like Faust. But in every case catas-
trophe is the result, which is inevitable.

Goethe's *Faust* is the story of a partnership between the
devil, Mephistopheles, and a member of the human race,
Henry Faust, the scholar. Faust is not a happy man. Even
though he believes that he will be satisfied by experiencing
actions in his life (e.g., interactions with women and the obser-
vations of a tavern) he is so unhappy with life's slim benefits
that suicide actually becomes a viable alternative, until he joins
up with Mephistopheles. According to their agreement, if
Faust becomes satisfied, his desires become minimal, if at all.
He is too smart for his own good.

Another book we read this semester is *Crime and Punishment*
by Fyodor Dostoyevski. Raskolnikov feels he is superior to

Partisan Review (Spring 1988).

human conduct, like Napoleon, so he kills two old ladies, one who deserved it but the other didn't. By the end of the novel he is wrong and in Siberia. If he was really superior that wouldn't be the case, but he must learn the hard way. Although it is true that some men are better than other men, they are only so much better, and after a certain point they are no better at all.

On the other hand, the situation in *Oedipus Rex* is completely different. He can be blinded by rage, and commits two sins, parricide (killing your father) and incest. The question comes up, which is worse? The answer is parricide. The worst that can happen from an incest relationship is that it may cause a family member to become emotionally upset which is not against the law while parricide is. Also, someone who is practicing incest can walk away from it at any time while in parricide the victim is dead forever. I must agree with his sons by their decision to drive him out of the country, and I agree with Oedipus himself by poking his own eyes out.

Scientists claim incest can ruin your genes, although the Greeks didn't know that when the play was written. However, Antigone (his daughter) is a good example. However, Antigone (his daughter) is a good example. That is why I think Creon's punishment was too harsh, and he changed it by ordering his men to bury her in the vault outside Thebes. Although Antigone broke the law she is worthy of a better death than public stoning, he figured. The great humility that would arise from stoning is not deserving of Antigone or her family, who have suffered too much embarrassment as it is.

Antigone is only one of the many suicides in this course. Jocasta does it too, and Julien Sorel does not try to get off at the end of *The Red and the Black* by Stendhal. Julien was realistic and for this reason he was less naive than some of the others, including Candide, but then he also chooses to die, which I feel is a kind of suicide and immoral in my opinion. Although life may be difficult to bear, it is the ultimate, and there are no superlatives for it.

So we see that Faust, Raskolnikov, Oedipus Rex, Antigone, and Julien Sorel are all trapped in the same way. Some turn to suicide, some turn to murder or worse. It is ironical that Candide is the only exception because he goes through even worse catastrophes, such as the woman who lost half her buttocks, and Cunégonde who was beautiful but ugly when he married her, and Pangloss, and the many kings and dukes who have less than their poorest subjects, traveling around the world in Voltaire's *Candide* and winding up in his own backyard.

Criticism and Crisis

Let me begin by noting that "Criticism and Crisis," the title I have chosen for my talk, is both a perennial and an annual: it might have served a speaker's purposes at laid-back summer conferences or energetic yuletide conventions at any time from, say, 1939 to the present. I am risking it for my paper, because—speaking as the token nonacademic on this panel— I believe that the crisis in criticism today is in some ways unprecedented. It is different from, and more disturbing than, what a contemporary critical theorist would call the "crisis narratives" of earlier epochs.

But first I want to acknowledge that there are always exceptions to be found, people of good faith and noble intention— undoubtedly everyone in this room, for example—and that there is therefore a slightly ironic edge to my title, "Criticism and Crisis." The irony might become clearer if I were to quote a sentence or two from Dwight David Eisenhower's "West Point Address" of June 5, 1960, exactly thirty-one years and two days ago. "Now, tonight," said Ike in the spirit of hearty good fellowship, "we meet at a time of bewilderment, I don't like this term or the using of the term that we are living always in crisis. We are not." I don't think it necessary to deconstruct that sentence, since, as Paul de Man would have said, it has already deconstructed itself.

Which reminds me to remind you that Paul de Man was

This is the text of an address delivered at the ADE Western Seminar at Claremont, California, in June 1991—a conference of English department "chairs" organized by the Modern Language Association. Published in *Boulevard* (Spring 1992).

also the author of an essay entitled "Criticism and Crisis." In fact I should probably point out that "Criticism and Crisis" is the title of the opening chapter of de Man's influential 1971 book *Blindness and Insight.* Knowing that many in the audience love paradoxes as much as I do, I do not shrink from warning you against people who deliver papers entitled "Criticism and Crisis."

A moment ago I referred to myself cheerfully as a non-academic. I am by profession a writer and editor who often feels—and I say this with the requisite irony—excluded from the hegemonic critical discourse in the academy today. As a professional author, I want to express my relief that none of the speeches today—none that I have heard anyway—have spoken of the death of the author. I realize, of course, that I am not supposed to take that ominous phrase personally. I have done my homework and know that Roland Barthes, the author of that phrase, meant to liberate the text from the presumably tyrannical author's intentions. He was proposing a more extreme (and more sensational) form of what used to be called "the intentional fallacy," but also a kind of literary corollary to Nietzsche's pronouncement of the death of God a century ago. I know that for Michel Foucault the author is a historical invention whose time may have come and gone, while for Jacques Derrida the author seems to be fundamentally a function of the sign for quotation marks on a computer keyboard. I realize, in other words, that "the death of the author" is meant figuratively, rhetorically, as a speculative gambit, a theoretical proposition. Still, deconstruction itself teaches us to be suspicious of figurative language, for within those walls where theory is king and tropes are trumps, wishes have a way of substituting for deeds and predictions may be prescriptions in disguise. The "death of the author" is not merely a metaphor, or not yet a dead metaphor; the hostility of such a doctrine to the lives and works of individual authors is real.

In any case, I think it only fair to point out that authors in general resent the imputation that they are obsolete. And I think you can expect more and more working writers to take issue with the academically fashionable notion that art is the gratuitous by-product of power struggles. To obliterate the qualitative distinction between *The Wings of the Dove* and a TV commercial for Dove detergent—to regard both as equally under suspicion—is on the face of it an odd thing for a practicing critic to want to do. It suggests an implacably adversarial view of culture, and I do not believe that the effect is to raise our esteem of popular culture—for which I am all in favor—but to mount a frontal attack on the very idea of greatness and high art. To put it another way, my sense is that the much-discussed assault on the literary "canon" (for want of a more exact word) is not so much on the specific makeup of required reading lists but on the idea that there should be required reading lists.

But to return to the alleged demise of the author, I do have a modest proposal to make, not so much in the interest of solving a crisis as for the sake of assuring civility. I happened to be in Cleveland a few weeks after a "death of the author" conference in April and the people there were still buzzing about it. My proposal is that speakers who allege the death of the author should agree, in simple decency, to have their own names removed from the conference's program. In this way they would prove that they take their stated ideas to heart—that, contrary to first appearances, not everything in the academic discourse is said for the sake of an argument or to register an effect.

The widening gap between the academic and the nonacademic literary communities is, I think, an important aspect of the contemporary crisis in criticism. More authors and journalists than you'd perhaps expect were trained in graduate school, got out, and now regard academic goings-on from a safe but troubled distance. Many of us think that critics addicted to the autotelic delights of theory have at one and the same time turned their backs on the wider literary public and abandoned their proper mission: namely, to illuminate literary texts, teach them, render them accessible, determine their value, and assess their quality as works of art. What I have just said is sometimes written off dismissively as "Arnoldian nostalgia," but it seems to me a simple job description, and if I had one wish for the direction that literary studies should take, it is for the restoration of literature as the prime focus of pedagogy and criticism: the text in its complexity, as a moral document and as an aesthetic experience; the text and not the theoretical pretext or the materialistic context; the text—the work of literary art.

Let us give literature back to the people who love it—not unreservedly, not uncritically, but at least without the bias against art and aesthetics that characterizes so much critical theory. That such a bias exists must strike everyone here as obvious. The critic Walter Benjamin, whose stock right now is at an all-time high, linked fascism and aesthetics in a famous essay, and that has become a doctrinal point, common to deconstructionists and to theorists who oppose deconstruction. *Aesthetic* has become a veritable term of abuse, so that, for example, critical theorists who reject deconstruction sometimes do so on the grounds that it is "aestheticist" in the hedonistic manner sent up by Gilbert and Sullivan in *Patience*. At the same time, those who practice deconstruction—even those who pay lip service to "the pleasure of the text"—hold no brief for the work of art, which they regard as mystifying and corrupt, an expression of false consciousness. Critics will duke it out over whose theory is more epistemologically accurate, ethically enlightened, and politically right-on, but nobody just now wants to have anything to do with aesthetics, and it has been fashionable to call for "the death of literature" ever since the British Marxist critic Terry Eagleton did just that in concluding his primer on *Literary Theory* back in 1983.

Gerald Graff can and does make the argument, in his institutional history of the study of literature, that quarrels between rival dispensations and factions are the routine stuff of the MLA. But I believe that the crisis today is of a different order of magnitude from the controversy generated by the New Criticism in the late 1940s. The crisis in literary studies today, though it centers on the problem of theory, is not a merely theoretical problem. It is bound up with the fate of those very abstractions so lately under critical assault: authors and art and literature. The crisis in literary studies today has, moreover, not been contained within the profession but on the contrary has entered the culture at large, where it has provoked a good deal of worry.

Like it or not, there is a growing perception on the part of the public as a whole that something is rotten in the state of the academic literary world. A ha-ha piece making sport of the MLA convention has become a journalistic standby—this year the story was done up memorably in the *New York Times Magazine*—and it is a seemingly annual feature in *The New Republic;* I published such a piece myself in *Partisan Review* five MLA conventions ago. Beneath the humor in these articles there is often to be found a degree of moral outrage—a sense that our literary heritage has been betrayed or abandoned and is going to waste, a casualty of some trendy imported theory of the sort that filled the author of *Gulliver's Travels* with savage indignation.

If trends in literary criticism anticipate or reflect what goes on in classrooms, the importance of the crisis in criticism—and the issue of its theoretical character—is underscored by the pressures of unignorable reality. We have basic problems of literacy and of cultural literacy that, if left unchecked, may someday soon give the lie to a college diploma. This is not a theoretical matter, this general public nervousness about the value of a college education, this gradual and seemingly irreversible decline in what we can expect our students to know. We see our students growing less and less fluent in our language and our literature while their most prestigious professors dwell in the aethereal empire of critical theory, and it is easy to picture them playing Nero's fiddle as Rome goes up in flames.

There is no denying that conflict and quarrel reign in literary criticism today, though attempts have certainly been made to put a happy spin on that piece of information. There are those who think that conflicts and controversies are healthy signs of a vibrant profession, evidence of diversity, vitality, and so forth. Gerald Graff even thinks we should teach the debate over critical theory to our students. Perhaps some of you have seen this article, either in its original form in *New Literary History* or as excerpted in the April issue of *Harper's.* Graff conceives the debate, or rather personifies it, as between an older male professor and a young female colleague, OMP and YFP for short. *He* thinks that "Dover Beach" is "one of the great masterpieces of the Western tradition" and *she* thinks it is an "example of phallocentric discourse." Graff's imagined dialogue between OMP and YFP is, you will have to take my word for it, considerably less fascinating than Arnold's poem, but that's not the point. Here's what Graff says: "My thought as I watched OMP and YFP go back and forth in the faculty lounge was that if OMP's students could witness this debate they would be more likely to get worked up over 'Dover Beach' than they are now." A novel idea: to quicken interest in "Dover Beach" by abandoning it in favor of a dull conversation about it. It is the point of view of one who assumes that no one ever read the classics in the first place.

Gerald Graff seems to think that critical methodologies, by being "controversial," will stand a better chance of holding our students' attention than poor old-fashioned literature. His idea of pedagogy by debate implies that convictions can be reduced to positions—and, in the persons of OMP and YFP, to stereotypes of age and gender as crude as those produced by Hollywood, where if you need a creep or two in a supporting role you might come up with a male instructor of English and his favorite female graduate student, as in the Debra Winger vehicle, *Terms of Endearment.* But what bothers me most about Graff's idea is that the form of instruction he seems to favor can resemble nothing so much as the debates between windy vice presidential candidates, who must curry favor with their audiences and whose every utterance is calculated for maximum political effect.

Pessimism takes different forms. Graff seems to be pessimistic about the capacity of classic literature to sustain the attention of students. I disagree. I believe our students are hungering for literature, for poetry, for great books. My pessimism has to do with the conformity and puritanism I see despite all the brave talk about the robust diversity in literary studies. I wonder whether I am alone in sensing an extraordinary professionwide loss of self-confidence. I was reading a book about William Carlos Williams's poetry the other day and I came across the argument that epistemological questions are based on ethical concerns. This is from Terence Diggory's just-published book *William Carlos Williams and the Ethics of Painting:* "Knowledge has come under critique because it plays a role in establishing authority, and the exercise of authority is condemned, from an ethical perspective, as violence." I paused over this remarkable sentence with its curious attitude toward *knowledge* and *authority* and *violence,* and then I read it another time: "Knowledge has come under critique because it plays a role in establishing authority, and the exercise of authority is condemned, from an ethical perspective, as violence." *Authority is violence* seems to me one of those tacit unquestioned assumptions of the age, and I wonder whether and in what sense any professor who says that really means it, since professors exercise their authority every time they convene their classes. Or is that somehow the point: is one to understand the academic rebellion against *authority* and *hierarchy* and *elitism*—the three dirtiest words in the lexicon—as evidence of self-loathing within elitist institutions of a strongly hierarchical character? (Perhaps the only institution more hierarchical than an Ivy League university is the United States Army.) I have friends in academe who think the key to understanding recent developments in the humanities lies in the academic humanist's inferiority complex vis-à-vis scientists and technologists, and there may be something in that, though more remains to be said, and in any event I think we had better proceed with great caution before we blithely agree that "knowledge" should be put "under critique," which sounds a lot to me like earlier moves to put history and literature "under erasure."

I cite Terence Diggory's book, because it so neatly exemplifies the ways and means of the type of theorist who does not altogether forsake literature but subordinates it to a species of speculative disputation. In Diggory's book, William Carlos Williams is treated as the site of a critical battle between post-Lacanian psychoanalytic theory in the person of Julia Kristeva on the one side, and the forces of deconstruction as embodied by Jacques Derrida and J. Hillis Miller on the other. Diggory favors Kristeva, and his argument, crudely paraphrased, is that Williams is okay because he can be seen to line up on Kristeva's side of things, which "can be called 'psychoanalytic,' as long as that term is taken primarily to designate a mode of discourse." Purely theoretical: theoretically pure.

What Diggory wants to do is to use Williams to strike against Miller and Derrida on ethical grounds. This entails the reduction of Williams's lines to illustrations of this or that critical axiom. "Danse Russe," the delightful poem in which Williams dances naked in front of the mirror and pronounces himself "the happy genius" of his household, is seen as "a reenactment of Lacan's 'mirror-stage.' " Williams's preference for Brueghel over the Italian masters—which Diggory attributes to an "excess of signification" in Brueghel—somehow corresponds to the difference between Derrida and Saussure on "the materiality of the signifier." In one passage in *Paterson,* the double meaning of *proper*—a word that can imply either propriety or identity—demonstrates the fatal linguistic oscillation that deconstructionists discern at the heart of every text. Indeed, according to Diggory, Williams "performs a deconstruction of the notion of the 'proper' similar to Derrida's analysis of the 'proper name.' "

It appeases me very little to know that the polemical force of Diggory's book is directed against deconstruction, for his engagement with deconstruction does more to confirm than to deny its power to dictate the agenda and the terms of the critical debate. And Williams the patient dies during the operation, for Diggory gives us no sense of the poetry as a compelling aesthetic experience. "Every attempt at applying a theory of reading to Williams turns into a reading of theory," writes Diggory. Nice of him to admit it. Poor Williams. That he has become a darling of abstract shadow-boxers and thesis-mongers is an irony that he, the most plain-spoken of American poets, would not have savored.

In the current issue of *PMLA,* Graham Greene's *Brighton Rock* gets the other kind of treatment available to great books and important writers today: in this case an article entitled "Revolt into Style: Graham Greene Meets the Sex Pistols" by a junior faculty member at the University of Texas at Austin. The main point of this article seems to be that *Brighton Rock* exists primarily as a forerunner of punk rock. I have tried to figure out why the piece got to me, since after all I'm not against pop culture, and the idea of basing an argument on a pun seems to me just dandy, in both senses of that word. True, the piece has little enough to do with Greene, who was, until the day he died in April, my favorite living novelist. *Brighton Rock* is approached through a thicket full of name-droppings (Benjamin, Lukacs, Bakhtin, the usual suspects) and without much appreciation of the novel's unique power and glory— the way it puts thriller conventions at the service of a theological mystery. No, the article didn't get us closer to the heart of Graham Greene's matter. But that's okay. What bothered me was something else. What bothered me was the sense that what was happening here was self-parody—life imitating a David Lodge novel. What bothered me was that it was difficult on some basic level to regard what one was reading as serious, and seriously intended. It was, to use the terms of W. H. Auden in his great poem "Caliban to the Audience," a little like what happened when you unleashed Caliban into the kingdom of Ariel. Contemporary criticism can boast of a great gain in scope—its purview can now take in soap operas and advertisements as legitimate objects of study—but that has come at the price of a critical, and I hope not fatal, loss of gravity.

Whatever else one may say of deconstruction, it is certainly an expression of skepticism taken to an extreme degree. The rise of deconstruction—or perhaps I should say the continued popularity of certain deconstructive notions and procedures— suggests that the profession is in, and to some extent knows itself to be in, a condition of extreme self-doubt. I was speaking recently to the dean of a fine liberal arts college and I mentioned that I admired the professors in the school's English department because they all believed in what they were doing, whereas at some universities people have grown skeptical about the very ends of knowledge. Oh, dear, replied the dean, do you suppose we're behind the times?

I am sometimes told that deconstruction is passé. I do not believe this is so. The term itself has become so elastic, coming more and more to designate a whole climate of opinion, that it would be wishful thinking to imagine that it could disappear without a trace. Ever since I published my book *Signs of the*

Times: Deconstruction and the Fall of Paul de Man earlier this year people have been telling me that the real problem in lit-crit today is political correctness and multicultural pluralism, the New Historicism and cultural materialism. Maybe so, but Jacques Derrida still tops the list of authorities—and I use the word advisedly—invoked most frequently in papers published in the *PMLA*. The editor's column in the March 1991 issue of this journal—the same issue that has Graham Greene meeting the Sex Pistols—is devoted to the results of an informal survey tracking citations in some 235 *PMLA* articles since 1981. Derrida and Roland Barthes had 58 citations apiece—they led the league for the second straight decade. Paul de Man pulled down 31 citations, incidentally, more than his ex-Yale School cohorts Geoffrey Hartman (21), Harold Bloom (20), and J. Hillis Miller (19), more than Stanley Fish (23), more than Fredric Jameson (30) and Terry Eagleton (17). I recently heard someone refer to Derrida as "the Jim Jones of criticism"—an arguably libelous reference to the ghastly episode in Guyana in 1978 when vats of Kool-Aid spiked with cyanide were drunk by crazed cultists—and I mention this only to show that deconstruction, far from being passé, is still capable of provoking reasonable people to fly into a rage.

I have been asked to say something positive, and I apologize for spending so little time pointing to things worth cheering, evidence that the tide is turning. But I do want to conclude by pointing to one area of literary studies that is sometimes maligned and right now may constitute the best hope for literature: I refer to the branch of English departments devoted to creative writers. On many campuses, the creative writing faculty enjoys a degree of autonomy from the rest of the English department, and in a number of these places the creative writers have led or are leading the resistance to critical theory. I do not mean to idealize them. We are all familiar with the criticisms to which writing programs are sometimes subjected; I have myself articulated some of these criticisms. Still, there is this to be said for the programs and the men and women who staff them. The best of them resist the theoretical dispensation in the most practical way: they assign books for their students to read; they value literature as an aesthetic experience; they teach authorship, which means taking responsibility for your words as an author. Not very long ago the idea of teaching creative writing was regarded askance by English department traditionalists. What an irony that it is now in creative writing seminars that the traditional values of literary study stand their best chance of being transmitted.

IV

Twenty Questions

Twenty Questions: An Interview

1) Could you tell me something about your childhood?

I miss it, though the humiliations of childhood are at least as vivid in my mind as the good stuff. I grew up in upper Manhattan, in a section called Inwood, near Fort Tryon Park and the Cloisters museum, just north of the George Washington Bridge. As a teenager I liked crossing the bridge by foot into New Jersey. I did that all the time with my next-door neighbor, Joel, my closest friend. He and I worked out a code: two knocks on the bedroom wall meant we were to meet on the fire escape that linked our third-floor apartments. We did a lot of talking on the fire escape, but what we did mostly was walk and talk, for hours at a time. I miss that; I miss the naïveté we had, which made true wonderment possible. City streets are unbeatable for long walks. My friend and I walked nights into the early morning hours—to Fordham and back, to Riverdale and back—across the bridges that remind you that Manhattan is an island, walking for the hell of it, not to get anywhere, just to walk and talk, mind and body moving at the same smart clip.

2) What was it like growing up in Manhattan?

New York City was a friendlier place in the 1950s and early 1960s. There was neighborhood life—choose-up softball

---

This interview was conducted by Nin Andrews in Cleveland in April 1991 and subsequently concluded and revised by mail. The form of the interview was suggested by the poem "Twenty Questions" in *An Alternative to Speech.*

games in the park, the Inwood branch of the public library where I hung out—though even at the time there was the general sense that the city was going downhill. The Dodgers and Giants left town before the 1958 season, when I was ten. The city was doomed from then on, said lots of newspaper columnists. On the other hand, the city remained king of the culture—a great place to be if you were interested in jazz bars, Zen bookshops, Broadway musicals, modern art, or poetry. You could go to the Museum of Modern Art with a hip Hunter High School girl who knew all about Paul Klee and was eager to initiate you, or maybe you'd go to the Village and see Marlon Brando in *Julius Caesar*. Culture had glamour in New York City. I went to Stuyvesant High School, a school for smart kids you needed to take a test to get into, and Hunter was our sister school, full of cultural sophisticates, back in those benighted days of single-sex education.

3) What sort of religious training did you have?

I was brought up to be an orthodox Jew. After kindergarten in the local public school, where I was almost expelled for misbehavior, my father enrolled me in the stricter of the two yeshivas nearby. In the yeshiva, the morning was devoted to Hebrew subjects, the afternoon to secular ones, and they worked you pretty hard—it was assumed that religion was the center of your life, as it was for my father, who came from a very devout family and liked nothing better than a Saturday afternoon session of talmudic interpretation. My father was unusual, a pious man but at the same time a tolerant one. He let me choose for myself. And I gradually defected from the orthodox fold from the time I left the yeshiva after the eighth grade. This was the religious drama that dominated my teenage years.

4) Are there powerful images that you have retained since childhood that still influence you?

There's a phrase I like in a recent poem of mine, "the thrill of homesickness." I associate that with childhood—the sense and sensation of homesickness—and not just childhood but the first twenty years of my life, when I lived at home with my parents. A couple of summers ago I went back to the old neighborhood and was aghast at how much it had changed. All the streetlamps in Fort Tryon Park had been smashed; the place looked sinister, deserted. I walked past the old synagogue and it seemed tiny, as if it had shrunk. And then one night I dreamed that the three-bedroom apartment I grew up in had become a brothel. Every place called home is different from the way we remember it, but in Manhattan the process is accelerated by a factor of three or four, and nothing in the neighborhood—not a store, not an apartment house—is the same as it was. So in a way I feel homesick for a place that no longer exists.

I also have a specific nostalgia for New York of the late 1940s, probably because I was born then, in 1948. I have a great appetite for the popular songs of that period, I love the hairstyles and fashions, the movies, and I'm never surprised to learn that something I have great feeling for—my favorite Auden poem, "In Praise of Limestone," for example—was written right around the time of my birth. Also, as my mother reminds me unfailingly, I was born a few weeks after the creation of the state of Israel and the birth of the future king of England. I suppose some of us romanticize the specific era in which our parents courted each other and conceived us. I have an almost voyeuristic interest in the period of my birth. In part it's because of a kind of natural solipsism, the doubt that anything in the world could have preceded one's existence. Also the lure of the ultimate taboo: the impossibility of being on hand to witness one's own creation.

5) *Alice Fulton, reviewing* Operation Memory, *writes, "Lehman's historical conscience dwells upon the Holocaust." Is that an apt description?*

I do regard the Holocaust as the great catastrophe of our century and as therefore in a way our moral and historical touchstone, the episode we return to whenever we get down to first principles and basic values. I have personal reasons for feeling this way. The two most important facts of my child-hood were, one, that Hitler killed six million Jews, and two, that according to the Bible the Jews are God's chosen people. My parents were refugees from Hitler's Europe. My father came from Germany, my mother from Vienna, and they met in New York City in 1939. My father and Henry Kissinger came from the same hometown in Germany, Fürth. My father went from Germany to Italy to Paris to Cuba to New York, an Eric Ambler itinerary. I was twenty-three when he died, and it hit me hard. My mother lives in Miami now. She is a great woman, a survivor with the great gift of laughter, and also a tragic figure, a witness. She was able to express for me, in telling me her story and the story of her relatives, all the suffering and the anguish of the Jews in this century. My mother's parents were deported by the Nazis and killed in Riga in 1942.

6) What was it like to grow up in the shadow of the Holocaust? Did you—can anyone—experience the Holocaust secondhand?

The Holocaust, for children of survivors, comprises history and mythology, philosophy and theology. The problem of evil. The story of Job. The Antichrist. The question of nihilism. Mob psychology and the persistence of anti-Semitism in Europe. A debate in philosophy class between the pacifists and the proponents of a preemptive military strike against the Nazis. And so forth. A whole college curriculum could be organized around this quintessential episode of twentieth-century history: the Nazis against the Jews. And the danger is that a research industry can be made out of the Holocaust—in our culture you could wind up with Holocaust T-shirts and Holocaust weekends at Catskills resorts. I don't know what can be done about that problem. But, yes, you *can* get the experience secondhand. I used to dream about it—about Nazis with machine guns on watchtowers in concentration camps. For my mother the historical nightmare was so vivid that a knock on the door late at night—the sound of boots on the stairway—meant the Gestapo. My father hated talking about his life in Germany, but my mother would tell me her stories, over and over, with the same intense passion each time. And when my uncles and aunts visited, there were their stories, too—stories of escape and danger and terror and chance and sorrow. There's a line in an early Allen Ginsberg poem that always moved me: "the war in Spain has ended long ago, / Aunt Rose." But of course that war is still going on and will never end—as long as Aunt Rose is alive.

7) Do you think that "writing is an act of expressed moral responsibility," as Malcolm Bradbury said in his review of Signs of the Times *in the* New York Times Book Review?

That does sound very grand, doesn't it? But I believe it. I have very little patience for those who would do away with the moral dimension of literature—the theorists who insist that there's no such thing as greatness or genius, that literary reputations are entirely the result of power plays, that criticism is more important than literature, and so on. All that crap. One reason I've cast my lot with the resistance to deconstruction is that I believe in the very things that have supposedly been terminally deconstructed. I believe in what a deconstructionist would call "bourgeois individualism"—only I would call it freedom—and I am skeptical of any philosophical system that treats the self not as a moral agent but as a construction like a text that awaits dismantling. Wherever politics substitutes for morality, what very quickly gets eroded is not only the moral sense but the aesthetic sense as well: the ability to respond to art, to discriminate among our responses, and not to behave like the prisoner of our own resentment. If writing is an act of moral responsibility, it is also an expression of the pleasure principle. It must give pleasure. A writer's first responsibility is to his readership, and if you aren't going to hold their attention, it's immaterial how noble your moral purposes may be.

8) I think your work has joie de vivre. I also think that writing about the Holocaust is important to you—that maybe you feel a moral responsibility to keep Aunt Rose's story alive. I sense a tension between this joie de vivre, this pleasure principle, and the reality you write about, as if you're afraid to be seduced by illusions in a world that allowed the

Holocaust to happen. I also wonder how this relates to the way you like to use irony in your work, as in "Rejection Slip."

Maybe we wouldn't write as much as we do if we weren't subject to the tension between the principles of pleasure and necessity, since we write not only to find out what we don't know (or what we don't know we know) but also to clarify our feelings and try to understand our mysterious inner conflicts. The internal conflict between the impulses of pleasure and necessity—or call it art and nature, or perhaps love and death—is pretty nearly universal. I think of irony as the accomplice of complexity, and as the attitude of mind best suited to the presentation of an internal conflict. Irony is the literary mode of intense ambivalence. Irony also suggests a certain kind of literary structure in which oppositions coexist and paradoxes can prevail. Scott Fitzgerald said that the test of a first-rate mind was whether it could hold contradictory ideas and nevertheless continue to function. I think irony is what allows the mind to do that. And the spirit of irony is an important element of joie de vivre.

Various forms of irony entail a discrepancy between what you know and what you are saying. Within that discrepancy may lie an epistemological riddle, or a moral conundrum, or a theological parable, or a romantic illusion. In "Rejection Slip," the speaker says he is glad to have been rejected by his girl-friend, a prospective employer, a foundation, and so forth. You get the idea that he is stating the opposite of what he is feeling, but also the possibility that he may just talk himself into his "ironic" praise of pain. In poetry it is sometimes useful to take the opposite of what you are feeling, and exaggerate it. That way you might end up with the truth.

It seems to me that in any art the artist is always trying first and foremost to seek pleasure, his own and that of his companions, and there is often therefore an escapist element in even high art, since the objective is enchantment. Yet without the pressure of reality, the particular reality that must be escaped, the art may seem incidental or trivial. The imagination likes playing hooky or getting drunk but at heart is really a responsible citizen, and it instinctively knows that some subjects demand greater mental concentration than do other subjects. A poem about three oranges in the icebox can be beautiful, perfect. But writing about the Holocaust requires greater ambition, since there are so many ways you can fail. And failure here is a matter of some consequence. If you're writing about the Holocaust, the last thing you want to do is to desecrate it. You want to make it real and vivid. You have an obligation to the truth, to history, the survivors and the memory of the dead.

9) When did you know you would be a poet?

I must have been seventeen. I would write something every day in those days. And the next year, my first year at Columbia, was pivotal, because of all the literature to which I was exposed—the abundance of it—Dante and Shakespeare and Milton, Rabelais and Cervantes and Goethe, Donne and Coleridge and Stevens. That was in class—in these amazing required classes we had at Columbia. On my own I read "The Love Song of J. Alfred Prufrock" and *The Waste Land* and Arthur Rimbaud's *Illuminations.* I also discovered Frank O'Hara's poems in Donald Allen's 1959 anthology, *The New American Poetry,* which was the defining anthology of its moment. There was a great poetry scene at Columbia, with headquarters at the *Columbia Review* magazine. Probably the magazine acceptance that meant the most to me happened in my freshman year when the *Columbia Review* took a poem of mine. My most important book at the time was James Joyce's *A Portrait of the Artist as a Young Man.* I felt that the experience of the protagonist closely resembled my own, allowing for the exigencies of our specific religions: his confirmation, my circumcision, his hellflames, my Holocaust. I was as nearsighted as Stephen Dedalus and thought of myself as defiant in his manner. And like him I saw my life pretty clearly as a progress from the religious to the aesthetic way. From priest to artist. Joyce and Hemingway were my first literary models. I wrote prose poems before I wrote in lines when I was seventeen, eighteen.

10) Do you think that growing up as the son of Holocaust survivors had any impact on your need to write, to record your life story?

When you're a child you think everyone else's home is like your own. Only gradually do you become conscious of how rare and singular is that thing which makes your identity distinct from anyone else's. Then you become more eager to give that identity a lasting form. But parts of your identity are fleeting; you get older, your parents die, you're estranged from what used to be home. The greater the distance from the past, the greater the need for poetry and memory to ward off the dangers of forgetfulness, distortion, betrayal. I am naturally, instinctively, drawn to pondering the Nazi genocide, in which, after all, my grandparents perished. But about the need to write, and why I have it, and whether the Holocaust is the determining element, I can't say. I know that writing poetry seems to me today a perfect and natural extension of the way my mind worked when I was a child. There, that's nearly as Romantic a statement of the writer's condition as you'll get in Wordsworth.

11) What is your writing process?

I never have the whole poem in my mind when I start. When you're writing you're constructing, like a painter experimenting on the canvas: shall I use red there? You never know what you're going to come up with, and this is part of the excitement. If you knew, if you had the finished product in sight as you began, it would be much less fun. You're phenomenally busy when you're writing, and if it's going well, you don't want to stop and reflect on what you're doing. Some poems are written in a day. Some take ten years. At some point you know when it's right. I like revising. Revising seems to me a great joy, because it's easier to work on a draft than on a field of virgin snow. The act of revision spares you from "the blank paper defended by its whiteness," as Mallarmé put it.

12) How does a poem start for you?

I often start with the title, instead of ending with one. Anything might set me off—an overheard phrase, snatch of old song, stray thought, idle image. Or I might feel like writing in a form, a sestina or a sonnet or whatever, in which case the choice of the form usually precedes everything else. I start with a phrase and work from there, but sometimes there's a controlling idea or conceit that comes to me, like the idea of making a "Tenure" canto parodying Ezra Pound's "Usura" canto. I was sitting at my desk and it suddenly occurred to me that "Tenure" and "Usura" sound alike. Then I thought of the kind of "had it up to here" rant that one comes across now and then in *American Poetry Review,* and the poem ["With Tenure" in *Operation Memory*] just took off.

13) When you visited Leonard Trawick's workshop at Cleveland State University, someone—it may have been Leonard—asked you about the "difficulty" of some of your poems.

The question of difficulty in contemporary poetry comes up all the time. It seems that many readers or potential readers are intimidated by poetry, and I wish there were a way of assuaging their fears. (Maybe there is: one thing *The Best American Poetry* series has demonstrated is that the readership for serious poetry is wider than the pessimists think.) Kenneth Koch, who was my teacher at Columbia, liked to say that it is possible to enjoy poetry before you understand it, and I know that was true in my own case. In fact I'll go further and say it is possible to love poems precisely because they defy easy comprehension. Some of the poems I read, when I was sixteen or seventeen and suddenly filled with the determination to become a poet, were difficult by any standard; I was enchanted with the opening of *Paradise Lost,* for example, though I am quite sure that I didn't understand it. Something other than the plain sense of the words captivated me—the rhetoric, the lining, the syntax, the imagery, the sound of the words and their cadences. It didn't matter what the lines meant or didn't mean—I'd get around to *that* soon enough anyway. If it's a great poem you want to reread it and if you reread it often enough you'll understand it. That seems a decent criterion for judging poetry: does it make the reader want to reread it?

The other thing about difficulty is that sometimes (not always) it can be a virtue. People are talked down to all the time. Some of us like experiences that are not all that easy to comprehend—or maybe I should say you *can* comprehend them but they somehow resist an easy paraphrase. Maybe it's a matter of expectations. People associate poems with term papers. I wish they would read poetry for pure pleasure, unselfconsciously, the way they go to the movies or listen to music. No one listens to a rock song and wonders about its meaning—first you have the experience, then the meaning. I know that T. S. Eliot wrote, in an admonishing spirit, "We had the experience but missed the meaning," which is always a danger. On the other hand, having the meaning without having the experience first is probably an even worse idea.

14) Your poems are never confessional. One reviewer described you as "blessedly free of morbid self-preoccupation." Is this a conscious choice, an ethic, not to reveal your more personal self in the poems? Do you dislike the confessional voice in poetry?

Well, I have written autobiographical poems, accurate to memory and detail. And I greatly admire certain poets who are or might be characterized as "confessional." But no one would call me a confessional poet. In part it's a question of temperament: wit and irony are great pleasures for me, and I couldn't maintain a pitch of confessional hysteria in my poems if I tried. What I object to is the presumption that I as a poet must be writing about myself, my own lived experience, rehearsing the autobiographical facts. And that's ridiculous. A poet deals in fictions just as a novelist does. When you read a short story, the sophisticated reader knows that the "I" of the story is someone other than the author. Why shouldn't poets enjoy similar freedoms and employ similar strategies? Why shouldn't they use invention as well as memory?

15) I love the phrase in your poem "An Alternative to Speech," "recipes for staying hungry." How does this relate to traditional religious thought, which teaches us to transcend our appetites, our desires?

I wrote that poem in 1980 and I can't clearly recreate what was going on in my head at the time. I may have been thinking of the view that satiety is death, that the retention of appetite or desire is what keeps you young. The question is, how do you get to keep your desire and transcend it at the same time? Is renunciation required? I wanted the hunger of a poet, not the austerity of a monk. I was reading Goethe's *Faust*, and was very affected by that. Faust vows that he can never be satisfied. He agrees that he will lose the bet, and his soul, when and if he should ever declare to the passing moment, "Linger on, thou art so fair." I was always moved by that. Willing to wager on the limitlessness of his appetite for pleasure and for knowledge, sensual and cerebral, the Romantic hero achieves the conquest of nostalgia (and what is nostalgia but dead desire?). In Commencement Day language the search for the inexhaustible desire translates into the Victorian ideal of always striving, never yielding, and may your reach ever exceed your grasp. In, say, *Cosmopolitan* it's the perfect diet, food that delights but does not fatten, or the supreme aphrodisiac, producing desire that renews itself in the act of gratification: the orgasm without guilt or melancholy. It seems to me that language negotiates desire. Language is not—no matter what the deconstructionists say—merely a function and a record of its failure to negotiate desire.

16) "Operation Memory" is another of my favorites. How did this poem get started?

It was on my birthday in 1986. I wrote the first stanza, noticed that it was six lines long and that the end-words of the lines looked promising: "middle," "jobs," and "loaded" are all versatile, "bed" and "loaded" rhyme, and "when" is a great connective. So I decided to make a sestina out of it at that point. I liked the idea of making one of the end-words a variable, a number—though I certainly didn't know ahead of time that I would go from a "hundred" to "fifty" to "eighteen" in a downward progression, then "1970," the year of the action, then "ten," then "one / In a million" and finally "38," my age the day I wrote the poem. The title, "Operation Memory," was one that I had been saving up for a big occasion. It came from my interest in World War II code names for military operations: Operation Overlord for the D-Day landings in Normandy, Operation Torch for the Allied invasion of North Africa, Operation Barbarossa for Hitler's invasion of the Soviet Union, and so forth. Someone once said that military justice is to justice what military music is to music, and that pretty much applies to military language, but I thought these code names were pure poetry. It also seemed to me that Vietnam was the central experience in my generation's coming of age and that the war could do double duty as both the subject of the poem and as its source of metaphor—in other words, the poem is "about" the war but the war is also a metaphor for a generation that feels itself to be "between jobs / And apartments and wives," in the long hangover following a bad mescaline trip.

17) I want to ask you something about the Best American Poetry *anthology series. If you were reading through a lot of poems, looking for "the best," what would make one poem stand out, jump off the page, for you?*

You have to trust your instincts, your immediate response to the poem. If you read enough poetry, you will approach the new writing that you encounter with a certain salutary skepticism; if you really love poetry, you will be impatient with the vanity and pretention of much of the stuff that gets routinely published. So you begin with a certain resistance, which the poem must overcome. At the same time you try to be as responsive and receptive as possible within your own limits. To some extent it's a matter of connoisseurship—encountering a poem that may not speak to you personally, you might still be able to recognize that it is very good of its kind. When I started out writing poetry I avoided contemporary poetry that didn't seem to me, from the point of view of my own work as a poet, useful. Today I feel enough curiosity about what my fellow poets are doing to make me read the magazines that get sent to me, and that's a lot. Often, as Mark Strand put it, you can tell after the first line whether the poem has any authority or not. I said that in Leonard Trawick's class the other day and someone got hysterical about my approving use of the word "authority," but it's a perfectly good word, having the same root as "author."

18) In your essay on John Ashbery you delight in his playful use of language and meaning. For example, The Vermont Notebook *has nothing to do with Vermont. Meaning and language have a slippery relationship; signifier and signified are not related. And yet you dislike deconstruction, which talks about the unreliability of language. It seems to me that in his own way, Ashbery is commenting on this separation between reality and language, this unreliability. That perhaps in Ashbery there is an embrace of the possibility of meaninglessness.*

That must be a good question, because people keep asking it of me. I don't see any real connection between Ashbery and deconstruction. Ashbery (and I, for that matter) may hold certain linguistic and philosophical assumptions in common with the deconstructionists, but that proves only that we all inhabit the same *Zeitgeist.* It is what you do with those premises that is important. Ever since T. S. Eliot wrote that a "shadow" falls between the idea and the reality, modern authors have been obsessed with the gulf between desire and fulfillment, the disjunction between the word and the world. I know that the writers of my generation have contended with this set of problems for the last thirty years. Deconstruction is only one possible response—a very narrow response, with a whole set of harmful implications. What the deconstructionists do is to reduce language to one insistent paradox: the answer to everything is that nothing can be known. History is a linguistic predicament, signifying nothing; literature is the product of power plays, and morality is a conspiracy of the haves to enslave the have-nots. The stuff is utterly reductive. It is tedious. It is wrongheaded. What Ashbery does is something else. First of all, it seems to me that his poetry is affirmative, not despairing. It is, in a phrase Ashbery likes, a "hymn to possibility." It affirms the possibility of its own existence, the possibility that a high aesthetic project can be realized. That project is to capture the workings of a mind in motion, so that time itself is conveyed, not arrested. Ashbery does not discard mimesis, he extends it. Rather than mourn the inability of language to achieve desire, he celebrates what the writer can do in collaboration with a language that appears sometimes to have an autonomous existence, a life of its own.

19) You've written a book about murder mysteries. What is it about detective novels that holds a particular interest for you? Borges said that the detective novel is the perfect form. Do you think this is true?

I wasn't aware that Borges used that phrase, but in a Borgesian universe of coincidences and labyrinths I may have been unconsciously echoing him when I called my book *The Perfect Murder.* The experience of poetry and the experience of mystery are very close for me. And that relates back to the question of difficulty, and the idea that you can enjoy poems before you understand them. After all, what is a mystery? Everything you don't understand is a mystery. Childhood is full of mystery. Birth and copulation and death: the three greatest mysteries. And love is a mystery, and the end of love. Sure, I can see some area of overlap between murder mysteries and poems—the detective novel with its recurring conventions is a very *poetic* form. There are obviously major differences, however, and one of them is that in the detective novel it is assumed that the mystery is intolerable; we need to clear it up, so we keep turning the pages until we reach the solution. Whereas in poetry, we like dwelling in mystery. In poetry, as Keats wrote, it is possible to live amid uncertainties, mysteries, doubts, without any irritable reaching after fact and reason, so long as the poetry is intense enough.

20) Do you think that detective novels have influenced your poetry? That the kind of search for truth, the hunt for the criminal, is an aspect of your worldview?

I suppose so. There are clues to that effect in my work, I know. There's the poem entitled "Defective Story" in *Operation Memory,* and others, too, in which murder mystery motifs turn up. I just finished a poem, "The Escape Artist," dedicated to the memory of the late Graham Greene, who had a big influence on me, and maybe the thing in his work that I responded to most avidly was his sense that the conventions of the thriller, its pace and its locales, were absolutely apt for conveying—in however disguised a way—the essential facts and circumstances of one's own life as a modern husband, a lover, a father, a professional man, a citizen, and so forth. There is also a basic and I think maybe surprising resemblance between the vocation of the poet and that of the hardboiled detective as depicted by Dashiell Hammett and Raymond Chandler. With Sam Spade, Philip Marlowe, and all their descendants, we wonder: why do they persist? They can't be in it for the money, since they're underpaid, and it seems that everyone is constantly warning them off the case. It is a predicament that most poets are familiar with.

UNDER DISCUSSION
Donald Hall, General Editor

Volumes in the Under Discussion series collect reviews and essays about individual poets. The series is concerned with contemporary American and English poets about whom the consensus has not yet been formed and the final vote has not been taken. Titles in the series include:

Forthcoming volumes will examine the work of Langston Hughes, Muriel Rukeyser, H.D., and Denise Levertov, among others.

Please write for further information on available editions and current prices.

Ann Arbor   **The University of Michigan Press**